CW00409359

HERE'S WHAT PEOPLE ARE SAY
MAKING PERFECT:
A TEA WITH TERI BOOK ABOUT **WHAT EM**̲ ̲ ̲ ̲ ̲
FROM THEIR EMPLOYERS:

"**Making Perfect** is not a book to read cover- to-cover in a few sittings; it is a tool for business leaders to improve their connection with their employees. On nearly every page is feeling. The reader will realize that this positive dynamism is tapped by asking, listening and acting on employee input - resulting in customer satisfaction and company success. Using this book, not just reading it, can make a real difference in organizations."
-Anthony R. Patanella, Director of Human Resources, Snap-on Equipment

"**Making Perfect** is a book that should stay within arm's reach on any manager's desktop. It is a touchstone that will serve as a constant reminder to the most successful bosses that human capital is the most important component of any business, and that by listening to and learning from employees, an enterprise can and will thrive. Both market conditions and office cultures (Staffwell operates in Russia) vary, but Teri's tenet doesn't: always, regardless of the environment, have open, two-way communication with your people, at all levels, and implement the good ideas and proposals they provide, and then reward the resultant success.

Teri reminds us to have fun at work, too - we managers ignore that maxim far too often. Managers, present and future, will enjoy **Making Perfect**, and will refer to it regularly- its lessons are golden."
-Richard Witt, General Director, Cameron Russia Limited

"Employers around the world are finally recognizing that the Employee Experience and Employee Loyalty are just as important as the Customer Experience and Customer Loyalty. Companies that work to build lasting, mutually-beneficial relationships with each team member will undoubtedly keep their teams engaged and happy. Many companies have adopted the practice of creating the Voice of the Customer. In **Making Perfect**, Teri Lindeberg does a great job of building the Voice of the Employee and understanding how her team members "view" the company, as well as what they "get" out of the relationship. Every employer and every employee can learn a lot about themselves by applying this principle."
 -Michael Ruckman, President & CEO, Senteo Incorporated

"Although most leaders claim their organization's greatest asset are its people very few actively engage with them as individuals. The benefits of doing this - clearly charted in this real-life business story - are huge: critical issues addressed, real insight gained and knowledge about how to build a better organization. Like all successful entrepreneurs, Teri blazes a path here showing leaders that a successful organization with engaged, involved people actually starts with them."
-Marcus Guest, M.B.A - Global Strategy Group, KPMG

"Teri Lindeberg takes us on a journey inside the company she founded as a foreigner in Russia. We sit with Teri as she interviews every employee about a wide range of issues ranging from compensation to job environment. Through careful questioning and listening to her employees' responses, Lindeberg distills some unexpected nuggets about what employees want and need, and presents a road map for creating employee satisfaction, which in turn leads to a more productive work atmosphere. "Making Perfect" offers an interesting look into a company that, while weathering an economic downturn from external factors, takes the time to look internally at the myriad of issues that make up its ultimate survival."
-Jennifer Eremeeva, Writer, Blogger, Humor and Cooking Columnist, Photographer

"While unorthodox in its approach, **Making Perfect** strikes to the core of our human nature by revealing what most executives and business owners really want to know, but rarely bother to ask. Teri's discovery of the necessary ingredients to develop Staffwell to success and her observations in respect to them, are poignant, purposeful and profound. Though unique in its perspective, the lessons learned will correlate in most business environments and the book will be a valuable desktop resource for anyone managing human capital. Tops off to Tea with Teri!
-Melinda Rishkofski, Partner, Baker Botts, L.L.P.

"**Making Perfect** is one of the most unique books to have ever emerged on the Russian business and publishing horizon. Its genuine originality is multi-faceted and stipulated by a multiplicity of unifying successful factors, bringing to the Russian readership a truly unusual, yet extremely well-structured, manuscript that is also fresh, yet well researched, and profoundly practical.

What makes the book so unusual?

Firstly, it was written in Russia by an American entrepreneur, who has created her own business that grew to become one of the most influential and successful recruitment agencies in the country.

Secondly, because the book reflects the story, atmosphere, rich business and social context of a very sophisticated and vibrant organization - the recruitment agency, where a fantastic mix of industrial and functional cultures, views, values and behaviors inter-link and inter-weave as they evolve into a cohesive, well-orchestrated and superbly performing team, united by a common goal.

Thirdly, because with all its polyphonic nature, the book delivers a strong and unambiguous account of thoughts, expectations, values and symbols of a team and the company - very representative of the emerging Russian capitalism. In this quality, it assumes the thought leadership in one of the least researched fields - the development of a new generation of managers and entrepreneurs in a major emerging market evolving in front of our eyes.

While having been written with enviable mastery, the book provides an extremely valuable set of practical tools and means inestimable for managing and developing a multi-cultural and multi-lingual team, which will serve well to those who are facing the challenge that the author embraced back in 1990s.

Particularly captivating are the passages on how the author and the Team overcame the hurdles of the economic crises - the memorable Russian meltdown of 1998, and the Global downturn of 2008 that still haunts both economies and minds alike. Lessons that readers can learn from respective parts of the book can be very practical in the current conditions of economic volatility and its social and motivational derivatives.

Overall, the book brings to life a sophisticated, well-nuanced, and subtly drawn picture of the rich context, emerging and evolving in a real-life organization that (in its almost palpable existence on the pages) incessantly creates unique knowledge - the theme of knowledge (tacit and explicit, sticky and leaky) is not brought by the author to the forefront of the book, but it reveals itself in many connotations and allusions to the famous book by I. Nonaka and H. Takeuchi on the Knowledge-Creating Company. In its ultimate role, the book is all about knowledge, both developing in the Team that makes the centerpiece of it, but also - to a much higher degree - the knowledge that permeates and inspires the contemplation of the dedicated reader.

In its significance for the understanding of contemporary corporate life and its multi-faceted context with its values, emotions, stories, and insights, the new book inherits from the seminal writings of J. Collins, but it takes us to a new quality - not only Great, but truly Perfect. And it clearly succeeds in that due to its ability to penetrate into the psyche of the Team, and not only into the tenets of corporate strategy and optimal business processes.

The book is destined to become the must-read among those who want to get a lease of precious knowledge, scrupulously gathered by the author in her years-long effort on managing the organization while writing down the inspirational chronicles of its evolution and attainment of ever-elusive perfection.

And soon it will clearly divide corporate Russia (and then, perhaps, China, India, Brazil, and America) into two distinctive categories - those who embraced its wisdom, and the ignorant."
- Dr. Boris M. Volpe, VP Business Development & Marketing, Member of the Board, The SITRONICS Group of Companies

"One year in Moscow is equivalent to 4-6 years in most other parts of the world. Therefore, this book - covering 12 years of entrepreneurial experience, is really a source of experience and knowledge. Although you may believe you are reading a promotional booklet at the beginning, as you explore the different chapters you realize that you are exposed to an honest, simple and pragmatic guide to addressing the most important asset any Company has: its PEOPLE.

Even though we all have read and used some of Teri's findings and recommendations from time-to-time, her book provides a valuable and systematic guideline to uncover the realities of your Companies' work environment and what to do about it. All in all, I think we could all use **Making Perfect** to improve our Companies' life. Great and inspiring read!"
-Ing. Rostislav Ordovsky-Tanaevsky Blanco, President, Rostik Group

MAKING PERFECT

A 'TEA WITH TERI' BOOK ABOUT

WHAT EMPLOYEES WANT

FROM THEIR EMPLOYERS

TERI LINDEBERG

SUNSHINE PUBLISHING HOUSE

Copyright © 2012 by Teri Lindeberg

Making Perfect
Sunshine Publishing House

All rights reserved. Printed in the United States of America. No part of this book may be used or reproduced in any manner whatsoever without written permission except in the case of brief quotations embodied in critical articles and reviews. For information contact Sunshine Publishing House at www.solnechniysvet.com.

Attention colleges and universities, corporations, recruitment companies, executive search firms, and others: Quantity discounts are available on bulk purchases of this book for educational training purposes, book clubs, corporate team-building, fund-raising, or gift-giving. Special books, booklets or book excerpts can also be created to fit your specific needs. For information contact Sunshine Publishing House at **www.solnechniysvet.com.**

ISBN: 978-0-9891524-1-9

For Vladimir, Leonid and Savva:

May this book one day help you during your careers;

to speak up when you have ideas, to listen for good ideas from others,

and to never stop improving yourselves and the companies you work for or lead.

FOREWORD

This book is not a standard management treatise – chock full of abstract points for students, aspiring executives and top-level management to provide hollow "take-aways". Nor is it loaded with absurd euphemisms that could be transformed into the buzz words of tomorrow. In a market cluttered with books on theoretical management practices and often-conflicting reviews of case studies, this book differentiates itself in both its form and its thinking. Its central tenet is that business, particularly in the service-sector, is ultimately about people. This, unto itself, is hardly new or ground-breaking. However, amidst the Board meetings, strategy planning sessions, capital markets presentations and review of spreadsheets, the issue of people, how to motivate them, what they want and really need is too frequently labeled by top management as a "soft-issue" and shelved. The author reminds us that the focus on people is most often the single most critical issue in optimizing the success of a business and that this can be lost in the noise during both good and bad economic times.

This book represents a practical treatment of key management issues in accessible language that should appeal to a broad spectrum of business people, not just those who work in the service sector. It is an account about the experiences of one woman and her quest to improve the company she founded and runs. We are privy to an evolution in her thought process and how enlightening and rewarding it can be, in commercial and humanistic terms, to engage with co-workers on a more personal level. However, the book is not unilateral in its narrative. The author brings us into her workplace and introduces us to the people who work for her, and their respective personalities, by allowing us to hear the voices of her staff directly. This dual interaction is what will strike home for most readers and is what makes the book both unorthodox and, I believe, more effective than its peers. The issues and opinions of the employees are stated for all to read and I believe that most will relate to the vast majority of topics discussed.

It is a book written with remarkable honesty and self-awareness. The author has been brave in revealing her own short-comings but, also, does not tread lightly regarding the failings of others around her, when appropriate and deserved. No office is without its tensions at times and her company, Staffwell, is no different. However, the corporate culture the author created and has diligently maintained at her company is inspirational and a reminder to the reader that the conduct and attitude of the CEO sets the tone for all those below in the workplace.

While the author resides in Russia and Staffwell is headquartered in Moscow, this book is really not about the Russian workplace nor is it about how to manage Russians in a distinct way. In fact, one of the imperatives revealed within these pages is that human resource management should not be employed in a discriminatory manner – that there are certain universal principles that apply regardless of nationality or type of business line. Of course, we do get a glimpse, often humorous at times, about subtle cultural differences in the office and how these are discovered and addressed.

I arrived in Russia in late 1995 – approximately around the time Teri Lindeberg moved to Moscow. Expatriates arriving during that period were made up of a certain breed – some carpetbaggers, but mostly people who wanted a sense of adventure and to be a part, post factum, of what was perhaps the single most important historical event of their generation – the fall of the Soviet Union. The truly foreign elements and the sometimes difficult living conditions we faced served to cement strong bonds among groups of expats. It is remarkable, therefore, that I had never met Teri until 2011.

In spite of the late introduction, we became fast and true friends in a short period of time – much of which was based on our common experience of living and working in Russia over the past 16 years. However, there were, in some areas, differences in our respective experiences. Out of the conversations about the divergences came the topic of the book she was in the process of writing – "Making Perfect".

To be honest, when Teri mentioned that she was writing a book I let out a mental groan, believing that it was just another exercise, by yet another expat, in trying to capture the mood of Russia when the influx of expats arrived. I was wrong and delighted to be off-base in my assumptions when she described to me the topic of the book and its creative genesis. I was so struck by the uniqueness of its topic and approach that I basically forced my way into being a participant in its latter development. I am incredibly fortunate to have been able to be a part of her project and glean so much from the primary source.

Not without accident did I arrive at the same conclusions that many of Staffwell's employees came to in working with Teri. She is generous, kind and carries a fair and positive attitude – toward life and with regard to the business she runs. Russia can be seen as a graveyard of failed entrepreneurs and business people who have abandoned their ethics in search of profit. In a very difficult business environment, especially for foreigners, and doubly so for expat women, Teri Lindeberg has succeeded in building a thriving business on her own terms, reflecting both her personality and her scruples. This is a remarkable achievement and particularly so when seen in the context of her vast array of activities outside the workplace – not least of which is raising three boys. This commands respect and should point to a desire to listen to her story on how she came to manage all of this. As you will read, the lost art of listening was the key in unlocking what has transformed her company and her approach to other aspects of life.

Michael Sassarini
Former Director, Chase Manhattan Bank
Moscow, Russia

TABLE OF CONTENTS

INTRODUCTION

I am Teri Lindeberg, an American who has lived and worked in Moscow for over 15 years. I am the founder, owner and CEO of Staffwell, one of the top recruitment and executive search firms in Russia. This book is both a story and a case study with, what I consider to be, a set of universal lessons about the workplace and management-employee relationships. It is a book about how you can make the perfect company simply by spending some one-on-one quality time with your employees. Well, perhaps "near perfect" is a more realistic picture of what could result.

Staffwell launched its operations in 2000 and we reached our peak in 2008. That same year the global economic crisis unfolded, which hit Russia and our company somewhat later in 2008. My Financial Director and I both realized that we needed to act quickly as we were likely in for a bumpy ride that would last a few years. Accordingly, in late 2008, through a two-stage process, we quickly down-sized the company by 40%, revised our budgets and hunkered down.

By the winter of 2009, I had become a bit bored and anxious, to be perfectly honest, and needed a new, challenging project. It was then that I came up with the idea to sit with each of our remaining employees, in a one-on-one format, in order to try to get to know them better and to hear their thoughts on the company itself, as well as about their careers within the company. I used our standard Staffwell exit interview questionnaire but omitted the first few questions that focused on why employees were leaving the company. I also left out the last few questions regarding their new employment and why they had chosen to work there. I then changed the tense, from past to present, of the remaining bulk of questions, entitled the project and the questionnaire "Tea with Teri", and was off to the races.

I sent an e-mail to all staff about "Tea with Teri" and explained my objectives, and that in the ensuing 2 months I would be meeting with each employee in my office - or in the conference room or via Skype. I attached the questionnaire so they could prepare ahead of time, if they so wanted, and explained to them that I was looking for individual input; that this was not a group gossip project; that there was nothing to worry about; and that I was truly looking forward to spending one-on-one time with each of them. I then started the scheduling and instructed that they bring a cup of tea or coffee with them to our meeting.

The idea and introduction of the "Tea with Teri" meetings were met with great enthusiasm from the staff and I was really looking forward to getting to know everyone - many for the first time. I had no expectations beyond that – other than it might be a potentially useful way to spend my time during the slow period that followed the global economic crisis.

In total, I conducted nearly 50 "Tea with Teri" chats. By the third meeting, I felt that what I was being exposed to would very likely be useful to others and, perhaps, convenient to place in a book format. The information that came out of them was so incredible, informative and useful, that I felt it had to be shared and, hopefully, help others in their businesses. I might imagine that consulting firms would likely charge a fortune for this type of an exercise, but in this relatively inexpensive format, everyone can learn something from what I learned and experienced, instill direction, and put it to good use.

In the end, this book is for everyone, anywhere who owns a company, manages in a company, or works for a company. You will learn a little bit about our company, Staffwell, and the world of recruitment and executive search. More importantly, you will gain insight into what employees want and what is important to them. You will also discover that, if you are armed with this type of information, it can be quite easy to figure out how to improve your company or division, make it a more attractive place to work and, in the process, a more desirable place for customers to do business with you.

Although the setting for this book is in Russia, and 90% of the employees are Russian, I think that you will find the information, story and advice applicable almost anywhere in the world.

Each chapter represents one of the questions asked. I have left the responses by the employees unedited, but categorized their replies under different headings within each chapter. I then added my impressions and my responses to their comments. Finally, I concluded each subject area with a general summary listing of what employees everywhere want.

I hope you find the story and content useful and, in reading this book, derive as much pleasure as I did in researching and writing it.

Enjoy.

TL

NOTE FROM THE AUTHOR

Each of the following 32 chapters is consistent in their format. They first provide the questions that I posed to each member of my staff during their 'Tea with Teri" chats with me. Next, I have broken down their responses into categories, which are delineated in topic headlines that are under-scored.

The verbatim responses from staff, taken from my notes during the chats, are shown in italics. These comments mostly have been left in their original dialectal form, as spoken to me. However, I have amended some comments for the sake of clarity.

My comments to their replies follow and then each section ends with bullet-pointed summaries of what employees want (at most companies).

Finally, I note that a certain degree of repetition has been left in the text in a deliberate manner. This was to emphasize and highlight areas of wider opinion and consensus from the team as a whole, on certain topics.

Making Perfect is a true story. All names except for mine, the author, have been changed.

Chapter 1
How Do You Feel About The Company?

I thought this was a great first question, as it is open-ended and, thus, felt it was more likely to solicit responses that gave a better, overall picture of what the team thought about the company. I also appreciated the term "feel" within the question itself, as I believed that it would trigger more genuine responses – from the heart and soul; more so than terms like "analyze" or "assess", which are likely to produce colder answers.

OWNERSHIP

"Like my child, built the department from zero"... "I feel a real part of Staffwell, coming in everyday is more than just work to me"... "Very important to me in my life"... "Love the company, been here a long time and enjoy our business –just great!"

Several of our managers and staff felt sincere ownership of the company. They had put time and effort into it, helped build it, loved what was created, what it is today and where we were headed. It felt fantastic as an owner to hear this: that some of our team had such strong admiration and love for the company they worked for and helped build.

Employees want:

- To have built or contributed to building a part of the company;
- To feel they are a genuine part of the company;
- To feel that coming in every day is more than just work to them;
- To feel that the company is a very important part of their lives;
- To enjoy the business the company is engaged in; and
- To love the company they work for.

POSITIVE CHANGE

"Before tough and selfish; now team spirit; share info and help each other; Directors closer to one another."

For some at Staffwell, elements of positive change came from certain management and staff turnover and the shifting economy. Prior to the global economic crisis that fell upon the majority of Russian industry in late 2008, Staffwell had emerged as a top 3 player on the market in placing mid- to top-level management professionals.

We were growing, busy and successful. When your company expands and moves at a fast pace it can be difficult to please everyone. You hire people fast, at times manage hard and erratically and, on occasion, relax the guidelines for some people and not others. This can result, for some team members with conflicting dispositions, in a more intense and tense atmosphere and, often, a seemingly unfair work environment.

It can be difficult to notice this when you are in midst of it and busy. However, it becomes crystal clear when disruptive members depart, allowing you to step back and notice the differences in people and their character. The departure of some of our management and staff, aided by a slower economy and a shift in work environment, enabled us to evaluate the past and improve the direction for our future.

Employees want:

- To see a change from tough and selfish - to strong and team spirit-oriented;
- To see a change from closed and uncooperative - to sharing information and helping each other for the greater cause; and
- To see a change from stressful, unfriendly internal competition - to healthy, friendly internal competition.

UNDERSTOOD AND ACCEPTED COMPANY DECISIONS

"We were stressed about redundancies but looking back now it is understood why we needed them - now everyone is ready to work and are in a good mood – the team feels good"... "Happy we reacted first - feel we are very strong as a company and very smart"... "Feel positive we will overcome all difficulties – in this company I learned one very important thing – there are no problems we cannot overcome."

This is the second crisis I had worked through in Russia. The first was the financial crisis of 1998. Recruitment is an industry that gets hit hard in such times and it is typical for revenues to drop by as much as 80%. It is not an easy process to go through and the only way for a company to survive is to cut expenses, of which the biggest is payroll (that is, in effect, people).

For many of the 20- and 30-year olds on our team, this was the first serious economic downturn they had encountered and their initial experience with its related down-sizing. As the owner and CEO of the company, I did my best to communicate to all members of the team what was happening and why, and what our future plans were.

I did this in both verbal and written email form in order to keep everyone in the know as often as possible. I acted fast and kept the best and longest-standing employees with the company, retaining more than 60% of our team - all the while knowing our revenues were due to drop by around 80%.

Employees want:

- To understand why redundancies happen in their company during an economic crisis, or at any time;
- To overcome the stress of redundancies in the company and push forward to new, happy, successful times;
- Fast, strong and smart reactions to external problems; and
- To know and feel that their company is capable of surviving external challenges and has the ability to thrive thereafter.

A GREAT TEAM OF GREAT PEOPLE

"I joined due to the people I interviewed with who were very positive and driving - I love to learn from positive people"... "Highly professional people make Staffwell a highly professional company"... "Friendly people, I missed the people when I left and it is why I came back"... "Highly professional"... "Great Directors"... "Love the people and how they get along and that you can really learn from them"... "The sales team helps me a lot to understand things"... "Very friendly"..." Great communications"... "High talented individuals with great English"

Having great people is the single largest key to the success of any company, especially ours. I was very happy to hear that our employees felt we had a great team. On occasion, we lose an individual here or there but it is always, at any given time, our core team and our combined core strength that keep us moving forward as a top-rate, developing company.

We do look to hire certain types of people, and every year we tend to put more and more emphasis on this. Some of the traits we look for are: significant business experience, sales and customer service-oriented mindset, highly professional, ability to multi-task, hard working, strong communication skills, sharp professional image, and a friendly, positive outlook. We train on the rest.

What makes us different from our competitors? Our team!

Employees want:

- To interview with positive and driven people;
- To work with and learn from positive people;
- To work for a highly professional company, staffed with highly professional people;
- To work with friendly people;
- To have great business development people working for the company;
- To love their team members and have a close, team-spirit environment;
- To be able to learn from their team members;
- To have helpful team members;
- To have team members who are good at communicating with them;
- To work with talented people; and
- To work in a multi-lingual environment with native and proficient English speakers.

TO LIKE THEIR JOB, ROLE AND INDUSTRY

"I love the industry sector I recruit for"… "Flexible, individual work procedures are given"… "I love the recruitment industry the most"… I love that we work for many industry sectors as it gives a lot of well rounded experience"… "It is the first time I am my own boss and can be creative"… "Recruitment is always new and busy".

It is hard to be successful when you don't enjoy what you do. I was really happy to discover that most of our team really enjoyed our industry, company and the roles they had.

There is a lot of satisfaction from being in recruitment. It is a "feel good" industry where you feel you are truly needed: the client needs you to find, for them, exactly the type of person they seek, and candidates need assistance in being placed into a new career. When great matches are made, there is nothing like the appreciation received by both the client and candidate for the services you have provided them.

In addition, I feel recruitment is a wonderful industry to work in as projects are inherently dynamic due the fact that clients, client contacts, vacancies and candidates are always changing. It is never dull and there is a lot of independence given in managing one's time, projects and workload.

Employees want:

- To like the business sector they work in ;
- To like the industry sectors in which the clients work;
- To have flexible, individual work procedures;
- To have variety in their work;
- To be responsible for their own success or failure;
- The opportunity to be creative in their work;
- To have new projects; and
- To be busy.

TO EARN A GOOD LIVING

"It was the first time I had the opportunity to make more than just a base salary – and the bonuses here can be great"... "Very clear plan and compensation plan"... "A team that wants to earn well but also loves their work"... "I am earning money!"

Having a very clear and well-defined compensation plan is important. Employees appreciate knowing exactly what they are going to be earning in base salary and having a well-formulated bonus or commission plan. This allows them to precisely gauge what they need to do in order to achieve their compensation goals. Having a clear plan for employees also promotes fairness within the team and in the company, and makes it easy to calculate due earnings and construct budgets.

Often, when new team members join us, I am surprised to learn that the companies in which they previously worked, within our industry or others, did not provide lucid compensation plans. Their commissions and bonuses were subjective, and more dependent on their relationship with their boss, rather than on their actual performance. Such an approach is extremely dated and only fosters unfairness, negativity and resentment within the workforce.

Employees want:

- The opportunity to make more than a base salary;
- Very clear Key Performance Indicators (KPIs) and targets;
- A very transparent compensation plan;
- To work in a team that wants to earn a great deal, while also enjoying their work; and
- The opportunity to earn a decent living.

GOOD MANAGEMENT

"We have great management who care about the company"…"We give opportunities to the team to realize potential and ideas; independence given"…"Thankful for believing in her"… "Teri and Adam brought great people here – great attributes"… "Diana loves the company and wants us to be the best and the sector team is great"…"Management stick to their word".

Hiring and retaining great executives and management in your company is extremely important. I have always believed in a strong top-down management structure. If management is good, their leadership will be a big key in the success of the company.

Good executives and management adhere to the corporate vision and directives that are laid out for them. It takes responsible ownership to create these elements, roll them out, and then constantly hold company executives and management to task. When everyone is consistently in synch, from owner to executive, from management to staff, it is much easier to succeed and have a happy, well-coordinated, high producing team.

Employees want:

- Management that care about the company;
- Management that delegate and give opportunities to the team that enables them to grow;
- To be given some independence;
- Management that believe in them;
- Executives that hire great people for the company;
- Management that love the company;
- Management that want the team to work to their highest potential; and
- Management that stick to their words and promises.

ATMOSPHERE

"Friendly, hard working and very democratic compared to others"... "The team has fun at work and desires to work hard and create new services"..." Very structured and great people, great internal relations, and ability"... "Professional, stable, feels taken care of and watched over, not tense, very family–like, very open and honest –all questions are always answered"... "Worked for a huge company before and loves the smaller feel of Staffwell - in huge companies I got lost and my efforts didn't matter much - I like being able to see and feel my results at Staffwell"... "Very dramatic, polite and friendly"... "Still love having my initial feelings of being inspired and challenged and love that we are a Western company;, love the process of work"... "Flexible, client oriented, we don't give up in a crisis, positive attitude, survivors, try to keep our team, always creating new services"... "Always developing and moving forward"... "Enjoyable (people, relations, written procedures, and pay as promised: we keep our promises!), not stressful, soft welcome"... "Feel I get along with everyone, not just a few people"... "Do not fear to be a winner as I know everyone will appreciate it and not be threatened or angered by it; I feel free to speak and give ideas and contribute; our hard working team stimulates me to also work hard".

Having a great atmosphere takes time, work and good people. From the top down, I have consistently let everyone know that they can always come to me with any issue or problem they may have and any exciting news that they wish to share. At times, this also has helped keep management in check and has continually supported the practice of fair play, respect and innovation in the company.

As the owner and CEO of Staffwell, I have always wanted the atmosphere in the company to include many elements: success, fairness, fun, happiness, talent, professionalism, customer service orientation, profit-driven, open-door, hard-working, helpful, respectful, ethical, growth-oriented and continual improvement. What I did not want were aspects such as: selfishness, theft, grumpiness, nay-sayers, procrastination, gossip, hierarchy, favoritism, depression, attitude and aggression. When people join our company I believe that they immediately notice the difference.

Atmosphere really does come down to the people you have in the company and their willingness to carry out and maintain the desired atmosphere. If they also buy into your vision and desire, then you have a high probability of successfully creating that environment for everyone. Having and hiring people that crave the same office atmosphere as you do is the best way to ensure it will be achieved.

Employees want:

- A fun, friendly, hard-working, structured and an equitable work environment;
- To work with great people, with great internal relations and ability;
- A professional, stable, respectful, open-door and honest atmosphere;
- To be known and be noticed (personally and on results);
- The occasional minor drama in the office, as well as entertainment;
- To be inspired and challenged;
- To work in a positive, fair, Western-style environment;
- To like the work processes and procedures in the company;
- To work for client/customer-focused companies;
- To work for companies that don't give up, that work hard and blossom in the face of any challenges;
- To work for companies that continually work to improve all aspects of their business;
- To be paid as agreed, and for agreements and promises to be kept;
- A welcoming, non-stressful induction when they join the company;
- To work for a company in which everyone gets along well and works well together - not just a few people or divisions here and there;
- To embrace being successful for the Company, not fear it due to others being threatened or angered by it;
- To feel free to speak, expound ideas and contribute; and
- To be stimulated by working within a diligent team.

PERSONAL DEVELOPMENT

"I am becoming more professional and learning more about the company and enjoy working in different sectors"... "A great school to learn how to deal with clients and candidates"..."We give a lot of professional development; time management, negotiations, communications."

The magic ends when you stop learning and developing. We provide a lot of training and on-the-job experience to our employees, and many in our team also self-educate themselves on their own time outside the office. A smarter team is always more likely to bring more depth to their roles and the company and, therefore, be able to bring better results.

I truly believe that the recruitment industry itself is very interesting and multi-faceted. It deals comprehensively with people and "people issues". Your clients are people, your candidates are people, your employees are people; and as no two people are the same, no two search assignments are the same. Everything is always changing and is always new, challenging, and exciting.

Employees want:

- To reach higher levels of professionalism;
- To learn more about the company they work for;
- To acquire and experience different roles and responsibilities in the company; and
- To improve their skills and abilities in customer service, communications, presentations, negotiations, time management and all other client/customer-related areas.

REPUTATION

"Good market reputation, good company name, best in management selection: I know a lot of people at other agencies and their rules, procedures and people, and their management do not compare to ours"... "Our team, people and business make me proud –it's all about our team"... "We were the best and we are now - we have clients who value us a lot, who call when they need us and call only us"..."We differ a lot from other competitors and it is thanks to our management, our trainings, our value of team work which makes us know exactly what our clients and candidates want"... "Great brand"..."Everyone knows Staffwell and Teri, great clients and searches"..."I feel our leadership in the market and that we will be very strong after the crisis as I hear this from lots of candidates and clients"..."Happy to be with a strong brand"... "Proud to work for Staffwell and that all systems are built here"... "All procedures are very professional"..."Great image of this company –gives pride to all"....Proud to work here, proud we are at the top."

I believe that reputation really is everything to a company. We have always tried to do everything better. I think this commitment to relentless improvement is one of the key reasons we have earned a good reputation within the company and in the market.

Furthermore, we always put the customer first – a directive that comes directly down from me, as this is how I have groomed myself professionally over the years. We do not take a position that is defensive nor ignorant; two elements that are too widespread in the average workplace at times. Instead, we admit our mistakes when we make them, with honesty, and work quickly to rectify and learn from them. I think this has been appreciated and welcomed from our clients and candidates, and by our own employees.

Employees want:

- To work for a company with a good name and a good market reputation;
- To be the best in their industry or be capable of becoming the best;
- To work for companies with superior rules, procedures, people and management, compared to their competitors;
- To be proud of their company, people and teamwork;
- To work for companies where their clients value them, and stay with them, due to the high levels of service and the results they receive;
- To work for a company that has a great brand, has market name recognition and has well-known leadership;
- To work for a company that has great clients with quality assignments, and a positive market outlook;
- To work for innovative companies that employ innovative people;
- Tight professional internal procedures; and;
- To feel proud working for their company.

OFFICE LOCATION AND OFFICE

"I am thankful we are a legal company"... "Great location"... "Democratic, very easy to give ideas, very fast procedures, nothing held up, a very productive company".

The Company and its office do matter. While there are always ways to cut corners, there are also risks associated with such, and if a company really wants to find a solution, then it will find one. At Staffwell, we do things on the up-and-up; for example, we pay full legal salaries and keep promises according to our compensation plan. This is appreciated by our staff and sets us apart from other competitors and companies.

We are housed in an old office in a historical building that I think is in a great location. Our team members, many of whom are nostalgic, love the office as much as I do. Of course, no office is ever completely perfect, but this one has worked for us as it is within our budget, is centrally located, carries good leasing terms and has an agreeable layout for us. We have tried our best to make it the best it can be.

Employees want:

- To work for a company that fully adheres to the law, especially with regard to their employee contracts and salaries;
- To work in a great location;
- To work in a non-regimented, easy-going office environment, where there are stream-lined procedures, little bureaucracy and it is easy and rewarding for them to express their ideas; and
- To work for a productive company.

NO DISCRIMINATION

"I was formerly a PA [personal assistant] *but wanted to be more, but nobody gave me a chance until we met her. Age discrimination is huge in Russia but Staffwell still allowed her through"..."It is the first time she is her own boss and can be creative".*

The recruitment industry in Russia has matured over the years, as have hiring companies and their Human Resource (HR) executives. It is no longer acceptable in the market to be interviewed, or be pitched business-to-business services, by a 20-year old.

Companies and job seekers with prior work experience want to know that the people to whom they are speaking have sufficient business and life experience, so as to understand them and their needs on a more equal level.

At Staffwell, we do not look at age or other discriminatory factors when hiring. We look for work experience, communication skills, language skills, professionalism, good manners, positive attitude, ability, and desire to join us and succeed. Everything else, and in-between, we train and develop on. This has worked for us and is another thing that, I feel, sets us apart from our competitors.

Employees want:

- To be given a chance, on occasion, to succeed by trying a new role or responsibility;
- To not be discriminated against due to age; and
- To be treated fairly.

Chapter 2
What Has Been Good/Enjoyable/Satisfying For You At Staffwell?

I felt this was a good question in order to find out more about what we were good at, and to induce people to be more forthcoming - if they were not already so when answering the first question. It also confirmed what we knew we were good at, while shedding more light on what our team liked about our company and what they felt our strengths were.

SUCCESS

"Seeing how the company has grown from zero"..."Success, want my team to be successful"..."Have really enjoyed the success that has been achieved"..."Revenues, frankly speaking, the first enjoyable thing was my first revenue, I never knew I could earn such sums due to hard work"..."The results of placing – very inspiring"..."Making placements"..."Big placements"..."Making my first placement"...

I am, and have always been, a salesperson myself and, as this a sales organization, this was music to my ears.

As mentioned in Chapter 1, recruitment can be a "feel-good" business if you do it well. Clients appreciate your finding them the employees they needed; candidates appreciate your finding them new employment; and, if you are with the right recruitment firm, you will appreciate being thanked, congratulated, and compensated appropriately for your successful efforts.

Achieving success has always been very important to me and I constantly strive to achieve it in everything we do at Staffwell. It comes a lot easier when you love what you do, and I do love our business - and it is apparent here that many of our team members also love our business.

Employees want:

- To see the company growing and developing;
- Personal, team and company success;
- To bring money to the company and to earn money; and
- To achieve success.

TEAM-BUILDING AND EVENTS

"Team-building in the woods has always been good"..."The team-building event when I joined was super and I got to know a lot of people"..."Team-buildings and parties"..."The number of social events –it really brings people together –helps people to get to know each other better"..."Team-buildings with Moscow and President's club trips"..."Birthday party of Teri's at her Taganskaya apartment, all team-building events"..."Very impressed by the team-building"..."Nice team – they go to parties and spend weekends together, and took a trip to the Moscow office last year"..."Best was team-building in September"...

I found it interesting that the team-building events that were mentioned here were the simple, local ones: a party at my apartment; a day in the woods together playing adventure games; our day creating theater skits; or just spending time at another office. No one specifically mentioned our big trips to the beach in Turkey, climbing Chamonix in France, whitewater rafting in Croatia, or sailing in Montenegro. Perhaps, simple and local is more convenient and provides more quality time in a lower stress, closer-to-home environment.

I am a big fan of team-building and we have always had good experiences, whether it was very low budget or on the higher end. The important thing was that we were together, having fun, became stronger and knew more of each other afterward.

It can be really beneficial to periodically spend quality time with your colleagues outside of the routine office environment. It allows you to see a different side of the people you work with and can give you a better understanding of who they are on and off the job, in casual settings.

Employees want:

- To spend informal, organized time together with colleagues outside of the office;
- Social opportunities to get to know their management, colleagues, and staff better;
- Team-building opportunities to get to know people in the company's other offices better; and
- Informal occasions to celebrate and have fun.

THE TEAM

"Now a very professional, very specialized team of people"..."I enjoy the team"..."All people working for the company are well-measured, intelligent, all on the same level – highly interesting and intelligent"..."The people!"..."Good people, strong team"..."Enjoys working with a highly professional team"..."Team is #1"..."Support from the team and company, everyone is friendly and close"..."The team make coming to work great and very helpful"..."Warm team and great skilled specialists"...

I cannot over-stress that it is definitely all about the team you have.

Again, hiring good people, and retaining good people, is the biggest key to the success of any company. To perfect that for Staffwell has become my focus over the years. Highly skilled professionals, good attitude, friendly, talented, smart, ethical and hard-working, are some of the traits our team members possess and that we seek. We part ways as soon as possible with those who, we later find, truly do not have these characteristic or are unable to develop them with us.

Having a great team is also one of the best ways to motivate and retain your employees. People like to work with great people.

Employees want:

- To work with a highly professional and specialized team;
- To work with intelligent people; and
- To work with a team that is supportive, friendly and close.

THE WORK

"Clients who changed jobs gave new work to us"..."Very enjoyable work"..."Confident at closing vacancies"..."First time in over 20 years where I had to have personal results to prove successful not only team results – I am thriving"..."Closed my first high level staffing manager position – hard to close but very satisfying when I did"..."I have always loved dealing with people and knew that one day I would go into sales, and thanks to our internal recruiters it was recruitment"..."The recruitment process and communicating with clients and candidates is very inspiring"..."Challenging recruiting projects will stay in my mind forever"...

The work is the work. To be successful it helps to find people capable of doing the work well and who also enjoy it.

Recruitment is fast-paced and challenging because companies typically need to hire quickly, and as the product (the candidate) is a human being, there are all types of people-related issues involved. Recruiters that are patient, understanding, convincing, able to multi-task, and handle a heavy workload, typically do well.

I am happy that our team loves the work and the job. I do too. It is challenging, fascinating, rewarding and fun.

Employees want:

- To enjoy the work that they do;
- To have confidence in what they do; and
- Challenging, inspiring work.

CAREER DEVELOPMENT

"Good career development and promotions, wants to help open new offices and start new services"..."Desire to improve"..."Learned a lot and I want to keep learning and developing"..."Professional growth, reporting and accounting; likes that she is developing here"...

It is encouraging that our team wants to develop the company and themselves. I live to improve and grow, and am happy our team does too.

Career development is important for companies and staff. It is a good motivator and an effective tool in employee retention. It is something that we must always examine in order to improve and expand.

Employees want:

- To keep learning and developing;
- To earn promotions;
- To help the company grow and expand; and
- To take on more responsibilities and challenges.

NETWORKING EVENTS

"I like attending networking events but feel evening events are better as there is more time to talk to people"...

This particular individual is comparing morning business club meetings (that have limited networking time before and after the meeting), to evening networking events that are devoted almost entirely to networking.

Business development is a critical part of our business and our team attends a lot of networking events. I support whichever networking events bring the most business opportunities per individual, and I am happy that the team likes and enjoys them.

In our business we can meet a potential new client or candidate anywhere, so it is helpful to be out meeting and interacting with business people in our communities.

Employees want:

- To attend useful networking events.

INTERVIEW PROCESS

"The interview process was very organized and professional, which is why I chose Staffwell over other companies"...

The interview process is such a crucial area for any company that wants to recruit good people into their organization. We put a lot of effort into our process and it has been well worth it.

I really want to highlight the point mentioned above, as it is really an over-riding, key one: candidates do compare and consider the interview processes companies have, and do use this as a part of their decision-making criteria when choosing between job offers. It may, in fact, be the only criterion a candidate has in which to make a decision, as they are unlikely to really know what they are entering into (the role, work life, the team, the company) until they are actually working in the job itself.

The interview process should be perfect. The people interviewing the candidate should know their roles in the interview process, be fully prepared on the candidate and for what role the candidate is being considered. The people interviewing should be highly professional, well respected within the company and friendly toward the applicants.

Employees want:

- An exceptional interview process to attract the best people into their company.

INDUCTION

"The induction was very helpful and stimulating and I was given the full picture"…"The lunches together during induction"…"Enjoyed starting at Staffwell, and in the fourth month I was sent to Moscow for training"…

Staffwell has a very thorough and well-structured induction program, which is the process of introducing a new employee to their role and the company they join. Everyone who goes through induction should end up with good knowledge of the company and the team, as well as a thorough understanding of their role and how to effectively perform in such.

It is important for us to ensure that new hires get up and running as soon as possible in order to quickly become successful for the company. I am really pleased and proud that we do this well.

Employees want:

- A professional and thorough induction to the company, their new role, and the team, when starting a new job at a new company;
- Social time during their induction to get to know the team in a friendly, informal way; and
- On-going training as part of the induction process.

LEADERSHIP/MANAGEMENT

"Good combination between motivation and encouragement" … "KPIs, but no major pressure – had time to find her personal style, good amount of flexibility given to Directors in choosing clients and working with Consultants"…"Diana is friendly and calms everyone down from stress"…"The leadership"…"Open door with Teri"…"The management is loyal to the team"…"I like how the management treats the staff"…"Management style"…

It is important to staff who they work for and how they are managed and led. From the top down, I feel we have a really good management and leadership team.

I would say that some of the key traits of our management team are talent (we have all been promoted ourselves throughout our careers, to date, due to our accomplishments); positive, forward-outlook at all times; friendliness; fairness; diligence; and we stick to the rules we set, for ourselves and for the team. This works for us and should work for most, if not all, companies.

In the past, we have had some senior team members who were, at times, tough, rough, manipulative, stern, lazy, or would always cause problems. Some of these people were fired while others just left. I feel that it takes having a good team in place to truly understand what a really good team is. I believe that we have a good team in place now and we will continue to develop it further.

Employees want:

- To be motivated and encouraged;
- To have targets and the independence to achieve them;
- Strong management who are also, when need be, sensitive, calming and understanding;
- An approachable, open-door management style; and
- Management who are loyal to the company and its employees.

ATMOSPHERE

"I like the atmosphere, everyone is very approachable; Teri, Diana and the Accounting team"..."Flexible hours"..." Competitive environment and I like winning"..."I like being the elder statesman of the office"..."Fun times"..."Family atmosphere"..."I feel I am trusted"..."Unique atmosphere inside the company"..."People atmosphere"...

So many things together create a great atmosphere: positive and fair management and leadership; a talented team of top professionals; a good balance of hard work and fun on the job; very strong operations; and a company that seeks perfection in what they do, and always tries to improve.

A great team and a great company make a great atmosphere.

Employees want:

- Approachable management and team members;
- To work a flexible schedule if needed;
- To work in a competitive work environment;
- To feel trusted; and
- To have fun and feel close to their team members.

TEAMWORK

"Good sharing of info between people, open-mindedness between people"..."Great communications"...

Success in our business depends on teamwork. Fortunately, most of the people within our company communicate effectively and work well together, which is essential to providing great service to clients.

Employees want:

- Everyone to get along;
- Team members to share information; and
- Good inter-office communication.

OPERATIONS

"I like SDS (Staffwell Digital System; our CRM system*)"..."Logical and clear procedures and systems"..."We always pay salaries and bonuses"..."Love that Staffwell has written processes (SDS), the process is very specific and detailed"...*

Having good operations, processes and procedures in place, greatly improves productivity, which in turn, benefits everyone.

We created our own CRM system, which tracks every detail of every client order and candidate with whom we work. We also have a detailed operations manual, and formal processes and procedures for each project step in the recruitment process for every client. Maintaining these strong operations helps ensure we do things correctly, systematically and consistently.

Always paying salaries and bonuses to our team when they are due is important for us. It demonstrates that we are reliable, honest and that we honor our commitments. Our team has always appreciated this in us and it does set us apart from many other companies. We have never once thought to do things in any other way than how we are now doing them.

Employees really appreciate strong operations within a company.

Employees want:

- Good CRM systems;
- Logical and clear procedures and systems; and
- To be paid as promised/outlined.

STYLE/METHODS/VALUES

"Feel the company treats clients and candidates well"..." Focus on quality service, reputation – other companies only about making money and targets – we work to please our customers first"..."Likes how Teri organized the company and its purpose, direction and structure"...

My own values are derived from a lifetime of experiences and from years of working for various employers. I have taken the good business practices and adopted them as my own, and anything bad that I witnessed or learned of, I tried to leave behind me.

It is all about customer service for me. We strive to constantly perfect everything we do within our company. Our clients, candidates and employees are crucial to our success, and so we focus our efforts on our operations: our inductions, trainings, rules, methodology, procedures, systems, databases, offices, marketing, public relations, human resources, and our management and leadership.

Customers really do feel the difference in working with us, as evidenced by continual client feedback we receive. Clients get a high-quality service when working with highly-trained recruitment Directors who understand their needs, who are helpful and who provide them with accurate and fast results. At the same time, candidates who come to us are pleasantly surprised to meet highly-trained recruitment Consultants who are respectful toward them and offer them assistance and encouragement.

I have never contemplated any other way to do it, and I sincerely feel it does set us apart in our industry.

Employees want:

- Customer- and quality service-focused employers;
- Employers who care about the reputation of the company and
- To work for companies with high standards and strong ethics.

PUBLIC RELATIONS (PR)

"PR activities are great right now – articles, conferences and events"...

Employees want to see their company, represented by its management and experts, in the media and speaking at conferences and events. It makes them feel that they, and their company, are important and instills them with pride. I can speak from experience that you really do not know how important and effective PR is to your company, and its business development activities, until you have it.

Employees want:

- Their company to be actively engaged in PR activities.

ABILITIES

"I did a very good hand over at my former company; I am good at this"...

I noted that this person inferred that they were caring and thorough, two qualities that I place value on. It is important to our business, and its success, that we have good hand-overs and hand-over procedures in place.

Employees want:

- To use their talent and experience to help the company in ways outside of their given role.

THE COMPANY/OFFICE

"I would like to be more involved in Staffwell; I love being involved in company discussions"..."Great office location"..."Corporate culture and business topic of recruitment is very interesting – listening to the team talk about the business is very interesting"...

I loved hearing that people wanted to be involved in the company as much as possible.

Employees want:

- To be more involved with the company and decisions made by the company;
- To work at a great office location;
- To work for an industry that interests them; and
- To work with people who really take an interest in what they do.

TESTIMONIALS

"Getting nice letters from clients and presents from them; all is good"...

Nothing feels quite as good as being appreciated for the good work you do. We always try to go the extra mile for our clients and it does come back to us at times in a positive way, such as in testimonials.

Employees want:

- To work for a company that makes its clients so happy that they hear about it directly from the clients themselves.

Chapter 3

What Has Been Frustrating/Difficult/Upsetting To You In Your Time Here?

The first two questions confirmed what we were good at, while this question began to tell me what we needed to look after, and or fix and improve.

UNEXPECTED TURNOVER

"Last summer when a few of our experienced team left us, and then having to explain to others what was happening and why and our future, but this is normal for companies"..."Departure of our GM [General Manager] *and other people, really liked our GM as a manager - losing him was the most difficult"..."Turnover of experienced people – but good is that it was my idea to return Polina to Staffwell as I spoke to the GM about it"..."I cried when our GM left, he was the heart of the company, maybe I am too emotional"...*

It is always hard when good people, sometimes unexpectedly, leave the company. Some of our staff did not have the years of experience to understand why it happens, and it can be difficult for management to explain it and, at the same time, boost morale.

In one instance, we were very fortunate that the key people who left us in the Summer of 2007, to either start their own companies or join others, had all failed in their new endeavors within a 12-month period after leaving us. As they say, the grass is not always greener on the other side.

Personally, I have always managed unexpected turnover very well. This is due to many years of experience and my firm belief that there are always better people to hire in their place. I have always seen employee turnover as an opportunity for a better start.

Losing our GM was hard for me as well because we were quite close, achieved a lot together and had and still have a lot of respect for one another. However, it was also the right time to part ways, and he did a good hand over, and we kept the door open.

Bringing back Polina, who was one of our Senior Consultants on our recruitment team in Moscow, was definitely a good move for us, as she is very strong and talented. She left to join a competitor and realized, within 6 months of leaving us, that we really were the best company on the market to work for. It is always risky to bring someone back into the company. However, in this case, it was a risk well worth taking and one that paid off.

Employees want:

- To minimize unexpected turnover of good people.

STAFF REDUCTIONS

"Staff reductions because I trained and hired them, but everyone understood it was due to the economy"..."Staff down-sizing"..."Redundancy period as it was visible as many seats were empty – but now all is OK"..."Beginning of crisis was very busy with changes of staff"..."Reduction of staff and second wave of reductions"..."People writing this is my last day letters"..."Crisis/redundancies as nobody knew what tomorrow would bring for themselves and colleagues"..."Reduction of colleagues because we were great friends with them – but have no doubt we will grow again"... "Need to improve high stress due to fears of being fired; need to create more stability"

Redundancies impact everyone: both the people leaving and the people staying. We were fortunate to have a sensitive and supportive management group and team in place. We did what we could to motivate and boost morale and knew we would get through it over time.

There is always a risk in allowing departing staff to write "goodbye letters" to the team they are leaving. These letters may depress the people who receive them. However, not allowing a departing employee to say their goodbyes could have an alternative reaction, and team members could wind up feeling that the management of the company is insensitive to those leaving. This is especially true in our company, where the people are, in general, close to one another and are, overall, quite often endearing and heartfelt toward one another.

Employees want:

- A stable economy that does not negatively impact the status quo;
- An office with filled seats and not one strewn with half empty workstations;
- To avoid receiving and reading goodbye letters from colleagues who have been made redundant and are leaving the company due to purely economic reasons (as this is a real downer to remaining staff who are likely friends with these people and may worry about their fate and chances in successfully finding new employment), and
- To feel stability.

TOUGH ECONOMY

"Frustrating is hard work and little results right now, even candidates declining offers"…"The crisis – hard to cold call and lots of 'No' responses and slow sales"…"Started with the company at the beginning of the crisis and it was hard to get it going"…"Did not make bonus, thought I could but had 2 cancelled invoices so I lost earning an extra $5,000"

Recruitment is typically hit very hard during times of major economic contraction. We were not different - our revenue decreased 80% and we had to fight and claw to get every little bit of work we did get.

I had to personally cover the financial costs of most of the team we retained during this last downturn, as well as all of the operational expenses. I was happy to do it as long as an effort was put forward by the team and they worked their hardest. Unfortunately, we did have to let go of a few people who, for whatever reason, after a while just refused to even try, and further decided to stop making the obligatory calls to clients. Even if cold calling was not their talent, it needed to be done and those that soldiered through survived and are now thriving again.

Employees want:

- Robust economic conditions and not downturns nor, especially, economic crises.

CORPORATE CORRUPTION

"Our former pharmaceutical/medical Consultant/Director stealing from the company –morals are very important to me"...

On occasion, every company discovers a bad apple in the bunch. In our case, it was our former Pharmaceutical Consultant whom, we discovered, had convinced a few small, local pharmaceutical and medical companies to pay our fees directly into her own personal bank account. We learned about this through the candidates she had placed with them while she was working for us, and unfortunately, we only found out about it as she was leaving us for another recruitment/search firm.

What really annoyed me about this was that, during one of my "Tea with Teri" interviews, a Senior Consultant who had worked in the same room with her told me that for a period of one year before she left, she (the Pharmaceutical Consultant) had continually complained about the company. I asked him, "Well, why didn't you tell someone about it (me or anyone in management) as we could have gotten rid of her a year ago and saved whatever time and financial loss we had now incurred"? He had no answer; maybe it had never crossed his mind, or it had but he just felt he could never act upon it.

This prompted me to make a note about revising our operations manual, induction and on-going trainings to request that everyone be observant about any employee who appears disgruntled with the company, or with anyone within it, and to report such to me or someone else in management. This would obviously help us to identify much sooner anyone whom we should be closely monitoring.

This particular pharmaceutical sector recruiter, who stole from us, was let go two years later from the competing recruitment firm she joined. We were unable to recover any of the money she stole from us, but she will always carry the worst reference from us, should any company ever call me about her performance. Again, most companies discover, on occasion, a bad apple in the cart - and she was ours.

Employees want:

- To work with people that have high morals and values; and
- Companies to more closely check staff for possible corruption, and to immediately fire those they find engaged in it (*TL: I confess that I may be mind-reading here but feel confident that this is wanted*).

INTERNAL COMMUNICATIONS

"To make direct communication channels with certain people – Consultants are tough: tough to motivate them and to get them to communicate"…"Some Consultants are challenging"…"Communication between offices is not as good as it could be, and some of the Directors in the other office keep some positions from us"…

This was a current issue at the time, which we could fix on an individual basis and company-wide. In our business it is important that there is strong communication within offices and between offices. This is an area that should continually be examined.

Based on these replies, I made a note to organize trainings on communication skills for the teams and management in both offices, and to look into the problem of "hoarding" recruitment projects between offices. I also recognized that our operations manual needed to be updated to address both of these concerns, with new policies and rules of working conduct.

Finally, I made a note to organize scheduled conference calls (either phone or Skype) between the management of the offices and between the Consultants and Directors' groups in both offices.

Employees want:

- Improved communication with those they are not communicating well with;
- Fair play: a share of work if it is supposed to be shared;
- Shared information between offices and departments; and
- Focused work and less drama between colleagues.

LANGUAGE SKILLS

"The level of my English"…

This was a good employee and if helping her to improve her English would make her happy (and would obviously benefit the company to some degree) then I thought we should look into that.

English is by far the most popular global business language and it is ubiquitous in our business in Russia. It is quite widely used by many of our clients, especially foreign companies that require correspondence, both written and verbal, be conducted in English.

Employees want:

- To speak, read and write more proficiently in English, in order to better communicate with foreigners; both colleagues and clients, alike.

THE OFFICE

"The office space is average, things need fixing"..."Everything promised came true; no problems – only thing is that Staffwell never moved office – but I think this is a good thing"

The epic and long debate about the office: do we move from our fantastic location, albeit in a somewhat run-down historic building, or stay where we are?

We have been in the same office now for 9 years and have expanded in the building over time: we started with one half of a floor but then expanded to occupy almost two full floors. The building is old and dated and so are the management and staff operating it. Most of us have a love-hate relationship with it. We love the charm and nostalgia, but we also desire the new and modern.

Moving would cost a lot of money in terms of relocation and real estate agency fees, as well as renovation costs, rent and deposits. While I acknowledged their comments, seeing as we were in the midst of a major economic down-turn, I ultimately felt that moving was something we should look into only after the market had recovered and our business was stronger.

I recognize that office space does matter to people and if things need fixing then we need to try to fix them - and if we can make the office better than average then we should try.

Employees want:

- A great new, modern office in an ideal location; and
- Things that are broken in the office to be fixed.

THE WORK

"Cold calling"..."To cover projects in many spheres in the beginning – advise not to have generalist recruiters when they start"..."Start-up of the department as the two who left the company left a big mess"..."Do not like split situations in the company as every time it is a conflict situation and relationships are not good after – I had a bad situation with another Consultant and the tension is still there and feel I was not treated fairly and did not like the behavior of the other Consultant"..."Candidate behavior when there are counter-offers, because it is difficult to influence the process"..."At the beginning it was splits, they were very unfair"..."Assumptions – when you are sure the candidate will be the one but sometimes the reality is different"..."Moving from legal to FMCG [Fast Moving Consumer Goods] – as it was unexpected and done abruptly, I knew nothing about FMCG but got great training and love the team there – it is a much less complicated sector, it is much harder to interview lawyers"

I was really pleased to hear this feedback as perfecting our work and operations is extremely important.

There are many aspects to recruitment. Foremost, we are a sales organization: to clients we sell our recruitment services, and to candidates we sell the job opportunities our clients engage us to fill. Accordingly, we must be highly skilled at finding, screening and interviewing people suitable for the roles proffered by our clients. This requires that we keep high standards in report writing, simultaneously managing numerous multi-faceted projects, and continuously updating databases and CRM systems.

Our priority is to serve our clients and candidates with whom we work. Internally, it is crucial we serve each other, as recruitment involves a lot of project work and working together in pairs or teams is the norm.

To stay the best at what we do, we must always look for ways in which to improve our operations and how we work. These comments are very telling and they show specific opportunities for us to improve upon.

I made immediate notes to consider focusing our new recruiters in one area until they get good at it and learn the business, to look into the fairness of the splits and our systems, and to create a more thoughtful and considerate process when moving people from one department to another (i.e., get their "buy-in" well ahead of time).

Cold calling, candidate issues and difficult interviews are all part of the job for our Directors and Consultants. It is what it is and they are either good at it and enjoy it, or they do not. The best we can do in this situation is to offer more specialized trainings in these areas to make our team more comfortable when handling these aspects of the job.

Employees want:

- To start a job by focusing in one area;
- The company to check that everyone is actively updating the databases - regularly and accurately (so that all company information is securely stored);
- More moderation and fairness on fee splits between colleagues;
- Companies (in this case from recruitment companies) to never counter-offer their resigning employees (*TL: wishful thinking, but highly unlikely*); and
- More involvement in decision making and the process of moving from one departmental role to another.

MANAGEMENT

"The only real problem has been my relationship with the former GM, I tried very hard to improve it but for whatever reason did not manage to do so – I am pleased, however, that I managed to get through what was, at times, the most difficult part of my career to date"..."Our former Commercial Director was crude in meetings"...

I was relieved to hear that these were the only two issues people had with regard to management, within this question, as I was aware of both of them. Our former GM, for some reason, did not like one of our top Directors. Even though both were expats and of the same nationality, our GM just did not like the Director. I suppose that they were just two different people and, sometimes, it really is as simple as that. I am so glad our Senior Director, who mentioned this, did not leave the company in spite of all the tension he endured. He stayed, was loyal and I really appreciate that.

Regarding the former (expat) Commercial Director, he was a somewhat experienced hire, whom we had to let go after 6 months due to poor performance – achieving only around 10% of tasked job responsibilities. His employment ended following a major argument with our GM, who then asked my permission to dismiss him – a request I immediately granted. Subsequently, we found out that he was trying to pitch one of our new clients (brought in by another

Director on the team) a million dollar project where all invoices were to be directed into his personal bank account – all the while being employed by us. He was our second bad apple in the cart.

Fortunately, we were able to stop this action in the proposal stage and our client completely shut him down. We were awarded the business and the client (a global bank with extremely high ethics) eventually became one of our best customers, in terms of revenue, in the following years.

Employees want:

- To be liked, listened to, valued and respected by their management;
- To be treated fairly by management; to be treated as all are treated; and
- To not have disrespectful, crude nor rude people managing them, working with them, or for them.

CHANGE

"Unexpected changes, maybe it is good or not good – but knows this is growth (compensation plan structures)"...

This comment referred to when we changed the compensation plan for our front office team (Directors and Consultants) a few years ago. What is important to note here is that, although this happened several years ago, this person still remembers it, and is still affected by it.

Change can really impact some people more than others. Some people need more attention than others during periods of change, such as deeper explanations and time for questions and answers. I made a note to keep this in mind for this particular person, and for the entire team, in general. I feel that it is always better to explain more, rather than less, and that it is important to allow more time, for those that need it, to understand changes that are occurring.

Employees want:

- Less abrupt changes (i.e., more time and explanation in order to adapt).

GOSSIP

"Gossip spreading about the company selling or folding"…

Since its inception 12 years ago, Staffwell has never even been close to folding and shutting its doors. In fact, up until the time of the recent down-turn, we booked solid and steady growth, in terms of client base, staff, revenue and profitability. Unfortunately, in our case (as with many others), it is often the people that have left us (not coincidentally, those that did not achieve the success they had expected in their new job), that have spread false rumors - most likely out of spite.

With regard to a sale of the company, since 2002 we have been, on occasion, solicited by companies interested in investing or purchasing Staffwell. We may eventually sell the company but, if we do, it will be to the benefit of everyone working for the company at the time, as well as those that join and stay in the interim, and those who stay on after any such transaction.

This is something that should be included in the operations manual and be updated on an annual basis. Namely, that if an employee hears gossip that affects them, they should go right to the top (i.e., me) and ask about it, as I am as honest, open, and straight-forward as they get.

From my side, I decided that I can and will address and update these topics with company staff more often.

Employees want:

- Less false, destructive gossip spreading around the office; and
- To know the truth (*TL: advice - go straight to the source or to the top*).

PROBATION PERIOD

"Start date, as there is a lot to learn quickly"…

I believe that the probation period should be the most arduous time of an employment term. That is, if workers are doing what they are supposed to do during this period. The harder one works during the first three months at a new job, the faster they will get up to speed in their role and the faster they will reach high levels of expertise and success in the company.

My advice to everyone is to always work your absolute hardest at the beginning of every new job you take on. Make it through probation period successfully and be seen by those you work with, and for, as a potential rising star, and then continue to work hard to become, and remain, one of the stars.

Employees want:

- An easy ride sometimes (*TL: but I feel that hard work leading to faster success is far more rewarding*).

TIME MANAGEMENT

"Nothing except getting here on time – but I know I need to do this"...

Timeliness is really important to me. We have given people flex (flexible) hours where appropriate, but they must show up on time for whatever confirmed hours of work have been agreed upon. It can really annoy others working around someone who does not show up on time for their scheduled work hours and it sets a bad example for everyone else working around them.

Employees want:

- To sleep in (*TL: but I don't let them!*).

Chapter 4

What Could You Do Better Or More For The Company If Given The Opportunity?

This was a question where I was expecting everyone to ask for a promotion.

OVERLOADED

"Too many now"..."I have enough on my plate now"..."I have a lot to learn still"...

Fair enough. I do believe that staying focused on present responsibilities, what you are currently doing, and being successful at it, can be a positive thing under certain circumstances.

Employees want:

- Nothing at all sometimes.

NEW SERVICES

"Help with out-staffing – new services creation"..."Out-placement is difficult to get going in this crisis, out-staffing is a new option too and I hope this works"...

I appreciate people that want to develop the company and have creative ideas, as this is how my mind thinks as well. Out-placement (formal job assistance for departing staff that companies sometimes have) was something we did start and sold as a service to companies and individuals, and it was a "feel-good" service during hard times for a lot of people.

Out-staffing (the hosting/transfer of a portion of a company's payroll to another legal entity) was something we went on to create and by one of the managers quoted above. We are developing this as client demand dictates (semi-actively as it is not our core business) and have several clients already.

Employees want:

- To help create, launch and manage new services.

MOTIVATING STAFF

"I worked in consulting before and I have the skills to motivate people to work long hard hours (while having fun), now Consultants skip updates frequently and do not put priority on my vacancies sometimes, also I love the way Maks works, lots of communication – he is a really smart guy"...

I am all for working long, hard hours as this is something I often do myself. Furthermore, I just really enjoy working. However, many people just do not share this drive to the same degree, and I understand that, so I let the first part of the comment ride.

Consultants skipping updates on a frequent basis is not acceptable as this is part of the job that places us a few levels above our competition. The Consultant that is not putting occasional priority on vacancies is something that also needs to be looking into, and a note was made to watch Maks, as it is possible he could develop into a top performer for us.

Employees want:

- To utilize what they feel are their own natural talents and skills; and
- To be given the authority to help others perform better.

SELL - IF SOMEONE WERE DOING THE ACTUAL SELLING FOR ME

"Doing what I can do but could do more cold calling and could do more and better if someone was doing the cold calling for me and the BD [Business Development] team"...

The job is the job. If we had to hire a new sales team to get clients for the current sales team – then we would have to either reduce salaries or put profitability at risk, or both. The top BD performers make good money and there are no caps on earnings. We eventually parted ways with this person as he simply was not "sales material".

Employees want:

- As much assistance as they can get, in order to do their job as best they can; and
- An easier ride, on occasion, at the same salary level.

COLD CALLING

"More cold calling"

This was music to my ears. I think my heart may have even skipped a beat.

Employees want:

- To try harder, and to work harder.

CREATE RESEARCH REPORTS

"I can create industry research; I like it, it is interesting and I come from a higher education background"..."Research, statistics, analysis, critical thinking, IT, can prepare full blown studies"..."Harder to sell right now but would be willing to make market analysis for PR"...

I was pleased to hear this and think it could be very useful for the company. I made notes on everyone interested in doing this.

Employees want:

- To try and help the company in different way, at times.

TRAINING

"I am very strong in conducting sales, I am ready to train all in sales and to share my skills"..."Trainings, anything to help develop the company"..."I can help with training new staff as I was a professional trainer"..."I teach at University in management and HR, and I can teach Staffwell on this"...

This was also great to hear. This is a very easy suggestion to accommodate and it would be highly useful in the development of the team. I made notes on everyone interested in conducting training sessions for the team.

Employees want:

- To train others at what they are good at, and have expertise in; and
- To share their knowledge for the benefit of the company.

HELP MANAGEMENT TO MANAGE

"Help the management to identify what the Directors and Consultants need, want to be the leader in my sectors but do not want to manage, I do not dream about the Commercial Director role, I want to be client-facing, I do like managing my sector team though and want to keep this in place"...

It is very satisfying to hear that some people love the exact role they are in. I also made a note that this person would like to assist management in their role and, as this would motivate him and he is a solid senior performer, we can create opportunities for him to do this.

Employees want:

- To be close to management;
- To help management; and
- Not always to have career aspirations in management.

MANAGEMENT

"I love to manage and build teams, but not to sell, but I can develop sales, I would like to develop the Consultants team to do more and go after top level clients and candidates, to make the team more assertive, to cold call to top level people"..."I believe I have a lot to offer in a sales-oriented leadership role and I believe my career to date supports this, we have discussed this in the past"..."I am an experienced Consultant and would love team leader responsibilities, to train new people and to mentor them"...

Two of the people quoted above were our two top performing business development Directors. They were asking for more and I felt they deserved it. Promoting these two people is something that I took into very serious consideration. In the case of our Commercial Director, she had already stated she was overloaded and it was clear to me that she was.

Employees want:

- To occasionally move into managerial roles (*TL: when they are ready, desire it, and deserve it*).

KEY ACCOUNT MANAGEMENT (KAM)

"I have already taken on an additional sector, but would also like KAM, more client work, but not the sales part of it"..."KAM for some companies –to provide more services to the clients and to be a Director to some clients"..."KAM, BD should focus on sales only and I should focus on dealing with clients and solving clients issues and negotiating with clients and I will even create a proposal and present it to you on it –this will help bring more revenue from the clients we have"...

This issue had been brought up before. Some Consultants want to be assigned a Director role as well, without having to do sales and cold calling. This does not exactly work for me. There is a reason we deliberately separated the two roles: in order to create a system of checks and balances for the client that, in the process, provides, I believe, a superior client service.

Once a week, the Directors monitor progress made by the Consultants, and then provide an update to the client. At the same time, the Directors check if there are any issues that the client may have about internal matters or with our work.

Having just explained my views on a combined role, I did listen to the comments and took into consideration what was desired: primarily, that the Consultant's team would like to introduce an official Key Account Manager role and title. This would create the most senior role within the team of Recruitment Consultants. While having some reservations, I decided that I needed to take this issue seriously, and to work with our management team to come up with a potential solution whereby we could continue to provide our customers with same, if not better, quality of service.

Employees want:

- To work more with clients;
- To help clients more; and
- To give clients better service.

BETTER CLIENT SERVICE

"I always try to do the best, and try to provide the best service to clients and candidates"...

My reaction: wonderful.

Employees want:

- To give clients better service.

MENTOR

"Mentor"…"I can also be a coach or mentor for new staff"…

This was great to hear and I noted this person's interest.

Employees want:

- To mentor staff in areas in which they have expertise.

HELPING THE TEAM

"Helping other departments when people are on holiday"…

I thought this was a good response as well, and I noted this person's interest in doing this.

This was a topic that I decided I needed to look into further, in terms of policies and other areas covered in our Operations Manual. This is because it is crucial to our business that clients receive a seamless approach when we render services to them, and that full coverage is always in place when our team members are absent, for example, on holiday or are ill.

Of course we do this now and have in the past, but it brought to my mind whether any of this had actually been formalized.

Employees want:

- To help the company, and other team members, by covering for them when they are on holiday or are ill.

LANGUAGE SKILLS

"Speaking French to clients and candidates, but not comfortable as a full-time focus as it is a little rusty"…

The Consultant replying here is willing to help, which is good. However, in this particular case, I thought we had to take a pass, as I felt her confidence level and abilities were insufficient.

Employees want:

- To help the company by using their foreign language skills.

COMBINATION ROLE

"Business development – doing more of it; Stas was a good example of a good recruiter and negotiator and attracted some of his own clients, he got to know all the candidates in his sector and I want to do this too; to become an expert Consultant and BD in my sector or other sectors, plus KAM and I want to be seen as a star and perfect mentor to be looked up to, to be a universal person and a future goal is to get an MBA at a Western business school"..."I want more responsibility to take on BD too, a combined role"..."I was given the opportunity to work in an additional sector and I acted as the client's Consultant and Director"..."I work well with clients and would also be interested in BD for my sector"..."I now try to do research to help the Consultants, I just started and I like it"..."I now have a lot of work and a lot of planned work, but think I can develop clients by going to PR/marketing/advertising conferences as I am a good negotiator, and to be involved with the website and new things"...

I was very happy to hear that many within our recruitment team also wanted to try their hand at sales - in order to help the company and to develop themselves. I have always provided this opportunity to everyone and was pleased that some felt they were ready.

Nonetheless, the reality is that some of the people above who mentioned this to me never summoned the nerve to actually dive in and do it, as they were encouraged to do. Instead, they just kept to their standard work that they had always been doing and chose to remain in their comfort zone. Having said that, I do believe that there is nothing wrong with employees staying within the confines of their assigned work (i.e., to the status quo). This is because the way in which our Directors and Consultants presently work is equally important to the success of our business.

I am pleased to note that one of our Consultants, who did indeed follow-through on her ambitions to take on a combined role, has really done a fantastic job in helping to develop and maintain a very strong industry practice group for us. We encouraged and supported her efforts along the way and we have all benefited from the success that has come from it.

Employees want:

- To take on more.

BETTER RESULTS

"I could do more if the Directors brought more retained, exclusive searches"..."My sector is very slow right now so I will go after in-house positions and focus on another sector and get the Directors to call into their clients for in-house positions I can close, and get our PR person to search for new vacancies and get the Consultant I work with to help me input candidates I have interviewed"..."Maybe close different vacancies in more lucrative areas"..."Contact ex-candidates and find out where they are right now and try to get them as clients as it might be easier for me to do this than BD"..."I can find leads from candidates I interview"...

This was great to hear: employees with concrete ideas and plans on how to get more business in difficult market times. Many of these strategies were successfully employed.

One of our success stories within this topic has been our legal sector team. Most of our recruitment work prior to the 2008 crisis was on behalf of law firms operating in the market. As many of our legal firm clients decreased, or even curtailed, hiring in 2009-2010, we instead re-directed, with great success, our energy on locating and placing openings for lawyers at corporations within industry sectors.

Within law firms, we focused on placing Partners capable of creating a valid business plan and bringing a book of business and team members with them. This also proved successful for us.

Our incumbent legal sector business, along with a focus on the two new angles within our legal recruitment sector, enabled us to more than double our results in this sector.

Employees want:

- More clients on a retained and exclusive basis; and
- To try a variety of strategies to enhance their success, as well as that of the company.

NOTHING

"I am quite satisfied with my role right now"...

This person left us within a month.

Employees want:

- Nothing sometimes, which could also be a red flag.

SPECIALIZE

"I really like executive search projects, preparing reports, etc. and I had two major ones that I closed successfully"... "I am an accountant in my soul so I would like to stay in that and keep improving and moving higher"

There was nothing to act upon here. It was just nice to know that some people really liked what they were doing.

Employees want:

- To focus in areas they enjoy and are good at.

NEW ROLE

"I like my job but would also like to try being a Consultant or Director, but know my English is not great"..."Our former HR [Human Resources person] *offered me, as an idea, a Consultant's role as a career growth area, so maybe I could do research for a sector team and eventually become a Consultant"...*

Indeed, both of the people commented above are good in the roles they have and would, potentially, be good as Consultants as well. I noted their desires and committed to speak to our management team about them for future consideration.

Employees want:

- To change roles on occasion (*TL: and if they are a good employee it can potentially be beneficial for everyone*).

Chapter 5

What Extra Responsibility Would You Welcome, That You Were/Are Not Given?

I was expecting some overlap here from some of the previous responses, which would confirm some things already mentioned, but I also believed that some further probing might bring some new insights as well.

OPENING NEW OFFICES

"In the future I would love to be completely involved in growing our branches – and organize everything"…

This was pleasing to hear from this person, as we are going to expand in the future and she has been an asset to our current branch expansion. Thus, I feel that her contribution to our future branch office growth will be essential.

Employees want:

- To be directly involved in their company's geographical growth.

NONE

"Too many now"…"Have enough on my plate with BD and running the office and opening new services"…"Prefer not to expand now"…"None, very busy"…"Currently have enough and supposed to have, but also with Elena trying to help them with lead generation by internet searches"…"Now I have BD responsibilities added on, so I feel I have enough"…"All is OK as it is"…"I have enough"…"I now have new additional responsibilities during the crisis, I have enough"…"We have a small department, so all is done"…"Now all is fine, in the future maybe can take on more – after crisis, or manage and event, conference or breakfast"…

Being busy is good, so I was glad to hear that so many people were content. However, I made a mental note about those that appear too busy from prior comments. In addition, I discerned that two people had begun to show a pattern of just not caring much at all about anything, and had consistently given neutral answers to the questions posed thus far.

Employees want:

- No additional responsibilities, sometimes.

INDIFFERENT

"Responsibilities just come"...

I felt this was somewhat of a boring, safe answer. However, this is fine, as it takes many types of people to form an overall very good team

Employees want:

- Sometimes, whatever they are given.

TRAINING

"Trainings for new or existing team members, or to participate in this; can also do insurance industry info session"..."I am very strong in conducting sales and I am ready to train all in sales, to share my skills"..."Never trained before but open to trying it, although not sure I would be good"..."To train or teach"...

Training is always needed and, in addition to helping further develop people, it adds something exciting and interesting to one's typical daily role - for both the trainer and the trainees.

Again, I was thrilled that our team wants to help the company by training others in areas in which they feel they are strong and where they can add value.

Employees want:

- To train others in areas in which they themselves have expertise.

ANYTHING

"Anything"…"Able to help with anything"…"I am always developing here, Angela tasked us all to get payments from clients, to cover for each other, to update our CRM and our finance database, and HR administration, I really like getting all these jobs, and doing the visas, I am open to new work"…

These were very encouraging answers in the sense that people are willing to take on anything they can or are offered, to help the company. I made a note on each of them for the future and their availability and attitude.

Employees want:

- To help the company in any way they can, as needed.

OPERATIONS

"Operations manual and systems review and overhaul"…

A perceptible pattern began to develop, based on this and previous responses, with this person, who was a good Director - but also had obvious interests in all things IT and systems-related. This was good to know and might be useful.

Employees want:

- To help in areas in which they have a personal interest.

INTERNAL RECRUITMENT

"Deciding who gets hired – working with the internal recruitment process"…"Screen candidates for internal Staffwell positions"…

For me, this was a great answer as our success really depends on who we have on our team, whether they fit in and if they can perform beyond expectations in their role. The interview process is crucial to getting it right most of the time.

I was very happy to hear that some of our team members really wanted to help ensure that we hire only the best people possible.

Employees want:

- To be directly involved in the internal recruitment process and decisions on who gets hired into the team; and
- Only the very best people to be hired.

PROFESSIONAL GROWTH

"All is good, would be interested in my growth plan"..."Should an opportunity arise in the future to be Commercial Director or General Director, I would welcome the challenge with open arms. You are one of the few people in my career that I have not been able to convince that this could be a good idea. I am not sure why and would welcome your thoughts"..."Assist the Consultants so that I can start learning that job and eventually move into it myself"...

Within this topic, the patterns are also clear - as they have been touched on in earlier questions: two people feel they are ready to be promoted and one is gearing up for it. That is good and good to know.

Timing has a lot to do with promotions. First, there has to be a vacancy or a need for a position to be created. Then, in order for there to be a promotion from within the company, there have to be people considered to be suitable, proven, and capable.

I felt that all three of these people were probably ready and deserving, so I made notes on all of them to later prompt me into looking into potential promotions for them.

Employees want:

- To grow professionally and move up within the company; and
- To be rewarded for good work and loyalty.

ANALYTICAL REPORTS

"Harder to sell now but would be willing to make analysis on the market for PR [Public Relations] and create analytical services for clients"..."I can provide great analysis, I am a great chess player"...

Once again, this was very useful information as PR was one of our new focus areas.

I also loved learning that one of our top Consultants was a great chess player. I grew up learning and playing board games, including chess, so I immediately wanted to play her (although I knew she would likely crush me). This particular person was one of our best producing Consultants: extremely focused, serious, and quietly competitive. I do not think it would harm us to consider hiring other avid chess players, as they, hopefully, will possess the same traits as the chess-playing Consultant we have now.

Learning about her hobby was a catalyst in my desire to learn about everyone's hobbies at some point in the future.

Employees want:

- To use their untapped skills.

NEW SERVICES

"Be a part of the management team to create new services if the market needs it"..."I would like to be involved in out-placement or new services"...

Anything new that would, or could potentially, be successful is exciting to me, which made it easy for me to understand their desires. However, what may be fun to create, may not always be successful or profitable for the company. I acknowledged their interest at the time and noted that they may be useful, where appropriate, in the future.

Employees want:

- To help with the creation and roll-out of new services.

KEY ACCOUNT MANAGEMENT (KAM)

"I have already taken on Pharma, but also KAM – more client work, but not sales"..."KAM for some companies - to provide more services to the company and to be a Director for some clients"..."KAM role, to work with clients directly, but does not want to do BD"..."BD, client work as an add-on, but not cold calling, but more client management, sometimes there are misunderstandings between the Director, client and the Consultant, so there are more communications between the client and the Director instead of the Consultant and the client"...

Here we go again: the desire to have Key Account Management without having to take on cold calling/sales responsibilities. As mentioned before, this slightly conflicted with our operational structure. However, at the time it seemed, on the surface, relatively easy to re-configure such a structure so that it would benefit all. This issue and how to make it happen with a balanced solution really sent my mind racing.

Without question, the team expressed a huge demand to create the KAM role, indicating to me how important an issue it was for them. So much so, that not only did I have to just acknowledge this desire but also really spend energy on what the specifics of the role would be and when it would be created and implemented. This was something to work on, and carefully decide upon, in order not to undermine the incumbent structure's advantages but, also, appease the demands of the employees.

Employees want:

- To give clients the best service they can;
- To have a maximum share in the most interesting parts of the job; and
- To grow and develop.

TEAM LEADER

"Satisfied right now, but in future to share experiences with new hires, to be a team leader motivating them"..."Would like to be a team leader, teach new team members, mentor and then be responsible for them"..."I think we do not need team leaders, only mentors"..."Increase activity of Consultants, leading them, coming up with better processes for them and to be more professional"...

Here is another pattern that was readily identified and is easy to implement. I do believe this would be highly beneficial for the team and company.

I am really impressed with the number of employees that want to train and mentor other staff members. To me it shows real team spirit and willingness, with selfless desire, to want to help others.

In most sales organizations, including ours, team members are always competing for the top spots, the highest numbers and the best results (KPIs). The replies to this question, and to other previous questions, make it clear to me that the great majority within our team cares deeply about our company, its growth and success, and not just their own personal aims. I am quite touched by this.

Employees want:

- To train, mentor, supervise, and lead new employees.

INDUCTIONS

"Induction trainings"...

Properly inducting employees, and in a quick manner, is an extremely important part of our success. If we can make someone happy through their participation (albeit, likely limited) in our induction process, which may also benefit the company, I see no reason not to do so.

I made a note to follow up with the potential inclusion of some employees into the induction trainings.

Employees want:

- To help introduce new staff to the company.

MORE WORK

"I can take on more vacancies, now it is boring and I like to be overloaded"...

With this employee, I felt sincere empathy as I also love to be busy and stretched to the limits of my capabilities - that is why I make sure that I always am. However, in this case, there was not a lot I could do at the time given the slowdown in our business which, in turn, was attributable not to our performance but to the recession that adversely impacted hiring and our industry. Only an economic recovery, which takes time, will remedy the situation and help allow this employee to work at the rate she so desires.

However, as this was a very good producing employee, I did make a note to speak to management about the possibility of re-directing some of the upcoming vacancy distributions toward her.

Employees want:

- To be busy; and
- To have a lot of work.

MARKETING-RELATED ACTIVITIES

"Organizing exhibitions, round table organization, assisting marketing"...

I believe, once again, that it would not take much effort on the company's part to include this person, who is part of the recruitment team, in a future marketing-related meeting. I made a note to do so. I see little downside in this as she may have some great ideas or, perhaps, just lend solid organizational skills to the efforts of the department. This is a very small gesture, and in turn, we would likely make a team member happy.

Employees want:

- To be involved in marketing-related activities.

TEAM-BUILDING

"I used to make a Staffwell newsletter and loved this, maybe for a team-building event we can do this again"...

I thought this was a good idea and it was one that I had recently been thinking about myself. It is a no-cost endeavor, if done electronically, save for a few hours of everyone's time throughout the year. As it does bring everyone together in a fun way, I agreed that this can be seen as a team-building activity.

Employees want:

- To bring fun, team-related activities to daily work-life, on occasion.

Chapter 6

How Can The Company Enable You To Make Fuller Use Of Your Capabilities And Potential?

I thought this was a good question as it attempts to uncover the problems the company might have that may be limiting people from performing better.

FREEDOM AND TRUST

"Now I have everything, even in this crisis with the salary default, what is important that I have freedom to create things, to open new offices and I can save us money"..."I am self-motivated, just for the management to trust me more, to let me fly more"...

The two people commenting here are valuable assets to the company. If it would help them develop more trust, respect and faith in their abilities, and in what they can achieve for the company, then I feel we need to provide them more space for creativity.

In addition, I believe that these two people were, in their own way, telling me that they were motivated to do and achieve more for the company. I took this as only good news and I am excited to see their potential developed.

Employees want:

- To be trusted;
- To be given more room to grow;
- To have less management controls on them when they are not needed; and
- To prove to management that they can make significant contributions without help.

IMPROVE OPERATIONS

"Our CRM needs to be improved and full documentation written on it, there is a useless function on reporting on statistics, update the operations manual"..."Anything! Participation in operations (operations manual and systems review and overhaul, and training, IT training not sales training, I can analyze if it is effective or not effective and I can make content of tracking programs and make them into measurable results"...

Fantastic! I am a true believer in strong operations so I support ideas people may have to enhance them. Operations need to be constantly improved, as they can become quickly outdated. We try our best, like most companies do, but realize it is a never-ending task.

For me, these were very useful answers as they gave specific areas of improvement that we can work on, fix, or implement. I made notes to follow-up on these issues and to include those commenting here in the process.

Employees want:

- Strong, optimally-efficient operations; and
- To help with operational improvements.

TEAM

"The team needs to be motivated and developed"...

I believe this to always be the case. This quote is from a top manager, indicating, I believe, what she personally needs to focus on to achieve success for the company and for herself.

I notice a pattern in her answers which I find interesting. She never answers in terms of herself. Rather, she focuses on the team and what we need to do to improve team members so that the company improves. These are very selfless, big picture answers and, to me, indicative of good leadership and executive management qualities.

Employees want:

- Employees to always be the best they can be.

STATUS QUO

"The new office and new services that we have now"…"I asked for a cold-calling room and got it"…

I was glad to know that these staff members felt taken care of.

The new office referred to here was in Saint Petersburg, where we down-sized into a smaller, but nicer office space. The new services were related to out-placement and gave our staff a brand new project to focus on and sell to clients amidst a slow market.

I personally like an open-plan office as I think it promotes teamwork, accountability and a group-bonding environment. However, it can get loud at times when everyone is talking on the phone or with each other. The cold calling room was requested to enable the team to occasionally have private, quiet, important discussions, when needed, with clients or candidates with whom they are working.

Employees want:

- What they ask for;
- On occasion, privacy - for important business calls; and
- Nothing at times, because all may be fine just as it is.

THE OFFICE

"My current seating location is not great and the room is too stuffy for me and hot and there is not enough light"

This is an easy aspect to fix and look into immediately, especially as it is a one-person issue.

Some staff members have specific issues that many others do not. This person was sitting in one of our smaller, darker rooms with a window looking out onto trees. Many people like that environment as it is cozy and quiet. However, she did not. Therefore, I immediately approved moving her to our largest and brightest room, which made her happy.

Employees want:

- A comfortable work station and environment.

EQUIPMENT

"A lighter laptop"...

All of our Directors use company laptops to give presentations to clients. We are the only company in our local industry that does this and it does differentiate us in terms of professionalism. However, the laptops became a bit dated and heavy, which can make it overly cumbersome for some of the female members in our Directors' team.

This was a high-ticket replacement item for us at that time but something we still needed to consider as the team's happiness and comfort is directly related to their performance.

Employees want:

- Equipment that is easy to handle and use.

TELEMARKETER/RESEARCHER

"Maybe have telemarketer/researcher to make me more productive as they can give me the names of people to call on"...

I agree with this suggestion as anything that can make us more productive is something we should look into.

We have never hired a person to simply collect names for the sales team as the Directors are responsible for this, as part of their defined role. However, this is worth considering and, perhaps, trying in order to see if we can increase our revenues.

Employees want:

- Assistance, in order to be more productive themselves and for the company.

TRAINING/DEVELOPING OTHERS

"Trainings for new or existing team members, or to participate in this and can also do an industry info session"..."Again, I am very good in sales and can train everyone in this, I am ready to share my talent with everyone"..."I can develop talents of others to provide better service"...

These comments came from three Directors and Consultants that are very good at what they do, and are high-level performers. It is encouraging that they are offering their time and talent to train others so that we may develop a better team and a better company.

I firmly believe that the best trainers can often be the talent within your own company. This is especially the case when they are training others about a role or task which they, themselves, already do very well. I made notes to take all three of these people up on their offer to help train others in the team.

Employees want:

- To train others, in their areas of expertise; and
- To share their knowledge to help the company perform better.

GETTING TRAINING

"Getting help on writing highlights, using the database, etc."...

This is someone asking for help in specific areas and I think it is great that this person wants to improve. I made a note to immediately follow up on this.

Employees want:

- To perfect their skills; and
- Training to improve their job performance.

CAREER DEVELOPMENT

"All is good, I would be interested in my growth plan"...

It is very clear that this person strongly desires, in a polite way, upward movement in the company - as she has mentioned this a few times in her responses. As I feel she is good at what she does, is smart and is respected within the team, I decided that I would definitely give consideration to her future career trajectory within the company.

Employees want:

- To grow and develop with the company.

MORE TIME FOR SALES

"I feel that the best use of my skills and experience is in front of clients and senior managers, presenting, selling and negotiating on behalf of the company, I enjoy this side of the job immensely. If I could be in front of clients more often I believe we would all benefit"...

This Director commenting is very good in front of clients and he just keeps getting better at it every year. There is a fair amount of administration that goes with the role of Director; all of which is quite necessary. However, I feel that the company would indeed benefit if this person was in front of clients more often.

This Director, in his prior submissions, is also seeking a sales management role, which I think makes sense as he is deserving and talented, and would necessitate that he be in the field with the team more often.

Employees want:

- To focus on what they do well; and
- To specialize in their areas of expertise.

ANALYSIS

"It is harder to sell now so I would be willing to create analytical reports for PR purposes and for clients"...

Employees need to feel useful, even in down-market times. I believe this person probably could create a very good analytical report containing recruitment-related information, such as compensation and benefits surveys, industry-specific analyses and market trends. I made a note to take action on this.

Employees want:

- To use other talents they have, and are not using, to benefit the company.

NEW SERVICES

"I would like to be a part of the management team to create new services, if the market needs it"...

Creating new services is a lot of fun at times so I understand this person's interest. Having said that, I am not sure if we are going to create any more new services in the nearest future as, at the moment, I am leaning more toward focusing on our core business areas. However, we do occasionally explore the idea and I made a note of this person's interest and potential participation.

Employees want:

- To be creative and to build and develop new products for the company.

KEY ACCOUNT MANAGEMENT

"Already taking on another sector, also KAM, more client work, but not sales, same as before, more opportunities to meet clients, KAM and trainings"..."KAM role"...

We do not have Key Account Managers, per se. We have Directors that sell, oversee client recruitment projects, update clients on our progress, and handle any issues that may arise during the course of a search. Our Consultants source, screen and present candidates to our clients, arrange client candidate interviews and assist with the negotiation process when job offers are extended. Both roles are extremely vital to providing our clients with a very thorough service.

It is clear to me from these responses, and those in earlier chapters, that the Consultants' team, overall, would really like a Key Account Management role created for their division.

As before, I made a note to look into this. Again, this requires some thought and a strategy in regard to potentially changing our current role structure, compensation elements and parameters - but I feel it is certainly worth considering.

Employees want:

- To provide better services to clients;
- To have more access to the company's clients; and
- To get out of the office, on occasion, and visit clients.

BUSINESS DEVELOPMENT

"Attracting new clients via candidate relations"...

This was an encouraging answer as it came from a Consultant who, while not responsible for new client sales, nonetheless is offering to assist with our sales efforts. I would point out that candidates are a great source of client leads: both from within the company they may currently work for, and from interviews they have with other companies in the market who are hiring.

Employees want:

- To help the company develop more business.

NONE

"I always use my full potential, even now during this crisis I am busy"..."All is fine"..."Staffwell has given me a lot of opportunity to grow and I am very happy with this, I have all I need"..."Nothing"..." Nothing needed"..."The company gives me new responsibilities and Angela often gives me new work when the accounting rules change"..."All is used now"..."We respect the staff a lot, there is no discrimination, I feel very comfortable at Staffwell, I am happy and will do anything to help"..."The chance you gave me to come back to the company is doing that"..."Now I am stimulated and it is important that people like my work and I am now working from 95 to 99%. The PR Director title was important for me and so was the salary increase, as it made me feel needed and appreciated"...

A lot of staff and management answered they were content with what they had and where they were right now. This showed me that, overall, we were doing pretty well in terms of employee motivation, and there was a fairly high satisfaction rate among the group.

Employees want:

- To be where they are already are, sometimes, and to have what they already possess.

HELPING

"I am able to help with anything"

I thought this was a great answer as it illustrates an attitude that I appreciate in employees. I noted this person's availability to assist with anything, and that I may use them, where appropriate.

Employees want:

- To help the company in any way they can, or as needed.

PAID SERVICES

"I would like to try up-grading my LinkedIn account in order to post vacancies"...

I think this is a reasonable idea. I am willing to try anything, within reason, that might help us increase business. LinkedIn is a very useful business tool for networking as one can see the career history of those within your contact base, and it is fairly easy to connect with people that you may otherwise not meet or become acquainted with.

We would pay for up-grading this person's LinkedIn account to see what the potential benefits are. If they are positive, then we will consider up-grading more of the accounts for our front office team.

Employees want:

- To try new avenues that may help enhance company results.

NETWORKING EVENTS AND CONFERENCES

"I would like to try networking events, but to go with someone else for the first time, the only thing that I know in theory is personal networking, I've never done professional networking but I think I could do it"..."I would like to participate in finance conferences, to understand the business and sector better"...

These comments are from two Consultants that are interested in advancing themselves, for which I can only have respect.

Professional networking, at business club events or at conferences, is a vital part of our business success and it does take practice in order to attain a certain comfort level. Most everyone we meet at such events may become a client or candidate; now, or at some point in the future. Accordingly, I decided that I needed to look into this for the first Consultant commenting above, as well as for others.

The second Consultant quoted recruits mainly finance professionals, such as Chief Financial Officers, Finance Directors and Chief Accountants. It would likely be beneficial to her and others in her sector, to attend a finance conference or meeting to better understand the sector - and also to meet potential candidates, or clients, they might not otherwise have known about.

Employees want:

- To try new avenues to help increase their results for the company; and
- To push themselves out of their comfort zone, on occasion.

EDUCATION

"I would also like additional education in HR"...

Unfortunately, for this particular person, this is something we are unwilling to offer. She is not currently in an HR position within our company and has never performed in an HR Management role. Furthermore, the cost of the program is not a minor issue to us, especially during this period of economic weakness.

In this situation, should this person really want an HR education leading to an HR Management role, I believe that she should attend night courses at her own expense. She may get much more satisfaction in having done it all through her own efforts.

Having said all that, I may consider mobilizing our own HR Manager to give some general HR training to the team, including to this person, to promote better understanding of the role that many of our clients have in their companies.

Employees want:

- Things that sometimes have nothing to do with their role;
- To enhance their education; and
- What they are unable to get, sometimes, or with their current employer.

MORE WORK/WIDER SCOPE OF WORK

"More positions"…"Take part in new projects or trainings or to work in other sectors, wider work"…"I am pro-active, I suggested to Nadya that I work with clients and I do now, I am open to anything the company gives me, plus I also act as the help desk guy for the office"…"I like very difficult recruitment assignments, or to work in Marketing"…"I would like to be given help with recruitment tasks, to get used to it"…

When the work-load is too light and people are under-utilized in their jobs, additional work and loading people up can, I feel, only benefit the employees and the company. I acknowledged this in the comments and requests above.

The very last comment above came from one of our receptionists. I further asked her whether she had ever been given any tasks from other departments to work on while she performs her reception duties. She replied that she does not get any requests for work or any offers to contribute, where appropriate and needed.

I was quite surprised to hear this. I then asked if she knew what her direct reporting line was and the manager to whom she is subject to – to which she replied that she did not.

I immediately sorted out both issues. I assigned her a direct report and instructed the recruitment team to give her some of their administrative work to do, to aid them – but also to help develop her.

As organized as you may think your company is, I believe that you always need to walk around and check to see if it really is that way. An even more effective method, I feel, is to have one-on-ones with your staff, as I have obviously done in this case.

Employees want:

- More work, if not over-burdened, and to be busy;
- Challenging work and to try different roles; and
- To be developed for growth positions.

ACCESS TO MANAGEMENT

"Working closely with Directors and Management team in all offices as we grow"...

This person would like to work more closely with our Directors' team and management, which could mean that one day he will also strive to be a member of one of those teams – or, perhaps, he may simply enjoy their company.

Regardless, I made a note to have Directors and management engage this person more and, out of curiosity, I also made a note to observe this person's career progression over the next few years.

Employees want:

- Closer relations and access to more senior members of the company; and
- To be a part of the geographical growth of the company.

Chapter 7
What Training Did You Like Or Need That You Did Not Get, And What Effect Would This Have?

I firmly believe that training is crucial to the success of our business. Accordingly, this was a question for which I was really looking for insightful answers.

PROFESSIONAL DEGREE/CERTIFICATION

"An ACCA degree is interesting, there are 14 steps and I have completed 1"…"In 1 year maybe get an MBA"…"External training would be management, I partly started an MBA at University, I would like to stay in a sales direction but also manage teams and processes"…"I now have no money myself to get accounting qualifications, but I would love this in the future"…"I understand Staffwell and our systems, but in the future I would like to be trained in systems administration"…

I am very much in favor of people getting advanced education and degrees. However, as an owner and CEO I have to take into consideration that there is a time and cost commitment involved that may not always benefit the company. Furthermore, the company may not garner any specific benefit from the learned expertise - unless such skills are targeted to our needs and the person stays with the company, which is impossible to guarantee.

At times, I have been really torn on this issue. On the other hand, sponsoring advanced degree candidates improves their skills and education, for which I completely support. In the event that someone you sponsored may leave your company, it is just as easy to hire someone new that has an advanced degree that was sponsored by another company. Therefore, in this sense it seems to balance out. However, the underlying factor remains: whether it is beneficial for our company (as opposed to the entire industry) to sponsor employees for advanced degrees. In general, I have to say that it usually does not make sense for us, given the cost-benefit analysis; however, I do feel it would be worth the risk at times, if the candidate is right.

Our Finance Director would like to get her ACCA (Association of Chartered Certified Accountants) qualification. I will fully support this financially and allow her the additional time off required, as she is top-rate and has been a loyal and highly-talented founding member of our company. Our St. Petersburg accountant would also like to advance her qualifications and this will be supported as well. Supporting loyal and great employees where there is a clear benefit for the company, like in the financial department, makes sense and is an easy decision to approve.

More generalized advanced degrees are harder to assess in terms of cost-benefit trade-off and risk. In the past, we have provided financial support to two employees pursing MBAs. Without doubt, these people have grown intellectually and in their confidence and abilities. However, our company could have benefited more from their improved knowledge and skills. This is not a condemnation of these individuals as much as it is a criticism of the nature of the MBA programs themselves.

Most MBA programs, I feel, are too theoretical in nature. Neither program attended by these two applied enough practical exercises that could have been useful to our company and, I am sure, many other companies like ours. For example, we would have benefitted greatly from a simple exercise such as "write down 3 things that are wrong in your company today; aspects that need improvement; and, as a group, work through them and then later present the proposed solutions to your company for their consideration". I believe that practical training would really benefit the students and the companies paying for these programs. When these practical trainings do not take place, the companies that sponsor such programs inevitably call into question their usefulness, and I am no different.

In a sales-oriented, people-centered business, such as Staffwell, the need to have employees with MBA-level skills is always going to be limited. For those employees that we consider to be executive management material, where MBA-level skills would be beneficial to our top management corps and to the company, I am willing to consider financial sponsorship. However, within this limited number I would still only consider it only if they worked for us, concurrently, on a part-time basis. I feel this would help ensure that their focus would not be completely on their studies while they were working. This may also mean that their role might be somewhat altered while they were getting their MBA but, in these ways, I feel that the company would enhance its chances of getting more out of sponsoring such programs.

In our hiring process, we look favorably on candidates who already possess advanced degrees, but it is not the degree alone that triggers our decision. Along with many factors, it depends on the practical skills such a degree may have in our workplace.

Employees want:

- To further their professional qualifications;
- To further their professional education; and
- To be the best they can be.

FOR SALES PERSONNEL

"Tough negotiations for our Directors"…"Selling techniques"…"Albert's networking training"…"Diana's training about how to work with clients"…"Interview skills and how to assess good candidates"…"Learn more about the Consultants' job and more tips"…"Internal sector info, industry info like structures, general trends for banking, insurance, and FMCG, just brief, not very detailed, maybe interview other executives"…"Effective negotiations and proper interview skills"…"Professional presentation skills such as when to lead and when to pause, time management, public speaking and getting confidence to do this"…"Project management and networking –especially with expats, sales training and stress negotiations"…"I am not very comfortable interviewing people outside of my FMCG comfort zone and rely purely on technique (open questions) to get by, I am also not good at taking the information and then writing highlights from them, Staffwell Advance training with you would be very helpful"…"Hard stress negotiations and quick negotiations, Nina gave one but it was not strong, and time management training, steps in time management techniques"…

This was extremely useful information for me. These answers told me exactly what our sales team wanted and needed. That is, instead of management always deciding what required training people need and should be given, it would likely be more beneficial to provide the team with what they feel would actually be useful for them. The comments also indicated which people were already good trainers within our company, and those with training skills and methods that are not as useful, or need to be improved.

I also found it interesting that our sales team expressed a desire to receive training about the role of our Consultants' team. Providing this, I believe, can only benefit the group overall.

I made notes to look into each and every area mentioned and to focus on creating new or improved trainings in the following areas:

Employees (BD and Sales Personnel) want:

- Tough, stressful, fast and effective negotiations;
- Selling techniques;
- Networking;
- Working with clients/client management;
- Interview skills;
- How to assess good candidates;
- Industry information (including corporate structures and organizational charts);
- Presentation skills;
- Time management;
- Public speaking;
- Project management;
- Working with foreigners and expats;
- Writing quality candidate interview notes/highlights; and
- People management/team management (*TL: taken from the first set of answers*).

FOR CONSULTANTS

"Different interview techniques for our Consultants"…"Sales, negotiation skills and how to get candidates to leave their companies"…"Cold calling and headhunting (clients and top candidates)"…"Sales training, negotiations with clients and selling services; to have more strength with clients, but I do not want to be a Director"…"Financial courses or seminars to learn more about the sector, attend conferences in finance"…"All trainings are useful, on the market, the job, and Albert's trainings are fantastic"…"Networking at conferences (OTJ), I had Albert's training but did not love it as I did not feel it was constructive – there was a ton of info but I did not retain it as it was not structured and was not consistent. Polina's training on how to interview candidates was very good as it was structured. Albert's training had a music box with different music playing? Shadow training for networking would be the best. I went with Eva but it was not helpful as I already knew a lot of the people there and we split up – shadowing is needed. I want to be proficient with contracts so more training with Angela on weaknesses we can meet when negotiating with a client, how to succeed, what areas of the contract we can negotiate, all types of contracts, I want to know all"…"Handling different communications and negotiations, communicating with mature, strong and overbearing people, working under stress and stress management"…"Time management probably, I have already passed this training but from my point of view this training should be held like once in half a year or something because this is really useful, but mostly as time goes by we again start forgetting these

issues"..."I already had a lot of training but using the internet for complex searches, selling to big companies, getting business from people you don't know, cold calling and sales techniques"..."Cold calling and networking"..."Additional sales training"..."Need trainings on how to assess candidates better, maybe with an external training company, we do formal interviews at Staffwell but we miss a lot of points in our interviews (real leadership capabilities of candidates are hard to figure out). Talent development, assessments and competitive interviews"..."Business development, negotiations with clients"..."Client communications as this will give more confidence to me and help me grow"..."I don't think I need training in recruitment, but training on management, motivating people, and building strong teams"..."Negotiation skills!"...

Once again, this was great to learn as it becomes crystal clear what the needs and interests are. I also found it interesting that there was a confirmed desire from our Consultants' team for training regarding the roles of the sales teams. I believe that this is something that will also benefit the company (as in the case of cross-training the sales team): that is, for the Consultants to also be fully well-rounded members of staff – some of whom may even develop into good sales people.

Learning that different people liked different trainers and trainings was also insightful. One method may not apply to everyone. Conservative, reserved and more intellectual people mostly prefer a more staid type of presentation delivery and one more analytical in nature. In contrast, people that are more out-going and "street smart" prefer a more entertaining and common sense style of training.

I made notes on all of the suggestions provided and where areas overlapped with the "Sales" comments mentioned in the prior sub-section. I also made notes to create new or improved trainings in the following areas:

Employees (Recruitment Consultants) want:

- Different interview techniques;
- Sales (see above);
- Negotiation skills (clients and candidates);
- Persuasion techniques (how to get people to leave their companies);
- Headhunting for different candidate levels;
- Cold calling new clients;
- Attending conferences and seminars (for knowledge and networking);
- Recruitment Consultant's role;

- The Market;
- Networking (including shadow training On-The-Job);
- Director's training (sales, including contracts);
- Communicating with strong personalities;
- Working under stress/stress management;
- Time management;
- Internet searching;
- Candidate assessments (including talent and leadership);
- Client management and communications; and
- Management (including motivation and building strong teams).

ATTITUDE

"How to stay positive; as I am naturally a negative person, I want to be positive and learn how to do this"...

I admired this person for admitting their weakness. We have a very positive environment overall in our company that, I believed, would help this person over time – and it did have some impact. However, in the end, people have distinct personality traits and outlooks and this is difficult to change – where it is the primary responsibility of the individual – not the company in which they work.

Employees want:

- To improve their personality and overall being; and
- To better themselves.

PSYCHOLOGICAL

"Psychological trainings, understanding different personalities and why they should not get along, I am upset that Zhanna, Kira and Kristina do not get along"..."Psychological training, Sofiya's trainings are very good and so are Albert's"...

I think this is a compelling subject for training and, ultimately, it may help our employees become more tolerant and understanding of others that have differing personalities and issues. I also believe it could help teach them how to deal most effectively with a wide range of personalities.

As should be clear, the three people commenting above do not get along well. They work in the same team but have vast differences in personalities, age, and dispositions. In addition, they compete with each other for their success. Of course, we could separate them into different teams but I feel that this should really only be a last resort and we have not reached that stage yet. I made a note to focus on these three - and training is a good place to start.

Employees want:

- Psychological training to better understand those they work with (colleagues, subordinates, management, clients, candidates); and
- Everyone to get along so they, and the company, can be more productive.

NONE

"No need but I would welcome any training"…"I feel I have all I need"…

I believe that everyone needs training, and continual training - even those at the very top. Furthermore, I think they should desire it and take it if offered. Those who feel they do not need it could, in fact, just be very busy, experienced poor training in the past and, therefore, feel it is a waste of their time. Perhaps, they also may feel over-confident in their abilities.

Employees want:

- No additional training sometimes.

LANGUAGE

"English language skills"…"English"…"English language skills, at lunch time and even partly paid"…"English lessons"…"The financial training is great by Angela, and I would like English classes"…"English classes on the basics"…

Being able to communicate effectively in English definitely has its advantages in the business world; both globally and in Russia. Thus, I understand the desire of the few people on our team who do not already have such skills, but would like to acquire them. It would certainly be beneficial to them within the company.

In the past, we have tried to help such people by offering group English language lessons in our Moscow office. Unfortunately, the excitement wore off over time and the participants stopped regularly attending the after-work class in our office. Therefore, we discontinued the lessons.

My belief is that if you really want something, you will be sufficiently motivated to go out and do it. This may mean learning or training at home or, for example, by having lessons on your IPad (or MP3 player, etc.) and listening to them on the way to and from work, instead of music. I have noted their interest, but I would first like to see more effort on their part before I agree to have paid classes with low attendance again.

Employees want:

- To have good, effective English language skills.

PR

"Attend PR conferences and events to stay up-to-date with technology, people and experts, and I would like to attend meetings with Directors to learn"…

This makes sense to me as something that our new PR person would want, and it would likely benefit her in the position. Shadowing our Directors would also help her in generating business leads for the company, which is also a small part of her remit.

Employees want:

- To stay connected with other professionals in their field, to stay up-to-date; and
- To learn more about the industry and company they work for, by attending client meetings with experts within the company.

ADMINISTRATION

"Recruitment, I never had induction for a Consultant or Director"…

This comment was from a good administrative person whom, I felt, deserved a chance to advance into a Consultant position in the near future. I thought that attending this training would be a good start along that path when the time was appropriate.

Employees want:

- To advance professionally within the company; and
- To be trained for higher positions within the company.

Chapter 8

How Well Do You Think Your Training And Development Needs Are Assessed And Met?

This is a straight-forward question meant to rate the attentiveness of our human resources and management team regarding staff development.

NOT APPLICABLE

"This does not matter for me"..."I do not think that training and development is a real issue outside of what I already mentioned"..."All are met"..."I do not need recruitment training, I was part of the team last year to create them, I had Diana's and Margarita's BD training but due to the crisis have not had time to use them in practice"..."Not yet"...

We have never really had sufficient time to assess the training and development needs of the staff and management of the company in a proper and professional manner. Therefore, my feeling is that many of our team did not correctly understand the question.

I was expecting to hear from all staff and management that they are not assessed at all, as this has been the case.

Employees want:

- Nothing at all, sometimes.

UNDECIDED

"Hard to say"..."Not sure"..."Hard to say"..."Not sure"...

I thought this reply was fair enough, however, I think it best for me to interpret this as "not well" in order that we still remain focused on improving.

Employees want:

- Something, but sometimes they are not sure what.

NEEDS

"We need to create training manuals for each sector – master classes, and create presentations on specific sectors"…"No needs but I would welcome any trainings, interview skills and how to assess good candidates"…"Consultants need a lot of training on selling candidates, headhunting and the importance of our clients"…"We need Master Classes focused on practice not theory"…"Most training is on the working process but master classes with peers would be beneficial"…"New recruits really need a mentor or coach as people were left alone and afraid to ask questions"…"We need great sales people to train us"…"Additional sales training"…

While the responses did not properly answer the question, they did give more solid information and ideas about where we need to focus our training and development for the team. This gives me the ability to cross-reference these replies with comments given in the previous chapter to create a new, and very thorough training and development program, covering all of the above-mentioned ideas which, I felt, were all very good.

Employees want:

- Individual training manuals for different areas;
- Master class trainings;
- Training on industry sector presentations;
- Training on interview skills and how to assess good candidates;
- Training on how to sell candidates to clients;
- Headhunting training;
- Better client customer service training;
- Master classes with peers (for the company's top performers);
- Master classes focused on practice - not theory;
- Mentors and coaches for new employees; and
- Sales training.

INDUCTION

"Good induction training"…"Great induction training"…"The induction was very good and I asked a lot of questions"…"I think the induction training was super, Nina did a great training followed by assessments on interviews and highlights"…

This was encouraging to hear and confirms that we do have a great induction program at Staffwell. It is also good to hear that the Consultants were assessed on their interviews and the writing of interview notes.

Employees want:

- Strong training in the induction program;
- Strong induction programs; and
- To be assessed on their performance so they know they are doing the job right.

ON-GOING TRAINING

"Nina coming to St. Petersburg"..."On-going needs are met quickly"..."It is harder to assess networking training as nobody monitors it"...

Inter-office visits are crucial for the business and are interesting for employees. I think on-going needs are met quickly in our company as I cannot imagine someone asking for help and not getting it; this is just not our way, so this confirmation was good to hear.

Assessments are weak in our company due to time and staff constraints in completing them. However, they are crucial and we need to look into this and, especially, at networking skills.

Employees want:

- To be trained by people who are good at it and by those they do not see every day (e.g., people from other offices);
- Quick response to training needs; and
- Training results to be monitored and assessed.

MANAGEMENT

"Discussions with Diana are like training"...

There are always certain employees and managers that really enjoy and appreciate spending time speaking with senior management. Most of the discussions are business or deal-related. It is a way for these team members to obtain additional ideas and insights regarding the issues with which they face. It also allows them to learn from someone with more, or simply different, experience in business and with more breadth.

I have always encouraged an open-door policy in our company, where staff should feel comfortable to chat with senior management at any time about anything, and I will continue to support this.

Employees want:

- To learn by simply spending quality time with senior management.

OPINIONS ON TRAINING

"The training was OK, it helped a lot"... "Overall very well"..."It is very good for Consultants and only OK for Directors"..."I asked for sales training but never got it, although Boris gave advert and sales training and James on sales too, but I need more"..."Very good, Sofiya did a great training on the finance sector and Nadya did trainings in St. Petersburg that were very good"..."The trainings were useful but should be more focused on practice and less on theory"..."We had several good trainings, they were good, but I would like to be trained by an experienced trainer"..."Good"..."Needs are met, if I need it I can get it"..."One of the strongest points of Staffwell is the intense internal trainings"..."T&D is really great, I can't think of anything that I haven't covered already in our sphere"..."Ozzie was only theoretical not practical, we need great sales people to train us"..."I had a lot of trainings and am satisfied, and mentoring from senior staff is good"..."Yana and Ozzie did a great job training, it was close to real life and useful"..."We discuss needs inside and then get it from people in the office, we spent one week on this in the beginning of the year"..."Last year's trainings were good and my needs were satisfied"..."We have had a lot of trainings, Ozzie gave a lot and we have done our own St. Petersburg trainings, and Tamara and Nina did them on industry sectors"..."I have small trainings with Angela a few times a week so all is good"..."It's great"..."I attended all trainings by Ozzie in St. Petersburg and I am happy to have had Consultants training, I am always invited to the trainings there, also when I started Angela sent me for reporting courses"..."I am grateful that we understand that I need time to learn things and I try hard to learn quickly"...

From the responses above it seemed to me that, overall, our training was pretty good. It was useful for me to find out the specific areas where it was especially good and who deserved the credit for such.

However, there were also a few things mentioned that I felt needed to be looked into - such as additional training for certain people, and better training in certain areas. I made notes on every specific thing mentioned and to cross-reference with other comments made in this and previous chapters.

Employees want:

- More training, if they still feel weak in a certain area;
- Trainings to be more focused on practice and less on theory;
- Great training offered on an on-going basis; and
- Occasionally, to be trained by external trainers.

TRAINING NEEDS BEING ASSESSED

"Met, but not assessed, do we have assessments for this?"..."I was never assessed, I only participated in Master Classes"..."Assessed?"...

This response hit the point exactly. These team members also felt that we were not appropriately assessing people's training and development needs on a frequent basis or, at all, in many cases. This is a clear area for improvement. I also made a note on these three specific people - simply to ensure that they correctly understood the question.

Employees want:

- To have their training and development needs assessed on a frequent basis; and
- To have their training and development needs met.

Chapter 9

What Training And Development Did You Receive That You Found Most Helpful And Enjoyable?

This question was modeled to tell me exactly who was good at training – in terms of what topics, how it was good, and who was not good and why.

PROFESSIONAL

"Scala [an accounting software package] *training on implementation and ACCA"..."IFS, ACCA training was great from Angela"*

It is good to know that our vendors provide solid training and that our Financial Director ("FD") then does an effective job in transferring that knowledge to our team. That our FD takes the initiative to improve the members in her team, by sharing what she knows and learns with them, is one of the many reasons I really have great respect for her.

Employees want:

- Good training from vendors;
- Good training from professional associations; and
- Good training passed on from those trained by vendors and professional associations.

NOT APPLICABLE

"None"..."Not really applicable"..."Had none"

The first two of these comments came from senior management, which confirms the absence and potential need for senior-level trainings. After some thought, I concluded that this would be a new project for me, as CEO, to take on. I decided to train my high-level people on senior-related issues, or find a way to stimulate them by utilizing external training programs or conferences. I made a note to look into this.

The other person commenting was our fairly new PR person and to do good PR for us she should be properly trained in what it is we do. I made a note to put her through our Director's training program.

Employees want:

- Senior-level trainings designed specifically for senior-level people; and
- To be trained in various roles within the company, in order to help them perform their wider role, if they have one.

COMMUNICATION SKILLS

"Ozzie regarding communication skills: 1-day role playing, theoretical, business game"..."Ozzie on communications with clients and candidates (always sit with a straight back) – this was very interesting"

I believe that this is an important topic and I was pleased to discover that our HR Director (Ozzie) has it down pat.

Proper posture on an interview is a key to making a good impression. Sitting upright with a straight back, and walking tall, are important if you want others to perceive you as confident, interested, energetic and in good health. Slouching is seen as lazy, unhealthy, uninterested and unmotivated.

Good posture is important on interviews, in client meetings, in the office and out in public. Just writing this is making me think about my own posture! This is a very important training area to continue within our company on a regular basis. How we are perceived by everyone is very important to our success.

Employees want:

- Good training on best-practice communication skills; and
- Training on the importance of good posture.

INDUSTRY SECTOR INFORMATION

"Diana gave great info on sectors"..."Sector trainings in St. Petersburg by the team itself, was highly interesting and helped all to understand each other's sectors"

It is critical to our success that we understand our clients and the industry sectors they work in. We really try hard to help our team in understanding the companies within each industry, their size and structure, the latest news and trends, and what issues and challenges they are facing. I was glad to hear that this was part of our training program, and that it was done well and is useful.

Employees want:

- Training on the industry sectors they work in and focus on.

COMPANY INFORMATION

"Sharing successes of the month, it is useful to understand the success of our company to better sell to clients"

I completely agree with this comment. It is very important for employees to know about the company and to be kept up-to-date about it. We have monthly meetings that detail top recruitment projects that we have recently closed and highlight the top performing Directors and Consultants. We also announce and discuss any important Staffwell company information.

Employees want:

- To know about the deals and successes of the company; and
- To know the latest information on the company.

SALES PRESENTATION

"Helpful was the sales presentation with roll play – very needed and useful, enjoyable is Albert's training"..."Training on how to give a PowerPoint presentation and role playing. Might be a good idea to give this training or an intro to the presentation"

Looks like Albert (a top Director) is our man for training on sales presentations. Role playing is an instrumental part in sales training and I was happy to hear that this was a strong area within our training program.

I was curious to sit through this training myself, just to experience it, as it has evolved over the years since I first developed it. I was particularly interested to see if it had changed or improved much from the original.

Employees want:

- Trainings that involve inter-active role playing.

INDUCTION

"Induction with Diana"…"Our induction trainings are not good, we need to develop much better ones, we really need to check on the work of our team often, we must constantly try to create the best team and I want to achieve this"…"Diana on how to be a Director"…"Induction was great and new for me"…"Induction with Ozzie, but it could be more centered on practical areas and not as much on theoretical"…"The induction was very good – it was fresh and funny and resulted in a strong desire to work hard to reach goals"

In these responses, we have many team members that liked the inductions of our Commercial Director and HR Director, and one senior team member and high performer who did not. If there is room to improve, we need to do it and, in this case, it seemed proper for this senior member to join the team conducting inductions. As a result, I made a note to give her these new responsibilities.

Here we also discover that our HR Director is being criticized again about her training content being too theoretical and not practical enough. I made a note to speak to her about this.

Employees want:

- Great induction programs;
- Perfection (or at least optimization), including in their training programs; and
- Trainings that are less theoretical and more practical.

COUNTER-OFFERS

"Counter-offers with Sofiya"…"I really like Sofiya's training on counter-offers and writing highlights – it was very practical advice"…"Sofiya regarding motivation of candidates, counter-offers, psychology"

Sofiya is a star performer so it was not surprising to hear that she is also good as a trainer.

Counter-offers can be a very delicate issue in our business. A candidate may get an offer for a new job but when he returns to his company to resign, that company may implore him to stay. They often offer a better compensation and benefits package and, possibly, an upgraded role, in a bid to make him stay. When this happens it is a challenge for our client, and for us, as we all need to start from square one again – delaying the hiring plan of the client and our success.

We train our staff on how to best deal with counter-offers, including strategies on how to try to avert candidates from taking counter-offers from their company , and how and what is necessary to best communicate to our client when they happen. I am happy to hear that Sofiya is proficient in this area and trains well on it.

Employees want:

- Good training on how to deal with challenges to the sales process related to hiring new staff.

MASTER CLASSES

"Master classes are not useful as most is obvious"..."Master classes with Albert, on networking, was great"..."Master classes on sectors were good"

I am a big fan of master classes: an expert training others on their particular area of expertise. However, I do appreciate that it can be a waste of time for some people to be re-trained in an area that they, themselves, are already an expert in – especially, when their time could be better spent bringing in more business, for example. We may need to look closer at who is asked to attend which master classes.

Employees want:

- To have master classes trainings by the top experts in various areas, within their company; and
- To spend their time being trained, only if they really need the training.

NETWORKING

"Albert's networking training – good was where one topic was discussed by different sectors for brainstorming"..."I loved Albert's networking presentation, it is artistic and useful"..."Networking by Albert – it had role playing which was really good and fun"

It looks like Albert is our man for networking training too! Albert is definitely one Director that I need to watch as we continue to develop as a company. He is a good Director and now, through this exercise, he is known as a good trainer. He is always helpful, has drive and really loves the business. His trainings are perhaps so well-liked because he has theatrical acting experience and a passion for it, which makes him entertaining to watch and learn from.

I made a note to watch his development more closely and I forecast great things from him, and for his future at Staffwell.

Employees want:

- Good training on networking; and
- Training that is entertaining and inter-active.

CONFERENCES

"MIPIM conference in CAAN, was 15-16 hours of networking, it was the best OTJ training"

Margarita is a networking superstar. If attending more conferences makes her feel that she is better trained (self training, on-the-job at conferences), and she can bring in business at the same time, then I am all for approving it.

Employees want:

- To train themselves sometimes, just by working in new and challenging business environments, such as at international conferences.

HEADHUNTING

"Headhunting with Valentina"..."Sofiya's headhunting class"..."Headhunting training by Ozzie"..."Headhunting training by Ozzie"..."The most stressful issue in the beginning was headhunting for sure. I passed these trainings twice and remember them perfectly; this was not just theory but some games and case studies. That helped me a lot in doing such a stressful thing as headhunting, now it is really not stressful, thank God"..."Ozzie's headhunting training"..."Ozzie on headhunting"

Headhunting is crucial to our business and it needs to be done right, as reputation is everything. Headhunting is also hard, cold calling sales and can be stressful for Recruitment Consultants that are typically more intellectual than outgoing in nature. I am glad we have Sofiya, Valentina and Ozzie as proven trainers in this area.

I am also glad that Ozzie is often mentioned here as she was a former investment banking Recruitment Consultant with us before she was promoted into HR Management. She can train well on specific recruitment procedures because she was a former expert at performing them herself.

Employees want:

- Great training that is on-going, and in areas of the job that are difficult and challenging.

GENERAL RECCOMENDATIONS

"External trainings might be useful on communications with candidates and psychological trainings. I like trainings by Polina, Ozzie and Albert"..."Albert's #1, also Polina and Ozzie"..."I liked trainings with Ozzie because it had models and simulations of different situations – it was fun, interesting and useful"..."Non-interactive sessions were not great and were boring, those with sharing ideas were better. James and Albert's were good but they were only talking and not listening or inter-acting"..."Margarita, Albert and Jim on selling retainers, networking and sales skills"..."Our trainings are only for junior Consultants, we need trainings for senior people"..."I would like trainings on how to sell retainers"..."Also Albert's was very entertaining – he is artistic, vivid and a great orator"..."Not standard, needs more focus"..."Ozzie is most helpful"..."Diana's business development training"

This is all very good and useful information for me and confirms some of what was already mentioned in previous chapters. I noted everything - especially that people prefer stimulating, entertaining and inter-active training; and, not a one-sided lecture style format.

Employees want:

- Inter-active training sessions, where people have the opportunity to share their experiences and ideas with each other;
- External training, on occasion;
- Fun, interesting and useful trainings;
- Trainers to listen and promote inter-action, not just talk themselves; and
- Specialized advanced trainings for senior people.

ON-THE-JOB (OTJ)

"My best training was OTJ with Sofiya – Sofiya is a great mentor"..."Shadowing the Consultants, and in banking, Polina arranged for me to meet some client friends of Polina's who talked to me about the different divisions in banks"

Good mentoring and on-the-job training is critical to training people quickly and well. In our business we have new team members observe client meetings and every step of the recruitment process. This includes candidate interviews, headhunting, report writing, client communications and job offer negotiations.

We also provide refresher courses for our experienced staff members with OTJ exercises, alongside their peers, as there are always different team members that become new experts in the differing areas of the role. Learning these new techniques help us to continually develop and improve.

Employees want:

- Great OTJ training; and
- To be assigned mentors for on-going OTJ training.

INTERVIEWS

"I liked Polina's training about interviews as it was really good and systematic"..."Sofiya, she gave examples of her work, how she does it, methods, psychological aspects of interviews"

These responses reference two of our best people training in what they know best. It makes sense to me that they are so well regarded.

Conducting a great interview takes real talent and it requires learning and a lot of practice to become good at it. It is also a crucial aspect of successfully recruiting new employees for clients, or into your company. It is an area that we always focus on maintaining and improving and, happily, we do it really well.

Employees want:

- To be properly trained on how to conduct a great interview.

COLD CALLING

"Cold calling by Margarita"

This is a case of the fearless training the fearful. It makes sense to me that Margarita is well regarded in this area of training as she is great at it OTJ.

Cold calling is one of the most difficult aspects of the sales cycle for most sales people. It is with purpose that our best cold caller is training her peers and new staff members in this area.

Employees want:

- Training by proven experts on how to successfully cold call.

WORK360

"Your blog articles"

I am glad that I have had a positive effect on our team and it gives me the motivation to keep it going.

Over the years, one of the things I have learned about myself is that, while I have a lot to say and to teach, I can express things better in writing. As a result, I launched a career magazine called "The Well", a blog site entitled "Work360" and, of course, have authored this book – with more to come!

The team at Staffwell also gets a kick out of all of these things. They find it cool and impressive that I do it, and, because of this, I have become somewhat of a public figure in the market.

Employees want:

- The occasional training and advice from the person at the top.

OFFICE VISIT

"Most enjoyable was my visit to our Moscow office"

Office visits can be highly useful for direct and subliminal training, and provide a big mood and motivational boost to staff and management. It is extremely important for us to stay in direct contact with each other in order to keep our offices close and so that they are helpful to one another.

Employees want:

- To visit branch offices of their company to better understand their company, its employees and the business.

ACCOUNTING

"Only with Angela, very helpful"

I really believe our Financial Director is a star with her accounting team. She is always training them - just another reason why she is considered a super executive for us.

Employees want:

- To be trained by superiors they respect.

Information Technology (IT)

"SDS [the Staffwell proprietary CRM system] *and induction from Roman"*

Our CRM system is very important to our work and follow-up training should be on-going. This is something for us to constantly look at.

Employees want:

- Proper and frequent training on IT and CRM systems of the company.

RECEPTION

"Reception training by Ozzie and Diana."

We have always believed in training our reception well - as they are one of the first points of contacts for our clients, candidates and guests. It is vital to us that they make a great first impression to our guests and that they are knowledgeable and helpful to our staff, clients and candidates, and others.

Employees want:

- Proper and thorough training for their given role.

Chapter 10
What Can You Say About Communications Within The Company/Your Department?

Building and maintaining good communications is very important for our success. This, I found out, was a great question as it really pin-pointed where we are strong and who was strong in communications, and where we had opportunities for improvement.

ACCOUNTING DEPARTMENT

"Accounting department is OK and very friendly and we rotate if someone is absent. They work for the sales team and give every opportunity to make more money for the company"..."In our department it is very strong and we understand we need to help the sales team and to keep high standards"..."The accounting team is great and we rotate functions"

This is a small, tight team with a fantastic leader and manager heading it. I love that they understand their bigger role in the company in serving the front office team to help improve our success. All is well here!

Employees want:

- To have strong communications within the company and, in the process, to help the company make more money and maintain high standards of service.

IT DEPARTMENT

"It is not great, there is a lack of information"

This comment pertains to our former IT Director who did not document anything on the systems we used before he left the company. This left our new IT team with the burden of spending a lot of time not only getting up to speed but in documenting everything as they did so.

This was a mistake of ours and one we will not repeat again. Our new IT team has been documenting everything so that, should anyone new join the team, it will be easier and clearer for them to get up to speed quickly on our systems.

Employees want:

- IT systems and procedures to be fully documented and kept up-to-date at all times.

FINANCE RECRUITMENT DIVISION

"Finance is not great"..."The finance sector team is screwed up and plus with Albert we are different people, I am flexible and Albert is odd, he complains that I do not communicate with him and then he never communicates with me after that, but now he is doing it. I am a real action person and Albert likes to talk too much and I find this annoying, but now all is OK"..."I have the hardest team of people in the office to communicate with and I try to get them to speak together"..."All is OK but last year there were some changes with Sofiya going to legal. People are different, me and Kira are very good and help each other, but with Kristina it is very different. We have different positions we work on and interests. For me it is very important to close positions and in the most professional way and with placed candidates. Kristina is closed from us but we need people too who can be a team together and get along, but I do not need or want to have lunch together with her"..."The culture overall is nice but in the finance department there are problems, as I am older I feel this is the problem. Everyone wants to succeed so teammates are fighting or in conflict and I do not like conflicts. Zhanna and Kira only want senior vacancies where I am open to taking all vacancies right now and treating the candidates right. They need to be more positive and enthusiastic. They treat me like a junior and there are problems with splits. They feel all candidates are theirs and they never want me to interview candidates after them, but they need to. They work together on projects a lot"..."Zhanna and Asya are good but Kristina is not good as she only communicates with Albert, she does not want to communicate with the rest of the team, and she takes candidates and does not answer e-mails sent to her"

These comments make it very clear that we have issues here. This is a team of extreme, polar personalities but also a solid, high-billing team; successful and hardworking. On the BD side, Albert is extremely outgoing and enjoys a bit of drama (and may even encourage it at times). Asya is new, extremely particular, a bit serious and structured/systematic. On the Consultants' side, Kira and Zhanna are more intellectual, reserved, skeptical and suspicious/cautious, while Kristina is more outgoing and flexible.

We cannot force people to like one another. However, we can implement and enforce tighter and more standardized rules and guidelines for people to work within - particularly in regard to use and allocation of candidates and vacancies, and fee split scenarios. I made a note to immediately work on this and to review and update the policies and procedures in our operations manual.

We could also move people into different departments, if needed, but I see this as a second to last resort.

Employees want:

- To work with people they can communicate well with;
- To work with people that are helpful and team-oriented;
- To not argue or have conflicts with their colleagues;
- To have equality and be treated fairly within the team;
- To work with positive and enthusiastic colleagues and management; and
- Quick, timely responses to the emails they have sent.

ST. PETERSBURG BRANCH OFFICE (SPB)

"We are very close as we have a smaller office"..."Good and flexible"..."SPB is very good as we are a small, close office"..."No problems as we are all now sitting in one room"..."Great as we are all working in one room"..."The SPB team is perfect and working perfectly together; regarding Moscow, we hope they love us too"

There are major benefits to having open plan offices and smaller teams/offices: communications can be great in this environment, especially with the right team and leader in place. Moscow loves you too Saint Petersburg!

Employees want:

- Easy to navigate, open-planned office spaces in which to communicate better; and
- Good communications between offices and to know that their other offices know and appreciate them.

INTER-OFFICE COMMUNICATIONS

"Moscow and SPB offices can be improved, more frequent, we do not know about events and things going on"..."Sometimes I speak with Diana and the Directors from Moscow but sometimes answers take too long (1- 2 days)"..."With Moscow I talk to Kira and Alyona but there are not a lot of needs, however, once a month a conference call would be great and by recruitment sector"..."No problems in SPB but I feel distanced from Moscow"

Based on these comments there clearly is room for improvement here. I made a note to work on improving communications between the offices and, specifically, to include faster response times and scheduled, frequent conference calls between management and recruitment departments.

Employees want (between offices):

- Improved and more frequent communication;
- Faster response to enquiries;
- Monthly conference calls between offices and divisions; and
- To feel connected to their other branch offices.

FMCG/RETAIL/B2B RECRUITMENT DIVISIONS

"Very good, everyone is close in my room and in the company, and there is fast feedback"..."It is good in the company but some people in the FMCG [Fast Moving Consumer Goods] department are not active communicators, but the atmosphere is very good"..."In the FMCG department James is very open and with very good advice"..."As for my department, we seem to be one big happy family with James at the head of it, it's all perfect, we are a great team really"..."In my department James is very useful, like a coach"..."Very good within the department"

Overall, I think it looks pretty good in this department and the comments came with a free assessment on James and some of his capabilities and strengths.

Employees want:

- Close communications and fast feedback;
- Everyone to be active communicators to improve business results;
- Open management; leadership with good advice; mentorship to offer; and
- Good teamwork.

BANKING/INVESTMENT/INSURANCE RECRUITMENT DIVISIONS

"Good, all is great and it is easy to talk to everyone, and it is the same within the entire company. Polina does a good job of keeping the sector strong and tight, there is a friend and mentor system in the department"..."The banking department is great"..."I feel no weaknesses, great, and great chemistry. Everyone is in contact and negotiating. Most of my time is spent in banking, but when I need to go outside of that all is OK"..."Good – I have all the info I need and the senior team shares info. Directors and Consultants should share more"

This department also looks to me as if it is in great shape. Once again, the comments contained another good assessment of Polina and her success and strengths in running this department.

Employees want:

- Easy communication between colleagues; and
- Good access to, and sharing of, information, within the team and company.

REAL ESTATE AND CONSTRUCTION RECRUITMENT DIVISIONS

"Pretty good"..."Everything is perfect now because we are small and we go to client meetings together with Directors"

This appears to be another department that is fine with regard to communications.

Employees want:

- To work in teams, in order to boost their own results and provide better service to clients.

LEGAL RECRUITMENT DIVISION

"Good, James is good with providing feedback and updates"

I did not find this surprising as James continually strives for perfection and always follows our formal system of working.

Employees want:

- Timely feedback and updates.

THE COMPANY OVERALL

"There were no communications when Adam was here. I feel lucky to be your friend to get the communications. My advice to you is to communicate often to the team, bring back values that are personal to a driving sales business"..."Well organized and democratic"..."The company is good but between sectors there are few as there are not on many shared projects"..."Democratic corporate culture, people like to work here and there is open-door management"..."It is good that you are chatting with everyone"..."Would help to get to know new people when they start and I agree with you about having lunches together with people I don't know well"..."As for the company, I haven't been dealing much with the finance recruitment team as they are not very communicative from my point of view, and I almost haven't been discussing anything with you so this chat seems to be a good start"..."Not good, we need to have more team-building and fun times together"..."The company is quite good"..."It was a good idea to have quarterly updates with Diana"..."High-level, very good"..."When we were bigger not everyone knew the names or people or their roles. I think everyone should be trained on other recruitment sectors, especially to cover for people when they go on holiday"..."Good"..."I think it is good, but because people are separated by different rooms they are distanced"..."Very comfortable and easy and everyone helps and gives answers, I communicate more with those who get back to me fast"..."Good, I have never had any problems with our team"

Overall, the responses lead me to believe that our communications are pretty good and it was good to hear where our strengths lie. However, there are a few things mentioned that I will follow up on - including my communicating more with the company employees, encouraging shared projects, the team getting to know each other and new hires better, more fun team-building time together, and cross-training in different recruitment sectors.

Employees want:

- Communications from the President and CEO of the company;
- Open, democratic-style communication;
- Introductory information on new hires and communication with them;
- To get to know the people in the company that they do not already know well;
- More time to get to know their colleagues and management on a social basis;
- Open plan offices, ideally; and
- Fast response to communications.

Chapter 11

What Improvements Do You Think Can Be Made To Customer Service And Relations?

This question was really important to me because I have a real passion for customer service and believe it has to be the focus of any business in order for it to be successful. Therefore, I was very interested to hear what the team had to say about this.

INVOICING

"What we in the accounting department do is prepare documents and call clients to get paid faster. We try to do everything perfectly and in fact clients say that we are the best company on the market with documentation"..."I would like Directors to be more attentive with getting agreements back, and then updating the server when they get them – many Directors forget to do this"...

Once again, our accounting department proves to be exceptional! They get it and they understand their role in the company. They are very focused on success and in helping the company to achieve it - by providing fast and accurate documentation and follow-up.

I made a note to follow-up with the Director's team on getting agreements back faster, and updating the server, and to check whether our current operations manual reflects those initiatives.

Employees want:

- Faster response by sales teams in getting documentation submitted for processing; and
- Faster response by sales teams in updating the servers on completed steps in the sales process.

CUSTOMER SATISFACTION FORM

"An idea is that if it is a new client, we should give them a satisfaction form to check the work of our commercial team"..."Satisfaction forms for clients"...

This is a great idea to re-establish. We used to do this in the early days of the company but then let it slide when we were growing very quickly, due to manpower and time constraints. I decided that I would personally look into this matter.

Fortunately, we do get a lot of feedback, via email from clients and candidates who use our services, so we hear a lot of positive remarks about our work. However, it is also very important to hear any negative feedback that may be out there so that we can improve on any weaknesses we may have. Customer satisfaction forms are a good way to cover both the positive aspects of our work, and to identify areas and opportunities for in-depth improvement.

Employees want:

- Customer satisfaction forms for clients, to provide feedback on the strengths and weaknesses of our team and the service they provide.

CRM

"SDS"..."We need post code searches on SDS to visit multiple clients when out on calls"..."I think all is fine but it is helpful when we can see accurate info in SDS, usually it is not updated by Directors"..."I think SDS can be improved to be more customer oriented"...

SDS (Staffwell Digital System) is our internal CRM system. We are continually improving on our system and these comments were very helpful.

The postal code searches are a great idea as Moscow is a very large city that is quite geographically spread out. If a Director has a call in one area and can then organize another client meeting soon before or after, then this would be a very effective use of their time. I believe this would benefit our St. Petersburg operation as well.

Having up-to-date and accurate information in SDS is crucial to our success and I made a note to check our operations manual about this, as well as to speak to our management and Director's team.

Employees want:

- The ability to search clients by post code in order to schedule more sales meetings in the same area, making more efficient use of their time;
- Accurate and up-to-date information in their CRM systems; and
- CRM systems that are more customer-oriented.

CLIENT REVIEWS

"We are very good; we work individually with all clients and meet with clients quarterly to discuss the work, results and plans. We should make this an official plan (quarterly reviews with clients)"..."Directors need to have face-to-face meetings with clients every 2 months or every quarter"...

Most of our business is repeat business, so it is imperative that we stay ahead of our clients' needs on a regular basis. This requires that we periodically update our information on clients, in particular on matters like: how our contact is doing; what is new with their company and local operation; any significant, material changes; updates on current searches; and going over new search requirements.

This prompted me to check our operations manual to see if this, in fact, was an explicit requirement for our Director's team.

Employees want:

- Company representatives to meet frequently with their clients.

FORMS

"Fix the highlights form"...

I believe that we are one of the few companies on the market that actually interview every candidate we meet, and then write interview notes to provide to our clients. We call these interview notes "highlights", and utilize a standardized form or template when constructing the notes which, with a CV, we present to our clients.

I am not sure what is specifically wrong with the highlights form, but decided that I would review it myself, and with our team, to see how we can improve it.

Employees want:

- Forms to be perfected.

NEGOTIATION SKILLS

"Consultants need to learn how to convince candidates better"...

Our Consultant's team is responsible for locating candidates that suit the hiring requirements of our clients. This includes, among other things: interviewing candidates, presenting them to clients, arranging their interviews with our clients, and assisting in job offer negotiations. On occasion, these negotiations involve trying to convince a candidate not to take a counter-offer that may be extended by their current employer.

Negotiation is a part of our job. Clients hire us to find them very specific profiles of people they want; most of whom are usually employed at other companies at the time. Our job is to convince candidates to go on the interviews with the clients we are representing, and convince them to take the offer, if one is extended. We always let candidates make up their own mind, as it is their life and their career. However, we must be excellent in selling our client's opportunity to entice a candidate to take our client's offer. I made a note to add this to the list of training areas for Consultants.

Employees want:

- A strong sales team that is competent at negotiations and handling impediments, such as counter-offers.

ATTITUDE

"Good overall but Consultants are too choosy about the vacancies, this effects customer service, it is less of a problem now due to the crisis, but soon it will be over and they might be back to old ways of being picky – it would be good if this could be overcome"..."More enthusiasm and connection with clients and candidates, better eye contact and better confidence"..."Be friendly to all"...

I see both sides of the coin in the comments made above. Directors want the Consultants to work on any vacancy they bring in - no matter how difficult or at what level it is, with all of their attention devoted to filling such vacancy. At the same time, Consultants prefer to work on vacancies that are likely to yield higher commissions and are easier to place.

The earnings of a Consultant are greatly impacted when a Director assigns them vacancies to work on that are impossible to fill, or cases where clients later cancel a vacancy after a lot of work has been booked by the Consultant. On the other hand, it affects the earnings of a Director when a Consultant refuses to work on vacancies they see as a waste of their time. I did not have all the immediate answers to this trade-off at the time, but vowed to look into this as a company and try to find a way to make it better.

Employees want:

- Team members to be more helpful and agreeable with regard to working on projects brought into the company; and
- All team members to be more positive, friendly and out-going in their communications with clients.

COMMUNICATIONS SKILLS

"Consultants need to be friendlier with clients and candidates, some of them are too emotionless, the team can be too cold and dead-fish to clients and candidates (Kira, Sonya and Kristina)" ..."Consultants need to be more pro-active in their work with clients and candidates, not wait until they are told to do something, and be more polite in business language (Kira, Sonya and Kristina), we need to create training programs and track results by systems"..."Consultants need to understand customer service, Kira is weak at talking to clients and one client even complained, e-mails are also very bad from her, cold and unfriendly"..."We need to have lots of feedback and communications with clients and candidates"..."Be in touch with clients and candidates whether we have vacancies or not"..."Client service is individual but when Consultants work together they have to share a joint project but still have different views. We need to have a more united front – the Director and Consultants on communications with the client"..."Closer communications with clients, more reports to them more frequently"...

One-half of the complaints mentioned here are directed at three individual Consultants. Accordingly, I made a note to speak to their direct management reports about this and to get them focused training in these areas. In our business it is crucial that our team always communicate well with our clients and candidates.

If their personalities are too dry, then we can easily create templates for e-mails and narrative speeches for use in their phone conversations. The people commenting here are all high-billing individuals for the company, so I would prefer not to lose them. Instead, I would like to come up with some creative solutions and intensive training for them from some team members that excel in communication.

Strong communications with our clients is essential and every comment written above by our team really triggered deep emotions in me and provided the impetus to focus immediately on improving our team in this area.

Employees want:

- All team members to be friendly, polite and pro-active in their communications with clients;
- Frequent communication and feedback with clients; and
- Improved communication between departments, for the benefit of clients.

<u>NONE</u>

"All is done well here"…"Customer service is good and we are doing what we can –James and Miron are on top of clients and sometimes Consultants. The crisis is good for giving clients more attention"…"All is fine"…"Thinks it is good now as we have a very professional team"…"I am not involved in this but I think it is great how our team now communicates with clients and candidates – at a high level"…

It is always good to hear the positive with the negative. Thus, I was happy, and somewhat relieved, to hear that many in the team felt that we were quite good and strong in our customer service and communications with clients. However, I am always more interested in the areas with opportunities in which we can improve.

Employees want:

- Their company to provide good customer service and communications to their clients.

RECEPTION

"Training for reception"…"I think reception is great, but not sure about the other areas of the business as I am only in reception"…

Most effort is focused on our core team of Directors and Consultants. However, we also need to lend attention to our other departments, including reception, which is important to us. Reception is the first point of contact for clients and candidates visiting our office, as well as for vendors and every one of our employees at the start of their day.

I made a note to have the performance of our reception assessed, and then to have them trained in areas in which they may need improvement, or could assist the company.

Employees want:

- Reception staff that is well-trained and customer service-oriented.

IT

"Training for IT too"…

IT departments should be trained in customer service and communication, and ours is no exception. Every employee in our company is their client, as are our clients, candidates and vendors. Indeed, I promised myself to see that they would be given this training, and I appreciated that they asked for it.

Employees want:

- Their IT departments to be trained and be adept in customer service and client relations.

NEW SERVICES

"Offer more analytics to our clients, maybe a newsletter, and provide out-staffing"...

I thought these were valid ideas and noted that they were consistent with what others had mentioned in previous chapters.

Employees want:

- To proffer additional services to clients in order to provide higher levels of customer service and relations.

CUSTOMER SERVICE

"Customer service is a very important part of Staffwell, we must be communicating constantly. If there are no vacancies during the crisis we need to be able to call clients with news and information and reasons to call them"... "I am interested to be involved in sales relationships and customer service, Consultants need to learn how to sell to the customer and what customer service means"..."Provide a high level of service and stay on top of everything"..."Be attentive to all customer needs"...

Again, I would like to point out that customer service is extremely important. Therefore, I was very glad to hear that many of our team members feel the same way. I believe that this is an area that we should frequently discuss within the company and provide continual training.

Employees want:

- Their company to provide high-level customer service to their clients; and
- Training on selling to customers and customer service.

KAM

"Clients to only have one Consultant work with them – an Account Manager"...KAM, one point of contact"..."As for customer service I think that the idea of Account Manager is rather interesting, this way we can always answer all the clients' needs"...

As discussed in previous chapters, Key Account Management is a role the Consultants would like us to create for them - for the more senior members of the team. However, under the current structure, that might mean taking certain responsibilities away from our Directors' team, as the Directors are responsible for checking the quality and progress of our work with clients on a frequent, scheduled basis.

I need to know what our clients would like in respect to this issue and whether or not they are satisfied with our incumbent structure. Feedback from clients on KAM should be taken into consideration, and I made a note to personally solicit their views on this before taking any decisions.

Regardless, I hear very clearly what the Consultant team members are saying and what they want: some form of a KAM role created and put into their team structure, as indicated in earlier chapters. While I do not see anything wrong with that, as anything is possible, I do need to look into it very carefully as not to compromise the service to clients or disrupt a flow of work that has been fairly efficient to date within the existing structure.

Employees want:

- More autonomy when dealing with clients and projects; and
- KAM titles and roles, if and when they have earned them.

HOLIDAY COVERAGE

"We need better coverage for clients when the team is on holiday"...

If this is indeed a problem, then we need to look into it and fix it. It is very important that we always stay focused on the recruitment projects of our clients - whether people are on vacation or not. In addition, I thought we needed to look into the distribution of vacancies within this context, as staff that are about to take holiday certainly should not be given new vacancies caseloads. Instead, such vacancies should go to others who are scheduled to be at work over that period.

Employees want:

- There to always be sufficient coverage for client projects and orders.

DOUBLE EFFORT

"We need double the effort on projects; the idea is to have 2 Consultants on each search"...

We tend to assign one Consultant per recruitment project and then share fees with anyone who may end up assisting in the process: for example, if the assigned Consultant located a candidate in our internal data base that had been placed there by another Consultant stemming from a recent interview.

I am not convinced that having two Consultants assigned to every project is a good idea, as I think it would likely cause a lot of friction within the team. Most Consultants prefer to work alone, with focus, and without conflict. It is possible that this may work for certain projects in which the required work is clearly more than one person can handle. We do this on occasion - but not for all projects, as per the suggestion above.

Ultimately, it is something I decided to look further into at some point - by circulating a simple questionnaire to the team about it.

Employees want:

* Faster results by sharing the workload.

INTERNAL RECRUITMENT

"Hire great people for us who are team oriented and proactive – as they are more successful"...

I agree with this comment. We have all types of personalities at Staffwell and many of the various types of people have been, and are today, very successful with us. However, we always prefer to have as colleagues, people who are naturally team-oriented and pro-active. Overall, these types make our company more successful and give us the strong positive reputation we always strive to achieve and uphold.

Employees want:

* Their employers to hire great, team-oriented and positive people into the company; and
* People hired into their company that will be successful.

SALES

"More selling to get referrals"...

When the market is thriving it can often be difficult to keep up with the incoming business flow, partially a result of years of our having built up a good reputation on the local market. On balance, this is a good problem to have. Conversely, during periods of economic down-turn or crisis, we need to do everything we can to source new clients with hiring needs. Accordingly, the recent focus has been almost completely on sales. This includes, among other things, tips from candidates during their interviews with us; that is, those who are interviewing at other companies provide us with information leads and referrals for our sales team.

Employees want:

- Sales leads and referrals in order to enhance success.

SPEED

"Must be faster due to competition"..."It takes too much time to start on the vacancy, Directors are slow at getting started, too much time is wasted"..."We need to give fast feedback to clients and candidates"..."Match the speed"..."Be faster"...

Speed is always a critical issue in our business, especially certain projects in which a client may give the vacancy to several recruitment firms at the same time. I am not a fan of cutting corners and providing sloppy work. It is why we created a system, adhere to it, and why we have, I believe, been so successful on the market. However, I acknowledged that I needed to look into what the issues may be behind some people feeling certain Directors may be slower than they think they should be in getting clients projects started.

Employees want:

- Client projects and orders to start faster; and
- Client projects and orders to close faster.

CLIENT MEETINGS

"Going to more client meetings, Consultants must do this to be able to close more vacancies – it is a huge help, if not office visits then conference calls are highly useful"…"Directors need to take Consultants to meetings more"…

When the market is strong we do not always have the time to take Consultants to meetings due to their workload and their need to focus on it. However, it is very helpful for Consultants to visit clients and hear directly from them about what their hiring requirements are. It is also very good training for them and useful when they get similar vacancies from other clients. Because of weaker economic conditions, Consultants have had the time that allows them to go to client meetings and enhance their training and learning.

Employees want:

- To have the opportunity to meet with clients that the company works with.

CLIENT NETWORKING

"More networking events with our clients, the roundtable event we had last August was really great to improve customer relations"…

I agree entirely with this statement. While our operating budget has been at a bare minimum due to adverse economic conditions, as soon as the market picks up again we will invest more in expanding client networking opportunities.

Employees want:

- More opportunities to network with clients by hosting or attending events catered specifically to networking.

INTERVIEW NOTES

"Consultants and Directors need to work closer on presenting candidates in a better way, the highlights need to be flawless and really selling to the clients, I think the Directors need to be reading the highlights before they are sent"…"Quality highlights, it is very hard to write about Staffwell's impression"…

Not everyone has the skill and talent to write well. I feel very fortunate that I have some skill and talent in writing and, perhaps more importantly, the interest and will to write well and improve. The quality of our written correspondence is an assessment and training issue and I made a note to focus on it. It is an area we must improve on as it greatly reflects on our reputation.

Employees want:

- High-caliber, written communications disseminated to clients.

TIMELINESS

"People should get to work about 10 minutes early to be there to get ready for candidates who arrive early"...

My immediate reaction to this reply was: "Are they not doing that already?" Timeliness is a huge issue for me, especially when it comes to client meetings and candidate interviews. The operations manual needs to be reviewed on this subject and management needs to monitor this more diligently and take corrective action where and if necessary.

Employees want:

- Their colleagues to be on time for any meetings they schedule, or are assigned to attend.

PLACING OUR OWN GREAT PEOPLE

"An idea is to place staff that want to leave into an in-house role"...

I think this is a good idea for those whom we have asked to leave the company, or for those that will be leaving without a new job lined up. By placing them in an in-house recruitment role at a company outside of our industry, we stand a better chance than our competition in getting future recruitment work from the company they join. In addition, providing this would also enhance the likelihood that our company would maintain good will and cordial terms with the exiting employee.

Employees want:

- To assist exiting employees in locating a new job; as a matter of good will - but also in that it may bring potential business to their company.

TEAM MANAGEMENT

"The division of responsibilities is not great (Directors managing the Consultants), I like how Polina is working with the banking team, thinks a former Consultant like Polina is better to lead them"...

Finding ways to improve on our current structure is always useful and requires an individualistic approach due to the array of personalities we have in our team of Directors. We would look into this over time.

Employees want:

- The occasional review of roles and organizational structures in order to improve upon them, where and when possible.

CUSTOMER APPRECIATION

"All is perfect in St. Petersburg (SPB), everyone puts their hearts in their job and how they speak with clients and candidates, and all are smart psychologists and very client oriented. It would be great to give small gifts to clients at the holidays in SPB"...

Our St. Petersburg team is a small group of very close people and I was very glad to hear that they are all working well together to the benefit of our clients and candidates.

The recruitment industry, including Staffwell, was hit hard during the 2009 economic and financial crisis. I personally invested a lot of money back into the company in order to keep as many of our top people employed and on salary as possible. We did not have an extra dime to expend on gifts for top clients when this comment was made but I am hopeful we can resume client gifting soon, with an uptick in the market.

Employees want:

- To show their appreciation to clients by giving them small gifts at the New Year holiday.

Chapter 12

How Would You Describe The Culture Or Feel Of The Company?

I was not expecting too many surprises here. However, I thought it was an effective question to re-direct people back into the reasons they like the company, or not.

STYLE

"We have good corporate style"…"Western Style"…"Best in style"…

That we do! I sincerely believe that we maintain a good, Western-style corporate culture. It does help that I was raised in the United States and started my career there, as I was able to bring much of what I learned about "best practice" into the company from its inception.

Employees want:
- To work for companies with good Western styles.
- To work for companies with good, Western-style corporate culture embedded into the business and operations.

LANGUAGE SKILLS

"We have good Russian and English correspondence skills and communications with the market"

Overall, I believe that we do. However, some of the comments mentioned in the previous chapter indicate that there is room for improvement in this area as well.

Employees want:
- Their company and employees to effectively operate and communicate in a bilingual environment and market.

CORPORATE CULTURE

"When people who leave look back and love our culture, I only worked for one company and they had no culture, they were just a company. We have teambuilding"..."Client-oriented, we are a high service level company"..."Professional, disciplined, authoritarian (army style), organized (all positive) and knows it works"..."Democratic and fair, openness and fairness, not authoritative"..."We are a very active sales company, unique is selling us, clients, candidates to the clients, achievements to the market"..."Open company and communicative, friendly, care about people and successes and feelings of people"..."Family-like"..."Democratic, very good and friendly, helpful team, all ready to learn, very open people, I look forward to work – very good mood in the office now"..."Staffwell for me is a great place to be and to work, the culture is friendly and relaxed, maybe too relaxed at a time when we do need to get the best out of everybody in whatever way that can be achieved (carrot and stick)"..."Flexible, dynamic, client oriented, positive"..."Very positive culture, no pain no gain"..."Best in family atmosphere and approach, but still adapted to the Russian reality and culture"..."Competitive, but not cut throat – he wants to keep up with the better performers"..."Unique – assertive but friendly, polite, positive, professional"..."Friendly, but we focus more on individual results than on the team"..."Western management, professional, friendly team, client oriented and try to be top on the market"..."Loves the corporate culture-very strong open, democratic, positive attitude, great work done and teamwork"...

I believe these comments provide a very accurate portrayal of our corporate culture. We are very friendly, positive, professional and hard working - but we also drive the business in a very structured way. We are very open and fair because equality and fair treatment of employees is very important to me. The rules and policies we have put in place enable us to maintain that environment in our company.

Corporate culture is often a factor in the decision of whether a person will remain at a company or leave. I am glad that the majority in our team feels very positive about our corporate culture.

Employees want:
- To work for companies that are democratic in nature, friendly, helpful, caring, communicative, positive, fair, team-oriented and professional;
- Team-building; and
- To work for companies that have very strong operations, are very organized, and offer a high level of service to their clients.

COMPANY DYNAMICS

"We went from a small company to a big one – a lot of turnover, now a great team that we don't have to be strict with. Everyone is experienced although some are young, and everyone is loyal to each other"...

Going through a major economic crisis is a difficult thing for a company and its employees. However, as mentioned above, there can be benefits as well: in our case we scaled down to our very best Directors and Consultants, and became a very lean, mean, surviving machine.

Employees want:
- Teams of employees that are really strong and close.

MANAGEMENT

"Lack of control, nobody really fixes everything, actions not taken"..."I think that more communication with the staff will be essential, we have and have always had a lot of staff leaving due to different reasons, but some really experienced people left because they felt they were not valued, those who are left feel the company needs and maybe would like to feel that they are a valued part of the team, because there are a lot of rumors about further redundancies, about selling the company and many more, these rumors appear because Directors know much more than the Consultants, I guess that if we all know all the general issues – that could help us feel the company better and understand where we are going"..."At the beginning of her joining Adam was the driving engine of the company, but only aimed at results (A competitor is too tough where quality of service lacks) but now our aim is to reach results but to take into consideration everything, now we are more democratic – we are much better now –more flexible with time now"..."Democratic CEO"..."Jokes and rules"...

These comments underline the fact that there are definitely some issues with our management team and some areas that I, myself, need to address and improve upon. This should start with communicating more with the employees of the company on a more frequent basis.

I also see how very important it is that our team like and respect management and that they feel valued. We obviously need to do more here, and do it better than we are doing it now, and have done in the past.

I also feel that we need to reduce any gossip in the office and any feelings related to unfairness in corporate communications. This is easily remedied with a scheduled e-mail to update all employees on our status, news and future development.

Employees want:
- Things that can be improved or fixed, to actually be improved or fixed;
- Management to communicate frequently to the staff;
- To feel valued by management;
- To have balanced communication, so that everyone has the same information, and less gossip; and
- To have an atmosphere that is a good blend of friendly and fun, and hard- driving work.

REPUTATION AND BRAND

"I like the reputation of the company and the name of the company and you Teri"..." We care about our image"...

We definitely have a strong brand and reputation on the market and most companies know who we are and have heard good things about us - whether we have ever worked with them or not. In addition, many people also know of me, whether we have met or not.

I believe that we have a strong reputation and brand on the market because we always strive to improve our company and offer the best service we can to our clients. Our focus on this will never stop.

Employees want:
- A strong brand name, reputation, and CEO in the company for which they work; and
- The company they work for to care about its image.

PERSONAL GROWTH

"Now very happy – becoming more professional and learning more about the company, likes pharma and banking both and wants to do both together"...

It is very pleasing for me to hear when an employee really likes where they are in their career, what they are doing, and that they feel they are learning and growing professionally.

Employees want:
- To become even better at what they do; and
- To learn more about the company they work for.

TEAM DYNAMICS

"We do team-building now but she does not know everyone here, Polina is very closed and does not like to share, Albert and Diana made her feel bad about joining the Biggest Losers group"..."Great warm and friendly team, always developing, best way for recruitment"..."Communicative, a good place for Kristina and the team (except for communications on finance team)"..."Great people, varied backgrounds, great chemistry and communications – no weaknesses"..."Good high level of intellect, people are very strong"..."St. Petersburg (SPB) is very friendly and open, but does not know about Moscow, and SPB has very strong, friendly relations not based on money, there are no fee split arguments"...

Overall, we have very strong team dynamics, especially now within our top team. The person first quoted above, who mentioned some problems she had with team members, has a very strong and particular disposition about her. Nonetheless, I will have management speak to Polina about being more open and communicative with her colleagues. I will also speak to Albert and Diana about not razzing employees who want to join our company's weight loss competition - whether they need to lose a substantial amount of weight or not.

For some people, any form of someone sticking a fork in their side, even if it is regarding after-work activities, can really have an adverse effect on them. Asya may have only wanted, or needed, to lose 2 kilos, or may have just wanted to be a part of a social club within our company. Either way, we should support her, not harass her, about her participation.

Employees want:
- To work with friendly and sharing colleagues;
- To not be harassed for involvement in work or after-work related activities;
- To work in a very friendly, strong and supportive team environment; and
- To work with strong, high-intellect people.

IN GENERAL

"Good"…"Positive and dynamic"…"Young, professional, ambitious, goal oriented"…"Flexible, optimistic, and strong company, only good and great"…

With some bias, of course, I agree that we are a great company. While there are many things to improve upon, I feel that we are better than most, if not all, of our competitors. I think that the mere fact that we care to make ourselves even better, says something special about us.

Employees want:
- To work in a company that is positive, dynamic, professional, ambitious, optimistic and strong: in short – for a great company.

PERKS

"President's Club trip for best performers"…

We are a sales- driven organization and I firmly believe in rewarding top performers - not only through the commissions they earn, but with an annual trip together in order to celebrate their accomplishments for the company. These trips are also a fantastic way for me to be with our top performing team on a more social basis where I can get to know them better.

The locales and itineraries are also exciting. In the past, we have traveled to places like Chamonix France, the Dalaman and Antalyan coasts of Turkey, Croatia and Montenegro, to name a few. We have gone white water rafting, kayaking, sailing, swimming and sightseeing. I love adventure trips and get a real rush out of the competition, teamwork and camaraderie during these fun weekends.

Employees want:
- To be rewarded for top performance with a fun, long weekend away with their President & CEO, other top management and fellow top performers.

Chapter 13

What Could You Say About Communications And Relations Between Departments, And How These Could Be Improved?

We are a fairly small company at present, following a necessary down-sizing stemming from the global economic crisis. However, economic conditions will soon improve and we will expand our headcount once again. Thus, I felt it was best to make any needed improvements in this area now, and to get things right, before we resumed our growth.

MANAGEMENT

"In the past, heads of departments meet to discuss – to do this again"...

The management team must have let this initiative slip during the period in which we went through two restructurings. However, it is very important so I vowed to ensure this would be re-instated.

Employees want:
- To have regularly scheduled meetings between the heads of departments.

CONCERNS (OFF TOPIC)

"Small salaries for some Consultants and job titles, very worried about headhunting or someone stealing our database when leaving"...

This response has nothing to with the question posed regarding office communications. However, it is obviously important to the person mentioning it. This comment was made during what was clearly the worst year of the crisis for Russia and for recruitment in Russia. I felt that everyone working for us during that time should have felt relief in just having a paying job, as there were so many people on the market out of work, and many continue to be to this day. For those staff that did remain with us, we did not decrease salaries, like many others companies in the market did at the time.

My position is that if someone within our company gets headhunted and they chose to leave us, the stable job we provide, and the great company that we are - then, so be it and good luck to them.

Starting somewhere new in the midst of serious economic crisis is very risky for those already employed. Their new employer will expect great results during their first three months of employment and, if they do not achieve them, they will be let go without any severance pay. Furthermore, it becomes even more difficult for them to find another job in such a market. They will have a weaker resume and more explaining to do when being interviewed - during a period when competition for jobs is extremely high.

In such economic conditions, and given the stature of our company, it would be easy for us to hire replacements if someone chose to leave our company. We would have sufficient time and resources to train them properly so that the material impact would not be detrimental to us.

Concerns about someone stealing our database are a security issue for our IT department, and I decided to double check with them on this subject. There is a percentage in every population that will steal, so this will always be a concern for us and should be for every company.

However, the essence of our company has far less to do with our database or parts of our database. As a case-in-point, in the past we have had people copy parts of our database and then set up their own competing companies. They consequently failed and had to close their offices down and work from their bed mattress. This is because the business we are in is focused on client relationships and service – not raw data in a computer. We are, and always will be, so much more than a database.

Employees want:
- Fair salaries and job titles;
- Staff not be headhunted from their company; and
- Departing staff to be unable to steal their company's database.

NO ISSUES

"None" (x 11)…"We have better communications as we are small and more informal now"…"Great as we are now all on the same floor"…

About one-quarter of the company felt we had no issues regarding our communications. That is a share that I am content with at present.

Employees want:
- Sometimes nothing, as they feel things are good just the way they are.

BETWEEN OFFICES

Great in St. Petersburg (SPB) and team spirit, need more communication with Moscow"..."Have not communicated much with SPB"..."SPB advantage is that they are small and all sitting together, now it is great, would like more communications with Moscow"..."Exchange of people to different offices, that was great, plus SPB they share info on industries"..."Not a lot of communications between Moscow and SPB, but have Skype now"...

These comments made it very clear to me that we need more telephone and Skype communication between our Moscow and St. Petersburg offices; between departments, management, and between Director and Consultant groups according to clients and industry sectors. A good place to start would be a monthly or quarterly meeting. An exchange of people between different offices will have to wait until the time the market and our company recovers from the recession.

Employees want:
- Frequent, scheduled communications between offices;
- To share information between offices, in order to help expand their business; and
- To visit other offices within their company.

BETWEEN PEOPLE

"I like Boris and Diana, Albert talks too much, Margarita is aggressive, I get along well with Miron, does not know James well, I like Diana – like her a lot, Polina is very tough and she is very scary for Asya – mean and tough and no smile"..."I like Uliana"..."Can be improved, we do not know enough about people in the company, backgrounds, hiring experience at Staffwell, role, etc. getting all this info will be extremely helpful –In school have newspapers/intranet that can help with this, everyone could tell about himself, background education, professional career, this would help improve our communications and Q&A and personal questions – and if it is fun and interesting it will – Ivan is interested in developing this and thinks Gleb is too"..."We need to know each other better, have lunches with people we don't know"..."Good, but would prefer to feel more like it was one team – not separate and two offices"...

The first person quoted here seems to really like characterizing people and how they personally relate only to her – consistent with her doing this in other, previous chapters. I consider this to be a bit gossipy and not really properly addressing the question. I feel that one of my own strengths is the ability to appreciate all of our people and all of their varying dispositions. Some of the people she is dismissing here are some of our strongest and best performers. I see this as a weakness in her and an unfortunate one at that.

I really liked the idea about getting to know each other better via Intranet or a newsletter, etc., and decided to definitely explore that and make it happen. I think this would also be a useful resource to have when new staff joins the company, as they can read through the expanded employee profiles as part of their induction program.
In addition, it would help the staff in different offices get to know each other better. I made a note that Boris, Gleb and Ivan have an interest in creating this for the company.

I also thought it was a great idea to encourage people to lunch with others in the company that they do not typically dine with, and one I will also push to make happen. We seem to all be creatures of habit at lunchtime and eat with those we are most familiar and comfortable with, and I am no exception. But it is a good idea to dine with others at least once a week and expand our network and connections within the office.

Employees want:
- To know more about all of the employees in the company;
- To have the occasional lunch with people in the company they do not know well, but would like to know better; and
- To have a newsletter, via Intranet, created that would enable employees in the company to learn more about each other on both a work and personal level.

MEETINGS

"Need constant change, with immediate effect, not waiting for long meetings, need shorter meetings more often, maybe between Directors but without reporting at it"...

The subject of meetings seems to be an endless debate. Meetings are clearly needed but are often so disliked, and I am no exception. I prefer meetings to be short and to the point, and packed full of very useful, structured and well-prepared information, or discussion, for those attending. Nothing is worse than a long, boring, useless meeting full of irrelevant and boring information.

This is a topic in which I have a personal interest and seek to educate myself more about: specifically on how to create the ideal meeting. I will start by researching the web for books on the topic but also talk to other professionals in the market across various sectors. Until then, I will speak to those conducting meetings about making them shorter and more to the point, and to hold some meetings that just let people discuss general business issues and experiences they are encountering.

Employees want:
- Shorter meetings that are more focused; and
- Meetings that are sometimes not only about reporting on results, but just about talking through business experiences and issues people are encountering.

BETWEEN DEPARTMENTS

"There is not that much need for a lot of communications between departments"…"Likes banking and accounting departments"…"I cannot say that we communicate a lot between the departments – this probably could be improved by some corporate events, even small ones"…

There were some good points made here as well: we do not always need to be communicating between all departments and, if we did, we would probably get a lot less work done – something I will not let happen. Social team-building events, social lunches and the intranet newsletter ideas from this and previous chapters, can help improve communications between departments, whether necessary or not.

Employees want:
- Small corporate events, on occasion, to foster communication between departments that don't typically have a need to interact.

SPLIT FEES

"Splits need to be worked on – as they cause tension – maybe change the splits policy –if candidates added to SDS over one year ago then they should be free candidates"…"Biggest issue could be the split of bonuses – although the system works great"…

This is regarding commission splits within both our Consultant's teams and Director's teams. There should not be tension in this area and if there is it is likely due to there being too many grey areas in the guidelines – or, perhaps, not enough guidelines. I am actually quite good at these kinds of things, so I will analyze, fix and improve on this area of our operations myself.

My position is that candidates that have been entered into our database for over a year ago should be considered partially free candidates during a market recession, as we will not place as many candidates. However, at times when the market is buoyant, I agree that it is reasonable to impose the one-year limit on candidate claims by an interviewing consultant for purposes of calculating commissions.

Employees want:
- Commission and bonus split guidelines to be thorough and fair.

TEAM-BUILDING

"Bowling and team-building to bring divisions together"..."Organize some parties and events all together – communications are good"..."Now great but before bowling and team-building events, going to the pub, sharing funny stories and experiences, makes you feel the camaraderie and wants to get closer to Teri – the Boss"..."Works mostly with reports, not people, but likes team-building and when SPB team visits"...

Due to the recession and a tight budget, we have not had team-building events for a while now, but I agree we do need them. Our team understands this, but they are also a very fun and creative bunch of people that need and deserve such an outlet. Consequently, I decided to task them with creating some mostly very low budget team-building activities. I think that being assigned the task itself will be a huge mood-booster for them - and I could use a morale boost at times myself.

As for the comment about wanting to get closer to me, the big boss, I am for it and need to enable people to do this by making myself more available to them – which I intend to do.

Employees want:
- Frequent team-building events to boost morale and bring people together; and
- To get closer to their CEO, or top person in the company.

WORK IDEAS

"Think it all works fine, idea is to list fresh new vacancies so everyone can see and others can try to put candidates forward"..."Train others on other sectors, to make everyone better"..."Sonya tries to match her candidates with other vacancies – need more training on this with the team"...

I agree with everything that was stated here and feel that these are some valid ideas that we should always be doing. I made a note of all of the respondents and that I would speak to the management team about rolling them out to our Consultant's and Director's teams.

Employees want:
- To help themselves, and the company, be more successful by finding ways to generate more potential sales; and
- To improve the company by training and educating their colleagues in more areas of the company's business.

Chapter 14

Were You Developed/Inducted Adequately For Your Role(s)?

I already know that we have a very strong induction program. However, I thought this question would help reveal exactly what our employees think about it, and how it can be improved even more.

YES

"Yes" (x 30)…"More than enough, does not need guidance or babysitting – thought our induction was great, very helpful and useful and supportive (Diana and James)"…"I shadowed Chris when I joined which was very helpful, I learned a lot from Damian as you know which improved my performance last year, I have learned a great deal from you also and now feel that my business development strategy for right now is pretty good"…"Because she had promotions is very happy"…"As helped by Diana and Valentina"…"Yes because I used all this theory in practice and it helped me a lot"…"Yana gave a fantastic induction and feels can ask any question to Nadya"…"Angela helped her with mistakes and she likes the way Consultants are inducted"…"It was easy to begin as Diana and Vera were friendly and open"…

Two-thirds of the people in our company feel we have a very good induction program, which was rewarding to hear. Our team put this program together, led by two different HR Managers that we have had, and it involves many members of staff and management throughout the program, depending on who the new hires are entering the program.

Having a good and thorough induction program really helps new hires start in their roles with focus, passion and determination to succeed. We do this well as attested to in the responses to this question.

Employees want:
- Their company to have a very strong and good induction program for new employees, or employees changing roles within the company.

DESIRES

"Internally feels very grown up, great to good ideas, wants to learn PowerPoint and Excel"...

Learning PowerPoint and Excel are very useful objectives. I also would like to learn these applications better and will look for books or good online tutorials for the office to share.

Employees want:
- To learn PowerPoint and Excel, and how to be proficient in them.

IDEAS

"Had both Directors and Consultants training, just missing success stories in it – need to add these"..."Polina helped Ivan in cold calling – but should also add in business letters –how to write a letter to a client or candidate as many errors in both Russian and English languages"..."Larger training and induction is better"...

These are two very good ideas mentioned here: adding success stories to the front office team induction and training; and providing a section on how to write general business correspondence, with examples. I decided I would speak to the management team about adding these things in.

Employees want:
- Success stories to be added into the front office induction and training programs; and
- Training on how to write proper business correspondence for inter-office communication and external communications to clients and vendors, et al.

MIXED FEELINGS

"Yes and no, James gave good induction at the beginning, not skills, but outline of the direction need to go in. No skills gained but had them, but no further development of them, only on the job"..."Fine but it is not standardized for all"..."Good only that Ozzie was enthusiastic, otherwise it was dull material – too theoretical"..."Last year yes, this year hard due to being thrown into everything"...

Clearly, these replies indicate we still have some room for improvement. I think we should consider adding some skills training, review the induction program to ensure it is standardized to some degree, and make the material more practical in nature, and less theoretical. As most people are happy with the program as it is, this is not crucial, so we will look into it when we have the time.

Employees want:
- Some skills training added to their induction programs;
- Standardized induction programs; and
- More practical, and less theoretical, induction programs.

Chapter 15

What Improvements Could Be Made To The Way You Were Inducted/Prepared For Your Role(s)?

This question was designed to tell us everything we would ever want or need to know on this topic.

FROM MANAGEMENT

"None"...

This is interesting as we typically promote management from within, and we do not, in fact, have an induction program for management roles in the company – although we should. This is something for me to explore further.

Employees want:
- Sometimes nothing - although they may actually need something or find something useful but just do not realize it.

MARKET RESEARCH

"Bring back the news reports as she does not have time to do them herself"...

While this has nothing to do with inductions it is something we need to keep current. Our news reports are compilations of daily or weekly news highlights, pertaining specifically to business news from which we glean leads. They are sent to the Director's team in e-mail form for them to follow up on.

We stopped doing them because we had to let our marketing manager go, as part of our down-sizing to reduce overall salary expenses, and she was the last person doing these for us. They are easy enough to do, so either I can help with them, or our reception, or a group of us.

Employees want:
- Summaries of the latest business news, for use in chasing potential new leads.

MORE

"The process and information is great as Diana is experienced and professional, might need more for green people"…"Yes, strong part of Staffwell, maybe extend the induction period"…"Great induction with Ozzie but could have used more practical experience training in the induction by experienced Consultants"…"Longer training and induction is better"…"It was only one week of theoretical, we need more practical training and follow-up trainings"…

These comments confirm what was mentioned in the previous chapter: that we need training that is more practical, and less theoretical. The team also feels we should have longer induction and training programs. This is something we will also take under review, including follow-up trainings consisting of master classes for all front office staff.

Employees want:
- Training and induction programs to consist of more practical, and less theoretical, trainings;
- Longer induction and training periods for new staff; and
- Follow-up trainings for all staff that is mostly practical, such as master classes.

INFO SHARING

"With Adam had quarterly meetings and Diana tries but it is not enough for Albert, cannot go as deep as he can with Teri and Adam, Albert also likes to share info with James and appreciates James's experience"…

Albert is a strong Director for us and he loves the business and loves to discuss the business. Not everyone does to the extent he does. But he does, and we need to appreciate that in him, and give him what he needs individually: discussion.

Our Commercial Director may not have the interest or energy to get into long discussions with Albert about our business and work. However, I certainly do, and that is a role I will gladly take on to keep him feeling fulfilled and loyal to Staffwell.

Employees want:
- Attention and discussion at times from the top management and CEO.

TRAINING

"Negotiations training"..."More practical training/case studies and master classes needed"..."Listen in on the interviews of others to create a more well-rounded training experience, and sector trainings"..."More trainings, headhunting, highlights writing, communicating with clients, time management, I think that repeating some key trainings would be useful in order to not forget how we were taught to work, communicate and deal with clients and candidates"..."More practical trainings in the inductions needed and have mostly master classes ONLY"...

I thought these were great ideas and requests and I made notes on everything mentioned and intend to follow up on it.

I also find it interesting to note here that the experienced professionals, which are mostly who we have working for us right now, really only desire master class trainings. They do not have the time or patience for simple, theoretical training, in which they are already well aware of most of the material. They want master classes to be led by one of their peers who should be a proven expert in a particular area of their role. This they would find beneficial and a highly effective use of their time.

Employees want:
- Master classes training by peers that are experts in certain areas within their role;
- Shadow training for interviews, to acquire better interview skills;
- Proper business communications, time management, and negotiation skills training; and
- Headhunting training for recruiters.

ALL GOOD

"Good system – loved induction, very professional and fun and structured – all was good"..."Angela and Vlada inducted her very well, plus Luda and Snezhana were also great"..."Easy to join the finance team - was very welcoming"...

I am glad that some people were happy and content with the status quo.

Employees want:
- Sometimes, nothing at all.

IDEAS

"It was very professional, Ozzie had one week with her in St. Petersburg (SPB), thankful competitors do not have as deep, it helped working as a Consultant for the first 6 months"…"Experience in assisting the senior team in top level projects, even as a researcher, would greatly have helped him"…"More professional focus, less theory on stress management, team is mature and experienced – do not need theoretical trainings/inductions"…"As new Consultants sit on experienced team interviews to learn, experienced Consultants should also sit in on new Consultants' interviews to evaluate them"…"Having a coach or mentor"…"Consultants should be trained by senior Consultants who have working experience"…"English teacher told her the best way to learn is by constant repetition, so we need to re-run trainings frequently"…"Check on the results of the trainings by sitting in on meetings, interviews and notes writing and email writing"…"Angela should prepare an induction for her on who/which accountants do what in the company"…"Training on Director's and Consultant's role for back office people and admin"…

There are a few good, new ideas in here as well, such as having new Consultants with no prior recruiting experience, work as a researcher for a while in order to ease into the much more demanding role of Consultant. I also liked the idea of having an experienced Consultant sit in on the early interviews performed by new Consultants to ensure they are conducting proper interviews.

I think having a coach or mentor is also a great idea and it would also make a new hire feel more welcome and supported during their probation period – or, perhaps, beyond. I agree that some hires that do not excel in an area after an initial training should be re-trained again until they are proficient.

I subscribe to the idea that we need to periodically spot check everyone's work and, when time permits, we should train our back office and administration staff on the roles of our front office team, so that they can better support them. In addition, I think our FD (Finance Director) should prepare a section for our induction program and training for current employees on the function of the accounting department for the company. I made notes to follow up on everything.

Employees want:

- For new, inexperienced Consultants to start as Researchers or Assistants for a few months until they are comfortable taking on the higher demands of a full-time role as a Recruitment Consultant;
- For experienced Recruitment Consultants to sit in on the interviews conducted by new Consultants in order to check their performance and skills;
- To be assigned a coach or mentor;
- To be re-trained in areas where they continue to struggle;
- Frequent checks to be made on the work of all staff members, including outward business correspondence and report writing; and
- To be trained by all departments in the company on what they do for the company.

NOT GOOD

"All was OK but not structured – things only happened when thought of (getting his pass, etc) – then Lika and Lara showed him around"...

This response was interesting to me as it came from someone in our IT department that did not have a formal induction (we do not have a program for back office staff). However, we should initiate such as I am sure that he would benefit from our front office induction program and very likely help him in his role of supporting all of our employees - the majority of which are front office staff.

Employees want:

- A structured and welcoming induction to a company, even if they are not front office staff members.

Chapter 16

What Did You Think About The Way We Recruited You? How Did The Reality Alter From Your Expectations When You First Joined Us? How Could We Have Improved Your Own Recruitment? How Could Your Induction Training Have Been Improved? (Posed Only To Those New Hires In The Company For Less Than One Year)

Unfortunately, we had to let go of most of the more recent recruits during our down-sizing period amidst the economic crisis. However, I was hopeful that those that did remain on staff would provide some good feedback to this question.

PEOPLE LEAVING

"Very upset when Vera left – felt she was very positive – got great energy from her"...

Vera was our most recent Marketing Director. I liked Vera when I interviewed and hired her. However, over time I saw less of her as she made other alliances with different members of our management team. I have always had a strong, personal, creative interest in marketing. In spite of this, I have a very hard time qualifying the need for it in the case where I do not see steady concrete value coming from it – and, usually, I do not. Vera did herself no favors by distancing herself from me, to a point where I felt no connection with her. As a result, when it came time to further reduce our headcount, I had no hard feelings about parting ways with her. This was especially true given that we had to focus all of our efforts on sales and placements at that time, and I did not see any direct contribution from marketing to the bottom line of the company.

The pivotal lesson outlined here is that employees should always stay close to those they need to remain connected to, especially if that person is the CEO.

Vera was a high-salaried employee of ours and we provided a severance package to her that was equivalent to a few months salary at her termination – at a time of very tight company budgets. Therefore, I was very annoyed to learn that she had already lined up a new job by the date she left us and simply pocketed the severance payment, which we could not easily afford at the time – but gave to her, nonetheless because really we were concerned that it might take her a while to find a new job. I have absolutely no regrets that we parted ways.

I sympathized with this person being upset about her leaving and missing her positive energy. However, this was business and life during a major recession, and we all must adapt and move forward.

Employees want:
- Staff members, from whom they get positive energy, to remain with the company.

ALL FINE

"Recruited in a standard and professional way – would not change anything"…"Applied via a Moscow Times advert, then received a call from Lika, second interview met Diana and Ozzie, then lots more people – all were very professional, then a walk around"…"Darya found her – she sent her resume to Staffwell (was at a bank before and small recruitment company on a part-time basis) all was good, Darya was a great first impression"…"Ozzie, Adam, Diana, Valentina – process very professional and several stages"…"Headhunter.ru; with Lika had a good interview – then she invited Roman immediately (not waiting) then Roman sent tests to him. Feodor passed test and got offered, last interview was with Ozzie before/after he interviewed with many companies and found ours to be the best (nice offices, offered coffee and tea, good professional interviews"…"Reality was higher than the expectations, but when got offer from Teri and then spoke to Vera, felt a very high level of management. Fast offer and info given – was great!"…"Hired by Darya – so friendly and positive energy person – she gave lots of info on Staffwell. Darya and Lika were so positive – making Marianna want to work for us. Then Ozzie made her image of Staffwell even stronger – it was the first friendly interviews she had ever had".

I believe that we are great recruiters for ourselves and have a really good team and a great company. I was really happy to hear in the responses about the specific people mentioned, and to know how friendly, positive and welcoming they were to those interviewing for a position in our company.

Quite often we hear from candidates about how poorly they are treated during the interview process at other companies. This can really have a negative impact on the company's reputation in the market, as people tend to gossip about their experiences and the word then further spreads. This is an area for every company to monitor and improve on.

Employees want:
- A very professional, friendly, welcoming, polite and structured interview process in which new hires are recruited into their company.

Chapter 17

How Can You Be Helped To Better Know/Understand/Work With Other Departments For The Company To Perform More Effectively?

I thought this was a very good question that would, hopefully, elicit some useful feedback and ideas from the team on how to improve our performance.

MEETINGS

"Provide meetings, bi-weekly or monthly, or when new services or any change in the company"…"Would like Senior Consultant meetings on how the company is doing – like Directors have"…

Even when you are a small company, or a division within a company, and you see and talk to each other all the time, it is still necessary to have scheduled meetings to update everyone on the company's status, projects and future developments.

When it comes to meetings and driving results in a true team spirit manner, we have always put more focus on our team of Directors vis-à-vis our Consultant's team, This definitely needs to change and equal attention needs to be given to our Consultants. I made a note to ensure we do this and provide more frequently scheduled meetings and updates on our status for the company.

Employees want:
- Frequent meetings that provide updates on the company's news, status and future developments; and
- Fair treatment when it comes to meetings; to have the same types of meetings on the company's status that others receive.

ALL FINE

"All is fine (x 7)"…"Works well with most but can improve –but easy to call and email"…

Many replied that they feel that everything, at present, is fine, and this pleased me to know that people are content.

Employees want:

- Sometimes nothing, as they feel everything is fine.

SHARING EXPERIENCES

"More successful story sharing"..."Have presentations made by each sector and what are the specifics of each position – only our Real Estate and Construction division made this for people before – but wants to see others and understand all"..."No problems in St. Petersburg – maybe more visits to Moscow to learn more – have a shared interview with Klara"...

I thought this was another great suggestion and one that we certainly should do more often. Sharing business stories can serve many purposes, including: training and educating others; informing others and adding to their knowledge; and allowing acknowledgement and presentation opportunities to those who have helped create the successful stories, projects, sectors or divisions for the company.

We need to do this between offices as well, and I especially like the idea of shared interviews among Consultants between different offices, in order that they can learn techniques from each other they may not already know or use.

Employees want:

- To hear the details of successful business deals in their company, so that they can learn from them;
- Presentations by various divisions within the company detailing what they do, in order to be better informed and to be in a position to help them, if possible;
- Inter-office visits to learn from each other; and
- To sit in on interviews with colleagues to learn new and, possibly, better techniques to use.

MORE SPACE

"All is fine – is mature, needs space to get on with it – current setup is good"...

I recognize that some people need more space, time and freedom to get things done, and that it is something that requires individual assessment. Unfortunately, for this particular person, all the space in the world was not going to get him to perform better, so we eventually had to part ways with him.

Employees want:
- Less management, at times, and more space and freedom.

STRATEGY

"Every sector to develop a formal strategy that is then communicated to other departments, – then a marketing strategy to follow the divisional strategies"...

I believe that each sector should have a strategy, and that it should be communicated to other departments for the simple purpose of potentially improving the strategies of others sectors, if a strategy has useful elements, as a whole or in parts. The tactic in marketing - to follow the strategies of the divisions, seems amiss to me. In our business, we generate activity by getting on the phone and arranging an in-person meeting with a potential new client at their office or ours. We then give them our very nice and thorough presentation, and discuss their hiring needs together. That is the marketing strategy and I am happy with it.

I would have preferred to have read "the sales strategy of hitting the phones" rather than "to follow the divisions' strategies". We have not had great experiences with our marketing department in the past, as they have never proven that they bring a dime to the bottom line. As a result, I am not a fan of this idea for our business, especially now amidst a recession.

Employees want:
- Clear strategies to be created by each department as to how they will hit their targets and expand their division's business for the company.

USE OF TIME

"Do not want to spend time going after other Director's clients (into IT departments) due to having to split fees – I can get more on my own – my own clients are a better use of my time"..."I know how to process new vacancies too"

The first quote came from our Director who is assigned to focus on the IT and Telecommunications industry. He is responsible for going after all occupational vacancies, not only technical ones, within companies of that sector. The concept here was to have him also target IT departments within companies that are all our current clients, across all industry sectors. This would generate more business for the Consultants focused on closing IT positions on his team. These are very easy calls to make because we already have signed contracts with our clients, so it would be just a matter of calling the IT directors to see if they have any hiring needs.

He would have to split fees with the original Director who established the client or who is assigned to them now. However, it is debatable whether he could bring in more revenue by purely targeting new clients on his own. It would help if he was more open to trying new things, push himself out of his comfort zone and think a little bit more about the company right now, and not just about himself.

I like this guy a lot and he is talented. While he is not in the top echelon, he is near to it. He is not great at cold calling for new business, but he is very good at pitching business once he is in a meeting. However, during hard times, we all have to think "out-of-the-box" a bit more. I decided to let this go for the time being and see how he does following his same old strategy.

The final quote above is from our receptionist, who is offering to help the company by processing new vacancies for us, when needed. She has a great attitude and offers to do more than is in her job description. I made a note of her offer and to pass this information on to management.

Employees want:
- To act stubborn and self-centered, on occasion, and potentially not in unison with the team, or for the good of the company;
- To be creatures of habit, at times, and to not try new things; and
- To be more helpful to the company when they need to be.

NEWSLETTER

"Think we do this – I know about recently closed positions and news – a newsletter maybe"..."More info on colleagues from Moscow, not only business-related, and other people in the company that she does not know very well, explain all roles, etc, to know who does what, support teams"..."Have a corporate newspaper and share all info"...

This is a good idea and has been brought up in previous chapters. We have never done this in the company, but I think we should, as the staff are suggesting it and clearly would like it. It seems easy enough to do and even a lot of fun, and it would be interesting for me, as well.

Employees want:
- Intra-company newsletters to get to know their company, and its employees, better on a business and personal level.

MANAGEMENT

"Change KPIs and re-establish targets, Maks is ready for BD too, need Consultants to be more than they are (more BD)"..."TL to email everyone on a weekly basis, walk around, every two weeks have meetings"..."Strong team with respect is most important – likes how Nadya runs the team and is teaching this, when Nadya hires she really tries to find the right personality fit for the office"...

In the heart of a recession, we do need to change our KPIs and re-establish targets for the team. If some Consultants are also ready to take on a full, or partial, Director's role, then it would also be very helpful to the company.

I understand that the team would like me to be in touch with them more often, especially when there is much uncertainty in the market and they are nervous about their jobs and our future. I will walk around the office more and communicate more with the team.

A strong team, with respect for their company and their teammates, is extremely important, and I am very glad that, for the most part, we really do have that.

Employees want:
- KPIs and targets to reflect current market conditions;
- To help the company bring in business during hard times and to survive, even if it is not in their job description; and
- To work with a team that is strong and respectful.

TEAMWORK/TEAM-BUILDING

"Increase the number of shared projects with other sectors"..."Maybe to work on different assignments, parties, events, conferences, to share points of view"..."All is fine but does not speak to St. Petersburg (SPB)"..."Corporate events – hanging out together more – get to know SPB"..."Put list up of fresh vacancies"..."Working together on vacancies to help close them faster"..."Team-building"...

When times are good, we do not really have the time to share projects. But we have had the time recently and the more effort and speed we can put into closing our recruitment projects for clients, the better off we will be. Listing our active vacancies for the entire team to see is also a good idea, as some Consultants or Directors may have, or know of, the ideal candidate to fill a vacancy.

Bringing our offices closer together via communication and more social time together, such as team-building activities, is definitely on the list of things we need to do.

Employees want:
- To share work and projects, in order to get them done faster and with a higher degree of success;
- A published list of current working projects in the company, so that staff, if they can, may help in contributing to their completion;
- Frequent communications between offices; and
- Team-building events and social occasions to facilitate bonding in a more friendly and relaxed atmosphere.

OPERATIONS

"Easy to communicate now with Consultants, but with back office team would be useful to understand how holiday fees are calculated – when to write the request, who handles it, etc"..."I am strong in communications, and because of that I was encouraged to communicate with the team"...

The calculation of holiday time, and the proper procedure for requesting time off, is something that should be clearly explained in our operations manual. If for some reason it is not, then we need to add this into the manual. In addition, the accounting department should clearly detail this to employees that require a deeper explanation. I made a note of this particular person's interest and will have our accounting team follow up with her personally about it.

I was very glad to hear that one member of our accounting department was identified by their team as a strong communicator and then encouraged her to be the spokesperson for the department in communicating with the employees of the company. I thought this was very smart of them and well-organized.

Employees want:
- To understand how holiday pay, time off, and other benefits are calculated, and what the proper procedures are for such; and
- To use their untapped skills and talents for the benefit of the company.

TRAININGS

"I could give small trainings and advice to others"…"All sectors should make trainings about their areas – for the group, must share experiences we have all learned"…" (PR) listening to department presentations, very interesting to read the highlights of candidates and observing all in the office, wants to go on sales calls"…

Training is something that is needed and desired by our employees. I think this is a good time to engage in trainings as there is a lull in the business brought on by the recession. Furthermore, trainings can also be an effective way to lift spirits and motivate the team, while also learning new ways to approach their job.

Our Public Relations Manager believes that she could do better in her role if she were also competent in understanding all areas and departments of our front office business. I agree with this and am glad she is taking a pro-active approach and some initiative on this.

Employees want:
- To train, and give advice to others, in their areas of expertise;
- To share their experiences to the benefit of others; and
- To understand different areas of the company's business, in order to better perform in their role.

Chapter 18

What Can You Say About The Way Your Performance Is Measured, And The Feedback To You Of Your Performance Results?

This question should give some good insight into the performance of our management and the performance reviews of staff.

ACCOUNTING DEPARTMENT

"We are absent of any penalty for the company, we have no problems, all is good"... "With sales team she hopes everyone is happy with her, in the finance team Angela gives a test every year so all is known"..."Angela gives tests frequently and hopes Angela is satisfied with her and hopes to become a Deputy Chief Accountant and take on Snezhana's role"...She is measured by the accounting reports, hopes Nadya likes her work, and Angela is far away based in Moscow, but she is trying her best with the reports"...

I think they hit the nail on the head here: we have never had to pay a legal penalty in the entire history of the company, and what better way to measure an accounting department's performance, than that. A few times, we were issued penalties by the tax authorities, but our Chief Accountant fought them on it, held our ground in that we made no mistakes, and won. In fact, we were even issued a certificate by the Government, declaring us as one of best tax-paying companies in all of Russia, meaning we never made errors in our filings and always paid on time and with absolute accuracy. This is a team I love and have a lot of respect for.

I also think it is great that our FD tests the team. She was never told to do this but simply did it on her own initiative. My background is not in finance so I have never been much help to them or directly managed them. However, they have always been loyal, honest and true perfectionists - toward me and the company.

We have never had any member of our accounting team leave on their own accord: another great tribute to the leadership of our Finance Director.

Employees want:
- Perfection in their work;
- Their colleagues to like them and the work they do;
- To be tested on their knowledge and skills;
- To be promoted when they have proven their capabilities; and
- To have their performance measured.

MANAGEMENT

"None"..."Performance is results of the branch – if work is good, performance is good. Q1 results discussed with Diana, monthly results discussed with Angela (for budget) – also speaks to Diana several times a week about clients and vacancies – good communications with Diana"..."No feedback from Diana, no criticism – would love more management criticism, critique or lots of strict deadlines (just not from Albert). Would not like to report to someone just to 'discuss' things"..."Nadya measures performance weekly, monthly and every six months"..."Thankful to Margarita as she has a very structured report – she keeps on Uliana to make all KPIs and is very helpful with difficult clients, she also always has instant communications with Uliana – wherever and whenever it is needed"..."Teri and James give very positive feedback which is very important right now"..."Once a week Nadya speaks with Consultants and weekly meetings are in groups of people – weekly update"..."Nadya does very in-depth updates, all is good"...

Based on these responses, it seems that the team mostly appreciates performance reviews that are frequent, structured, to the point, offer criticism and deadlines for deliverables, and positive feedback when deserved. Performance reviews that are poorly structured, offer little critique, and are more conversational and chatty in nature, tend to be viewed as, more or less, useless and a waste of time for the staff members, which makes sense.

Employees want
- Frequent and structured performance reviews that offer criticism and positive feedback, where warranted;
- Performance reviews that are helpful, to the point and demand new goals with deadlines; and
- A very professional approach to their performance reviews.

KPIs

Measured in a professional way – KPIs are traceable and fair"..."Measured well but harder to meet due to the crisis – maybe adapted to crisis or for after"..."Need more discussions regarding that – need to really analyze KPIs as statistical entries (e.g., Asya needs to turn more calls into meetings – maybe Albert too)"..."The only KPI is money - Boris is very results-oriented and does not care about process – only results (commercial KPIs and actual KPIs)"..."By numbers mainly – sales should be the numbers – understands the importance of KPIs – she pushes Uliana to put 3-4 CVs into SDS every night before going home"..."KPIs are just quantity KPIs, show numbers but do not show quality of the work done"...

There were some positive things mentioned here regarding our KPIs for Directors and Recruitment Consultants. I believe that we do have a good KPI system but it does need to be adjusted to meet current market conditions.

When times are good, we have been very fortunate and business just seems to roll in; Directors are given a lot of active leads to follow up on and cold calling for new business is not that difficult. However, during recession, it is crucial that KPIs are met.

I feel that "Boris", who does not seem to care about the process, only results, is shooting himself in the foot with his comments. From my stand point, I know most of our Directors are not going to make their sales targets during recession, and I am prepared to cover the shortfall for a year, or more. However, the cold calls for new business have to be made and we must stay in front of our current clients and work hard to immediately find new ones. If I see from the KPI figure that people are trying their best and working hard, then I am satisfied. Those that display very little activity, and are just waiting for the good times to come back, may find they have little job security.

I think it is unfair that, while some work very hard to help the company survive by making those constant, necessary cold calls, others do not and are still paid a salary. The team and management notice slackers and recognize how unfair the situation is. Boris is a good guy, in general, but in order for him to make it through with us in tough times, he really needs to push himself out of his comfort zone, put in the hard work like everyone else, and do so in a way like the others.

I was really pleased to hear the comment about one of our Directors pushing a Consultant on her team to input 3-4 CVs, with highlights, every night. Not all the Directors work the same in this regard, but this Director has really shown herself to be a very structured and focused executive and I am gaining more and more respect for her working style. How she works and leads is commented on throughout these chapters.

Regarding the quantity versus quality issue, this has been mentioned in the past and we do need to address it. For instance, we may track how many calls are made, instead of how many meetings are set up, or how many CVs are input into the database, instead of how many CVs with perfectly written highlights are input. We need to rework our KPIs a bit and this is clear.

Employees want:
- KPIs that reflect current market conditions;
- KPIs that reflect both quantity and quality of work;
- To be motivated and driven to achieve their KPIs; and
- To be exempt, on occasion, from meeting their KPIs (*TL: but don't let them as it is not fair to others in the team who work hard to achieve their targets*).

PERFORMANCE REVIEWS

"Regular performance reviews – every week would be better than every month"...

I think monthly performance reviews are suitable for the vast majority of the team and it allows everyone, both staff and management, more time to meet their KPIs and responsibilities. However, I noted that this particular individual may desire, and need, some extra attention with regard to being held accountable on a more frequent basis, in order that KPIs are met.

Employees want:
- Frequently scheduled performance reviews; with some people wanting, or needing, them more often than the standard schedule provides.

OTHER MEASURABLES

"We are measured by financial results which is understandable but sometimes this does not reflect the effort and skills of employees, for example when candidates reject offers, etc. – discuss further"..."Only see results on the financial side, but we need to have more criteria – more performance criteria –Q4 shows low vacancies but it is not my fault"...

I understand the point here and it is something that has been brought up over the years. We have always only focused on the total dollar amount that people bring in or bill out. We also need to focus equally on the number of placements that are made.

By way of example, suppose that every Consultant works on an equal amount of positions. Consultant 1 may place only one candidate with one of our clients during the month, but at a very high fee. Consultant 2 may place five candidates with our clients but with a total aggregate dollar value less than that brought in by Consultant 1. In the past, we have given "honorable mention" to the highest billers, no matter how many placements they made. However, to me it makes sense and would be fair, to give equal mention to those with the highest number of placements, as they are working just as hard.

Regarding the issue of when candidates reject offers: well, unfortunately, that is sometimes just life and bad luck - and not an area I believe we should take into consideration when measuring actual, concrete results.

Consultants are always at the mercy of whatever vacancies the Directors can bring in, and then to whom they are distributed. At present, they are also at the mercy of the market, in general. The last comment, about low vacancies not being the fault of the Consultant, is valid. She did receive a low amount of vacancies to work on during the crisis and the subsequent hiring freeze in the market, but successfully closed the work that she was given. I let her know that I understood all of this.

Employees want:
- To have their performance measured by more than just a pure revenue total; and
- To feel that their employers still value them, even at times when business may be at an almost complete standstill due to a major recession.

ALL FINE

"Clear and responsible"…"It is good but now harder to make money – but satisfied with the system"…"All is fine"…"Measured well and lots of feedback on good and bad performance areas"…"Great and consistent and visually fine – and you see how others perform to try to do better"…"Get quarterly feedback – the system works"…Quarterly one-on-one with Diana, all is OK"…"An important point is the fixed % - and Senior Consultants' growth, and the opportunity for new projects and services"…

I was glad to know that a good part of our team seemed content with our current system of measuring performance and the feedback they received on those results.

In the last comment, the person mentioned "the fixed %", which refers to our commission and bonus plans. We have a very concrete plan, where there are no caps or limits to their earnings, in order that front office staff will know exactly what they will make. This has proved to be a great plan for our company and our team as it places more weight on results, but also has a fixed and concrete component, without exceptions. We have always paid our team what we have promised as set out in our compensation plan, and we have a very strong reputation regarding this on the market.

Employees want:
- Nothing, at times, because they feel all is fine; and
- Detailed, easily understood and concrete compensation plans, so they can calculate the exact amount of their earnings.

IDEAS

"Satisfied but maybe better to start every period from zero – even with less % is OK – it will still be motivating"…

Our compensation plan for front office staff is probably the best on the market when times are good, as it carries unlimited earnings potential, and no caps. However, in a down market like we have been experiencing of late, staff can go into debt under our draw system, if they do not cover their base salary. We could switch to a salary-based system with low- to no-upside or, as this person mentioned, lower the percent on commissions. However, I just cannot see the point in changing a really good system that is very motivating for many who want to make as much money as they can.

In addition, I have provided, through my own re-investment into the company, sufficient capital to cover any deficits that may occur over the next few years. This includes provisions for everyone's salary in the event that revenues are insufficient.

For every fiscal period (e.g., quarter or year) over the foreseeable future (in which recession pervades) we will likely re-calibrate balances to zero by forgiving their debt. This will allow a fresh start with new motivation and they will stay employed as long as they strive to meet their KPIs and demonstrate that they are really working hard for us.

Employees want:
- To feel job security during a recession - even if, for some, it requires a reduction in their overall compensation plan.

COMPENSATION PLAN

"We need to be more flexible as a temporary measure. The performance is measured fair enough, in fact our revenue scheme is one of the best among other agencies – I have a list of all the top agencies in Moscow and there is probably only one company that could compete in terms of total revenue, but there are other issues that would prevent me from moving there"...

I believe my comments to the previous topic sufficiently addressed the flexibility idea offered up here. I was pleased to hear that this person acknowledges our payment plan vis-à-vis our competition. I am sure that by now all the employees, through general office gossip, have researched the compensation schemes and structures of our competitors and concluded that we, in fact, have the highest paying plan.

It just goes to show that a percentage of employees working for you will likely be evaluating their career position on the market at any given time. Therefore, it is essential that companies always strive to improve and be the best that they can be - and certainly better than other options on the market. This is one area where my focus has never flagged.

Employees want:
- More flexible performance measurement during a period of economic recession and, especially, in a crisis; and
- To work for companies with the best compensation schemes.

<u>BACK OFFICE</u>

"Happy when I understand I help people, goes over performance on Monday mornings – likes this"…"Hear feedback and sees the publications – I like your comments in your 'PR People' blog post"…"Only had one assessment with Ozzie last August – do not feel I have a direct manager right now – thinks it might be Diana – but no orders or reviews ever"…

The second response here is from our PR Manager. She is referencing the comments I posted on my blog site (Work360.ru), where I explained how much I respect the value PR brings to a company and, more importantly, that its performance is measurable - unlike marketing, where it is often difficult for me to measure their contributions or results in any tangible way. Our PR Manager, and all of our staff, appreciates hearing positive feedback and acknowledgment for the role they perform and the good work they do.

The last quote is from our receptionist who has no clue as to who her direct report is and, apparently, has not known for the past nine months. I find this incredibly shocking and totally unacceptable. This, as was mentioned in a previous chapter, would immediately be sorted out.

Employees want:
- To help their colleagues, as needed, as it gives them a feeling of accomplishment in contributing to the company and its performance;
- To hear and feel positive feedback and re-enforcement for the work they do and the role they perform; and
- To be assigned a direct report, to know who that person is, and to meet regularly with such person to have their performance and role evaluated.

Chapter 19

How Well Do You Think The Appraisal System Works For You?

I know for a fact that, at present, we do not have a formal appraisal system in place at the company. We did have a system in place but it has been years since it has been applied. Consequently, I was very interested to hear how people might respond to this question.

ACCOUNTING

"Auditors are our appraisers – the people who check our work"..."We have annual tests"..."I like the way the tests are conducted as it helps to understand the weak areas"...

I thought that was an excellent point about how the external auditors are our appraisers on the financial side of our business. I certainly could not appraise our accounting department, but auditors, to a great extent, do perform that function for us.

I think it is fantastic that our FD tests our accounting team, as it is a very good way for her to appraise her team and their knowledge. Good answers!

Employees want:
- To be audited to confirm that their work is perfect, and if it is not, to point out what needs to be corrected, so that it is in perfect form prior to being submitted to the tax authorities; and
- To be periodically tested on their knowledge and skills.

STAFFWELL DIGITAL SYSTEM (SDS)

"Have KPIs via SDS"..."Good, all results in SDS and we discuss them every month"...

KPI figures are more of a performance review tool than an appraisal system. However, I do agree that it would be useful to have formal KPIs stored in our CRM (called "SDS") and have a monthly discussion about them between front office professionals and management.

Employees want:
- KPIs tracked in a digital format; and
- Monthly reviews of KPI results.

WHAT APPRAISAL SYSTEM?

"Not aware that we have an appraisal system – only the comp plan is understood"…"Only had one appraisal at the end of the second month, not sure we need it – it has to be understood"…"No appraisal system, we need one – would like to be a part of creating one"…"Wants an annual appraisal, have only had one appraisal by Adam and did not get a great deal from it to be honest"…"Ozzie did an appraisal system, gave motivation and instructions – no appraisal system since Ozzie left"…"No system, but if tax authorities like her reporting then I am doing a good job"…"None –there is none"…

Exactly! There is no sneaking things by certain people and I am glad they caught it. We do not have an appraisal system right now and need to implement one. The system needs to be superior to the one we previously had and be set up so that it runs like clockwork on an annual basis.

Appraisal systems are important for people to get feedback on their work, results, attitude, talent, skills and helpfulness. The feedback should come not just from their direct report, but also from other colleagues, support staff, other management and departments, and even the CEO of the company. If done correctly, the appraisal system should provide a full picture of a professional or manager, and clarify the future potential of the person within the context of the company.

For our Accounting Department, I do agree, as said before, that the Tax Authorities are the ultimate appraiser of their work. However, they do have other roles within the company that go beyond just reporting. I have no doubt that they would find it interesting to be appraised on these areas - and by a mix of many different people and departments within the company.

Employees want:
- To be appraised in a formal and professional manner on an annual basis.

KPIs

"Fair, very clear, just sell"..."Well, but not seeing it yet as crisis"..."Fine, fair, the company keeps its promises, KPIs were hard to meet with interviewing candidates (TL talked to him about why we need to interview often)"..."Clear, the more you do the more you make"..."We are judged on money, but we also need to calculate the number of positions closed"..."It works but we need to make more criteria"...

These replies do not really address the topic of appraisal systems. Nonetheless, I thought there were some interesting comments here. We are a two-cycle sales organization and it is our most important KPI: we need to sell our recruitment services to clients, and then we need to fill their recruitment vacancies, by successfully selling candidates into them.

We are a very fair company and we do keep our promises. This has been something that has always come from me at the top: if you work under our compensation and benefits plan, we are going to pay you according to that plan, without exception. Unfortunately, a lot of the candidates we meet claim they have not been treated fairly by their employers, and promises to pay them according to their comp plans, were not carried out.

At the beginning of the crisis, many of our Consultants had a hard time understanding why they needed to interview candidates in the market when it was more than likely that we would not be able to place them somewhere. They felt it was a waste of both their time and that of the candidates. I explained to them that we needed to interview as many candidates as possible now in order to have them in our database and be ready to place them when the market picks up. It would also allow us to pick up any leads about which companies were actively interviewing and for what roles, and to give emotional support and encouragement to these people, who are less fortunate than we are, in that we have current jobs.

Employees want:
- Their employers to keep their promises by paying what they earn according to the formalized compensation plan;
- More thorough explanation as to why they need to do certain tasks; and
- To have more than one criterion if needed, in determining KPIs, so that the system is fair for all.

FINE

"All OK, likes the mood here more – less stress, need to add more points to the appraisal system, Adam always had great appraisals – never confusing, Diana also good"…"100% as was promoted – the bonus system is good (SPB)"…" Fine" (x 8)…"This is a sales job and feels he controls the income – here you make as much as you want –and our appraisal system reflects this"…"Very good and attractive, career and professional growth and thankful for salary increases – and for new working schedule"…"Good, been given some clients to work with and some trainings to do"…"Generally it works – going from Consultant to Senior Consultant but the crisis stopped more promotions"…"Had the opportunity to choose sector more important for her and go on client meetings and the opportunity to teach their team – she loves it all"…"Every three months assessments are fine, but KPIs are only focused on quantity not quality"…

Our former appraisal system was not a bad one and people appreciated that we took the time to do them, as it made them feel that they were working for a really professional company. We need to bring appraisal systems back when we have the time, improve on them and then administer them on a regular basis.

I was also pleased to hear that people really liked being rewarded with our compensation and benefits plan, expanded roles and earned promotions.

Employees want:
- Appraisal systems that contain a lot of detail and criteria;
- To be promoted to higher positions, when they earn it;
- To be able to control their income by earning more if they produce more;
- To expand their roles in able to do more for the company and to make their own work life more interesting and exciting; and
- KPIs that are focused on both quality and quantity.

REVIEWS

"Quarterly reviews only – Margarita likes this as she always shares the results as soon as they come in"…"Need flexibility from the company during these times as I am working very hard but clients then freeze projects which is not my fault"…"Best appraisal system is nobody asking for him – sees this as his performance reviews (IT)"…"Works well but knows the future will be more – important to hear comments now"…

We have quarterly reviews in addition to our monthly reviews. However, the format is still along the line of performance reviews, and not traditional appraisal systems.

We do have flexibility and I do understand that it is not the fault of our team when clients freeze their recruitment projects due to the budgetary issues they face. However, I do not throw all my cards out on the table as I still need people working their hardest right now and bringing in as much business as they can. In other words, I have allocated enough of my own person money to re-invest back into the company to cover everyone's salary into the nearest future should we need it. However, I know people will work harder to cover more of the company's expenses if they are unaware of my tacit financial commitment.

One of the IT staff commented here that he thinks he is doing well if nobody asks for him. On the one hand, there is a lot of truth to this as our systems seem to be working well. On the other hand, I have to wonder if some people simply do not speak up when confronted with a problem or lack of knowledge in using part of the system. In order to find out, we should test staff in a pro-active way in the various areas of our Staffwell digital system, databases, network folders and websites.

I feel it is important for the team to hear immediate comments from me and other management. I understand that people need to know how you think they are doing in order to get a sense of job security, or know what to do to create more job security by improving their performance. Formal performance appraisal systems are a great way to achieve that.

Employees want:
- Monthly, quarterly and annual reviews;
- To feel sympathy and understanding when sales orders decline for reasons unrelated to their performance;
- To receive additional encouragement to carry on with their work and spark motivation, when sales orders slump due to exogenous factors; and
- Comments and feedback on their work, as often as possible.

Chapter 20

What Would You Say About How You Are Motivated, And How That Can Be Improved?

The response to this question was something that I really wanted to hear as people are motivated by many different things, and often we do not know what these things may be because we never bother to ask.

COMPENSATION & BENEFITS

"Motivated well now, but in future if we expand social package to include fitness membership"..."It was improved with salary increase already – I felt good with this."..."Monetary motivation system now that works good, although some people who left had a hard time with that – but this is normal and she likes our system"..."Fair bonus system – everyone works hard to close as much as possible – as quickly as possible"..."Motivated well – everyone gets what they earn – work little = earn little, work hard and successful = good pay, effective and clever motivation scheme – does not have a fix with little %"..."Salary and bonuses – very happy and thankful they got bonuses in the crisis, insurance and days off, team-building, payment for meals, environment is also important and understanding you are important for the company and internal development and trainings, etc."..."Broader social package in the future –paid lunches, fitness club discount, personal dream to work till 5pm on Fridays all year long"..."To be comfortable and she really likes the people, last year they tried to think of an award and gave her two extra days holiday instead of bonus"...

Financial assistance for fitness memberships, or directly providing fitness memberships, is a great idea and something I decided to examine more closely when earnings recover. I am also very focused on my health and would like for the Staffwell team to be as well. I am not a fitness club person myself, as I prefer outdoor and other types of exercise, but a lot of people do enjoy a gym environment, and I appreciate and respect individual preference on how they may want to get and stay fit.

The compensation system for our front office team is not for everyone. People that lack confidence and put little faith in their ability and what they can achieve, have a difficult time with it. This is because they are usually not as successful and, therefore, will not earn as much as others, which often makes them feel depressed. Our system is geared toward confident, high-level performers and achievers that do not want a cap on their earnings, and want to make as much as they can and deserve. These are the type of people we want working for us.

It is very important for me and our team that we pay according to our compensation plan, and that we always keep our promises regarding that. We have all heard from too many people in the market, too often, about how they did not get paid their due commissions and bonuses, and the negative affect it has had on them. I have a lot of integrity and believe that what I do and how I act, in business and in life, will come back to me in a positive way - and it almost always does.

Environment and team understanding are important aspects for the company as it is also a key in keeping everyone motivated and feeling good about where they are and what they are doing. As the CEO and owner of Staffwell, I see this as one of my most important functions in the company, and there is always more that I can do in this area.

A broader social package in the future is something we will definitely explore, especially when we are back to pre-recession revenues and are in high-growth mode again.

We let all of our employees leave work an hour earlier on Fridays during the summer months as a seasonal perk. It is unlikely that I would ever make it standard in allowing everyone to leave an hour earlier every Friday throughout the entire year, as our performance would surely suffer. However, I do think it is a great idea in the form of an award; to give to people who perform above expectations.

The last quote here came from the accountant in our St. Petersburg office. She willingly accepted two extra paid vacation days in lieu of a small discretionary annual cash bonus during the first year of the 2009 crisis. We really appreciated that she did that, as every little bit of saving back then really helped us.

Employees want:
- Fitness memberships (full or partial coverage) to be part of their benefits package;
- Salary increases, when they deserve them;
- A fair and competitive compensation system;
- To be paid, on time, according to their agreed compensation plan;
- A good office and work environment;
- Benefits such as insurance, paid holiday time off and paid lunches;
- To understand and know that they are important to the company;
- Internal training and development programs;
- To leave work an hour earlier on Fridays.

SOFT MOTIVATORS

"Likes to feel needed, team, people who work with relations in the company, no nasty people – great atmosphere, projects and prospective of the company, what's happening with the company, opportunity to learn and give to others around you and decent money and level of life – have things, best motivation is feeling needed"... "Successes could be noticed and highlighted"..."Success is her main motivation and likes being and then hearing that she is successful – needs to improve her English to work with clients"..."Now is learning and studying – new tasks encourage this"..."Self motivated and happy we have a strong team, likes to be first, tries to get results and pleasure from the process"..."Is motivated and proud she is working for a company placing great people"...

The first person quoted here is a member of our senior management team. Her primary motivational aspect is to feel needed. This is something, that if I am smart, I will pay close attention to, as she is a good employee. Naturally, the team will make her feel needed, as we are in a very emotional and demanding industry. However, I, as the CEO and company owner, also need to make her feel needed, and remember that this is what she needs most of all.

We do need to highlight and give more notice to our successes, which work not only as a motivator for the team that was directly involved in each of the successes, but as a good training tool for everyone else.

I believe that the fact we always have a very strong team, and that we always strive to be the best in our business, provide additional motivation for everyone in our company, including myself.

Employees want:
- To feel needed by the team, management and company ownership;
- To work with positive, friendly and team-oriented people;
- To work for a focused, dynamic and growing company;
- To learn and teach;
- To earn a decent living in order to live a decent life;
- To be successful and to be praised and acknowledged for that success;
- To be the best at what they do;
- To derive satisfaction and pleasure from the role they perform; and
- To feel proud about the work the company does.

MARKET AND MORE

"Want crisis over so we can really develop – want to prove to all we are the best"..."Difficult during the crisis but happy to have a job – coping, trying"..."New positions are motivating, her success and company growth"...

A booming market, with strong economic and financial conditions, are definitely good motivators. Similar to other people, I want things to be great again so we can grow quickly and reach much higher levels of success in the future.

Employees want:
- To work in an economy that is robust and growing apace;
- To keep their jobs; and
- Their company to attract new business.

LEGAL

"Feels comfortable now she is a fully documented legal employee, since personal life was not good she needed professional life to be good"...

In this situation, we extended the probation period of this Director as she was hired just before the crisis hit and we, therefore, deemed her a high-risk employee. She was relieved when we decided to give her a chance and officially put her on our books. This was very motivating for her at the time.

Employees want:
- To pass probation period; and
- To be legally employed by their company.

All FINE

"Motivated well, - good balance, she is very competitive"..."Typically a perfect system –but harder in the crisis –but fantastic – works for 99% of people – if work hard can earn a lot"..."Very motivated person, works as hard and as fast as he can"..."The system itself is great, it is achievable – if no crisis, all would be perfect"...

I was very happy to hear here that several people were very positive, motivated and, more importantly, self-motivated, content, forward-thinking, and able to see our future potential.

Employees want:
- A compensation system that is very good and provides motivation.

MORE MANAGEMENT

"Adam sitting with the team made Albert work harder and better – great training. Now things are weaker – more relaxed, could use more pushing – we all need it – need more control over everyone"..."I believe I am a highly-motivated individual, I want to win everything on offer and strive through effort to be the best at what I do, like everyone I want to hear good feedback – it helps, as you know I tend to worry a lot and sometimes get down, and need to be reassured – a personal weakness, don't hold it against me"...

I put into practice what I thought was a great system with our former General Manager: he would spend half of his time with me in an office that we shared, and the other half of his time sitting amongst the team. While sat with the team he would do his own work but he would also observe what everyone was doing, as well as listen in on what people were saying. It should be obvious that productivity would be high when he was sitting with the team, as few dared to goof around in his presence, and this really helped to drive our business forward.

As mentioned above, this was also great training for the staff, to see how effective management works in certain areas.

It was time to regain focus, restructure and motivate everyone, and all of the responses from this question gave me the necessary framework to do just that.

The last comment came from one of our top Directors. It was good for me to hear this from him as a lot of times I do not always take into consideration that top people may need to receive encouraging feedback, or that they get down and feel depressed at times. It reminded me that everyone needs attention, and attention from me, and I made a note to give all of the staff and management more of my time in the future.

Employees want:
- Strong management in place, that hold people accountable and keep people focused and working hard;
- To learn on-the-job from observing their management at work;
- Management that literally sit and work amongst them, and observe the team's work;
- Management that is strong, in control, and pushes and motivates people to achieve results; and
- To hear positive feedback and re-assurances that their performance is accepted and appreciated, and that their position in the company is stable and even advancing, when deserved.

MORE TERI

"Motivation decreased by crisis, low prospects and fees, Teri's meeting boosted motivation, on all company prospects - money is tight right now"...

It is clear to me, from this and from previous chapters, that the team wants and needs to hear more from me. I believe that I am a very motivating person: positive, driven, creative, out-going, happy, a bit crazy, caring, and I pretty much always know what we need to do, how we need to do it, and where we are going to be once we do it all. They will hear more from me, and more often.

Employees want:
- Frequent meetings with the company CEO, to boost motivation.

LESS MANAGEMENT

"Self motivated – does not like too much control, she is a control person herself and does not want someone on her"..."Self motivated – best motivator is Diana, Diana is very truthful (right or wrong) – always available for discussions with her"...

I do appreciate that some people are self-motivated and do not need management all over them. If these particular people are also high-achievers, they need to be given space to achieve more. People do need to be treated differently; all fairly under the same system, but occasionally in varying ways, according to their unique personalities and dispositions.

I was pleased to hear that some of our team felt our Commercial Director was a good motivator, truthful and available to the team. Honesty is really important virtue to me, especially in our management team. I am, and always have been, honest and straight-forward (almost to a fault!) and I strongly desire this in those closest to me in the company. My honest disposition has always worked well for me in life and in business situations, as most people really appreciate hearing the truth. Even when I, or Staffwell, mess up at times, I have always owned up to it and fixed it, and it is appreciated.

Employees want:
- Less management control on them, if they are greatly self-motivated and high- performing;
- Management that are honest and truthful, at all times – be they good or bad; and
- Management that make themselves available to the team for discussion.

MORE WORK/BETTER WORK

"Important to sell and make targets and money - tough market now which needs more clever work – more client oriented"..."Highly motivated to succeed and improve work, skills, knowledge"..."The number of vacancies and top vacancies"..."Wants to succeed and have potential for growth"..."Main motivation is to achieve something – needs more vacancies, which can be motivating"...

Our Consultant's team is motivated when Directors bring to them lots of solid, genuine, high-level vacancies. Our Director's team is motivated when our Consultants work hard and close the vacancies the Directors bring into the company. Everyone, including me, is happy and motivated when the company is doing well overall.

For me, and most at Staffwell, it has not just been about surviving the crisis and recession. It has always been about being better than everyone else through this period so that we have a super strong platform to quickly build upon once the recession ebbs and the market booms again. More clever client-oriented work is needed, as our business is all about clients: both our hiring client companies and our job-seeking client candidates.

Employees want:
- More clever, client-oriented work to be done;
- Sales teams to bring a lot of good business to the company; and
- Execution teams to close business in a quick and professional manner.

TITLES

"Titles, better titles"...

It is important to many people that their job title be properly aligned to the type of work they perform and to the level of success and contribution they have brought to the company. If better titles will motivate people, then I am more than willing to look at creating new, or better, titles for parts of the team.

Employees want:
- Better job titles, if they are needed and warranted.

Chapter 21

What Suggestion Would You Make To Improve Working Conditions, Hours, Shifts, Amenities, Etc?

Sometimes the small stuff is the big stuff for employees.

MIRROR

"A mirror!"..."Like my new room – was where I started. Would love a mirror in their room (as they are girls)"...

I was having my "Tea with Teri" with Alla, one of our accountants, and I got to this question and the conversation went like this:

> "So, Alla, question twenty-one, what suggestions do you have to improve working conditions, hours, shifts, amenities, etc.?"

> "A mirror", Alla said.

> "A mirror?" I asked, not sure I was hearing right.

> "Yes" she giggled, "a mirror. You see, most of the team work close to the bathrooms, but we have to walk all the way past all the interview rooms, past reception, past the staircase, and well, we are girls, and we just want to try to look good before we leave our room and walk around the office."

> "OK, so let me get this straight, all you want is a mirror, like so big (I held my hands up to an 8" x 10" size), like a ten dollar IKEA mirror, is that what we're talking about here? Ten bucks?"

> "Yes", she giggled, "that's all."

> "There is nothing else I can do for you, like a salary increase or...? Just a mirror?" I asked.

> "Yes", she giggled again, "Just a mirror".

> I said, "Alla, I will personally go to IKEA and buy you
> this mirror and you will have it within two weeks."

I have to say that this was one of the most, if not the most, touching moments of this exercise for me. It was just such a sweet and simple request and yes, of course, they should have a mirror in their room. It makes total sense to me and I think it is great that they care about their appearance in the office. I love it, and it still brings me to tears of endearment just thinking about it - like it was from a screenplay.

Employees want:
- Mirrors in their office area so they can check their appearance, to ensure they look presentable around the office.

AIR AND LIGHT

"Already have a good schedule now, need to think about air this Summer – open windows during lunch time to refresh air, early Fridays as usual – microwave could be good, but not necessary"..."Air and light issues, likes it light plus fresh air – has issues with things like this"..."Hard to sit in open space as hot or cold – she likes it cold and Margarita likes it hot"...

When it comes to air and light, different people like various working conditions. Some like it colder and darker while some prefer it warmer and brighter. Most like air conditioning but also like, on occasion, to open the windows for fresh air. These things should be taken into consideration when a seating plan is being designed. Sending out a simple questionnaire will allow everyone to provide their preferences.

Employees want:
- To open windows, on occasion, so that fresh air can circulate through the office; and
- To have their seating preferences taken into consideration with regard to bright lighting or low lighting, and colder or warmer areas of the room.

COFFEE MACHINE

"Coffee machine; want a coffee machine"..."Coffee machine, I like espresso"..."I like our office – a coffee machine would be great"...

We do have coffee machines in our Moscow office so, of course, we should have one in our St. Petersburg office. Perhaps it will not be an expensive espresso machine but we can surely provide them with a standard coffee machine. We need such, in addition to tea and water, for our staff, and visiting clients and candidates.

Employees want:
- Coffee machines in their offices.

FLEXIBLE SCHEDULES

"Good conditions, good office, some flex schedules for employees (Oksana starts at 8am) "..."Slightly flexible schedule – maybe some opportunities to work from home from time-to-time (save on gas and time traveling)"..."Would like an 8-5 work hour shift for me and Uliana"..."Company is flex with work hours"..."Flex hours every so often when needed"..."Flexible or floating hours with a nine hour total"..."Thankful for giving me 8-5, better for time management"..."Happy with the new flex hours"..."The occasional 10 to 7 would be good"..."9:15 start time due to my daughter's school"..."Leaving early every Friday all year long – not just Summer hours"..."all is good now that there are shifts for people"..."8-5 would be great"...

During some of the first few "Tea with Teri's" I conducted, our staff mentioned they wanted flexible work schedules. I immediately offered it as a benefit to the entire company. In addition to our formerly required 9am to 6pm, people were allowed to also work the hours of: 8am to 5pm or 10am to 7pm. I was really appreciated for it and it was very motivating for everyone.

We do let a few people, on occasion, work from home, but these are staff members that are high performers and always meet, or exceed, all of their KPI targets. The person that is requesting flexible work hours here has difficulty in meeting some of his KPIs on a regular basis. As a result, I am not comfortable in trusting him to work successfully from his home.

Early Fridays all year long is not going to happen! However, as I mentioned in a previous chapter, I do like this idea as a monthly reward for high performers.

Employees want:
- Flexible work schedules to be offered;
- To occasionally work from home; and
- To leave one hour early every Friday of the year.

UP-GRADE LAPTOPS

"Very organized already – all fine, up-grading laptops in the future (out-dated and heavy now)"...

We use laptops to deliver electronic presentations to clients when we are selling our recruitment and executive search services. I believe that it is a great presentation and really sets up apart from our competitors. We have had our current laptops for several years now and they are larger and heavier than the latest models. This can be especially burdensome for our female directors to carry around the city on appointments.

When we have the budget we will up-grade current laptops to lighter models.

Employees want:
* Lightweight laptops or similar, if needed for their role.

SEPARATE COLD CALLING ROOM

"All works very well, need cold calling in separate room"...

At Staffwell, everyone works in rooms where people are seated around them. I have always preferred this type of seating as it fosters a more focused and productive work environment. It leaves less opportunity for people to goof around on the company dime through activities like extensive internet surfing or chatting on the phone with friends.

However, I do appreciate that some of our team would be more comfortable and confident if they had some privacy and less noise when making important sales calls or follow-up calls to clients. I decided that I would look into dedicating a small office space for our Director's team to use for this purpose.

Employees want:
* Dedicated private and quiet rooms, in which to make important business calls.

MANAGEMENT REPORTING LINE

"All OK but people are still going to Diana instead of Albert – this is an issue!"...

Reporting lines do need to be respected. However, I need to look further into this to see what the real issues are. Albert may need some training on how to communicate more effectively with his team so that they do go directly to him. Alternatively, Diana may just need to set boundaries for Albert's team regarding which issues should be directed to Albert and which issues should be addressed to her.

Employees want:
- Reporting lines to be respected and followed by everyone.

KITCHEN

"Have a kitchen room, fridge and snacks"..."If we had a fridge and a microwave, it would be easier to stay out of expensive restaurants at lunchtime. Beer could be kept in the fridge also ☺"...

In Moscow, we are housed in an old historic building with no cafeteria, so our only dining options are city restaurants, cafes and food kiosks. If we had a kitchen in our office we would surely have roaches, so that is not an option. In spite of the sharp recession in Russia we did not lower wages and, therefore, I thought we could survive without a kitchen for awhile, and come back to this issue when the market was better.

I agree, having a huge refrigerator full of beer, and a wine cellar, hot tub, masseuse on staff, hookah pipes in every corner, a disco ball with a sweet sound system, and a roof top deck with 40 lounge chairs, would be great! However, we are not Google, and we have a lot of work to do in order to come out of this recession on top.

Employees want:
- Kitchens in their offices.

RENOVATION

"Remont [renovation] office; too cold and too hot in some places - make that better"..."Fix the paper towel holder! It is embarrassing for candidates to see this. All candidates think our updated offices are great compared to before"...

Employees care about the condition of their office and their working conditions in it. We cannot really make the office hotter or colder and this is not an issue, except for one person who is an above-average complainer. However, we can immediately fix the paper towel holder in the ladies' bathroom and I decided to see to it myself that it got done within a few days.

We did update our offices a year ago to the delight of all of our staff, visiting clients and candidates. We had limitations due to our offices being located in an historic building. Nonetheless, we put in all-new carpeting, painted all the walls and windows, created a proper reception area with proper reception furniture, and put up framed Staffwell motivational posters in all the rooms. This was done to create a really great looking and thoughtful office design which really brings good and positive feelings and feedback to all who visit us.

Employees want:
- Office air temperature to remain fairly neutral and not fluctuate too much;
- Bathroom toilet paper and paper towel dispensers to be in proper working order;
- Offices to be updated when they need to be.

FITNESS CLUB MEMBERSHIP

"Pay for 30% of sports club membership"...

Paying only 30% is better for us than having to pay 100%. Unfortunately, this is something that we cannot afford in the midst of recession. However, I have noted that it is of interest to several people and maybe in the future it is something we would consider as an incentive, or additional perk, for top performers.

Employees want:
- Partial payment of fitness club memberships.

SCHEDULE

"Create an electronic schedule in the system – not just a board in reception"...

Currently, in our reception area, we have a big board that shows which employees are in the office and which are not and why, and where they are. Our staff update it themselves, every time they enter or exit the office.

Creating an electronic version is a great idea and I am unsure why we don't already have one. I decided to look into that further.

Employees want:
- Modern, digital processes and systems.

MOVING DESKS

"Bad was too many workplace moves under orders from Adam – very disruptive"...

Some people just do not like change and, especially, changing their workstation location. We have to do this sometimes as it makes sense when we are trying to keep teams together. However, we should be more flexible in the future, and more considerate of possible disappointment by certain people in such moves.

Employees want:
- To sometimes keep their workstation location where it is; and
- To be consulted prior to any workstation location change.

IT/SDS

"After we hire a good programmer in the future, there are some up-grades needed with SDS – especially pertaining to the legal sector (specialties of lawyers)"...

We can always make our Staffwell Digital System better, and it is a constant work-in-progress. I think this idea is a good one and I noted to look into it once we have our new programmer on board.

Employees want:
- Their suggested up-grades made to the Company's digital CRM systems.

ALL FINE

"Hours are good now, great office location, not Class A like others, but likes this place here and the management"…"All is fine"…

It is just nice for me to hear that some of our team appears content with our hours and amenities.

Employees want:
- Nothing sometimes, because all is fine.

ENGLISH LESSONS

"English courses"…

We have very few staff members that do not already speak English. Those few that do not speak English seem very keen to learn and I think that is great.

A few years ago, we did offer paid English classes to staff. However, those who signed on for the course eventually started to show up less frequently for the classes, and we eventually cancelled them. However, when things are better I am willing to revisit them for those who are interested to learn, and willing to allocate the time commitment for the lessons during lunch or after work hours.

Employees want:
- English lessons, to be paid by the Company, if they need and want them.

DISCIPLINE

"Discipline helps, people need discipline.

I agree that people do need discipline and strong-focused management. I made notes to personally evaluate our management team on this and other areas mentioned.

Employees want:
- Management to instill discipline throughout the company.

Chapter 22

What would you say about equipment and machinery that needs replacing or upgrading, or which isn't fully/properly used for any reason?

Except for the heavy laptops our Director's team had been complaining about in previous chapters, I was not sure what I was going to hear from our employees on this one.

PRINTER

"Printer problem"..."Printer not working great"..."Printer"..."The color printer is very old and it takes a long time to print something from it"...

It looks like one of our printers needs to be serviced and the other needs to be replaced. I made a note to look further into it.

Printers are important for our business and they need to be working and working well. No one ever brought this to my attention before but I am glad people are raising the issue with me now.

Employees want:
- Printers, and other office machinery, to be serviced or fixed when they are not operating well; and
- Very old printers and other office machinery to be replaced with newer models.

LAPTOP

"Sometimes with Excel – needs a laptop! Small, not too heavy for homework"..."The laptops are out-dated"...

The first quote here is from our Finance Director, who was requesting a laptop so that she can work from home on the occasions in which she is ill or needs to work very late into the night, and prefers to do so at home. As I trust her immensely, I approved the request immediately, and even gave her one of mine that I was not using. She was thrilled!

In previous chapters I had been notified that people felt our laptops were out-dated and too heavy to carry around, so I added laptops to the tally of items we would need to replace when we could afford to do so financially - when the market improved and recruitment placements picked up.

Employees want:
- Laptops, so they can work at home, on occasion, when needed; and
- Laptops that are new and lightweight; i.e., the latest models.

SKYPE

"Everything is OK now but we could use Skype – are using it, Feodor is checking on this now – have everything we need at the moment"…"Skype does not work, need to figure it out"…"All is OK except Skype"…"Would love to have Skype"…

Skype is free, so I don't understand why everyone does not already have it and use it. I use it and love it. We could be video calling or messaging each other between our offices, and clients and candidates, who also have Skype.

I made a note to have our System's Administrator look into this, as well as the cost to provide cameras for everyone and whatever else might be needed.

Employees want:
- To be able to use Skype for work-related purposes.

PAPER WASTE

"We could re-use paper by printing on the other side – too many CVs get immediately thrown away without re-using it – feels a stronger hand is needed here – she can help with this"…

We used to be quite diligent in this area as this was one of the projects of our former GM. However, I suppose we have let it slide a bit since his departure. We do not seem to use a lot of paper anymore as things have increasingly switched to a digital format. However, if this person would like to help with this then I do not see why we should not let her. I also sent a quick e-mail to all employees mentioning the need to re-use paper.

Employees want:
- Companies and other employees to re-use and recycle paper and other materials, when possible.

WINE BOTTLE OPENER

"We need a wine bottle opener"...

Of course we do! Why don't we have them already is my question? We celebrate occasionally in the office and also give out wine to our top performers every month and fiscal quarter. I made a note to go out and buy one for each of the rooms where employees sit in our offices, and for spares to be kept at our reception areas.

Employees want:
- Wine bottle openers, for use at the occasional office celebration.

HEADSET

"Wants a headset for calls"...

Our rooms often can get loud, especially when many people are speaking on the phone to clients or candidates, and to each other, at the same time. I would definitely approve a headset for this person, and would have management check with everyone to see who else would like one.

Employees want:
- Headsets so they can hear better when on the phone, especially if their office is noisy at times.

SCANNER

"Scanner for business cards"...

I see these being advertised all the time but I am just not confident that they effectively work. At present, we just manually type business card information into our database. In addition, we often use LinkedIn as a lot of people's contact information can be found there. Nonetheless, I made a note to look further into this and find out if it is a good idea or not.

Employees want:
- A scanner for business cards, or other potentially easier ways, to input business card data into their CRM systems.

PCs and SOFTWARE

"PCs are sometimes slow and not state-of-the-art; Boris has lots of windows open all the time"..."All is OK with SDS, would like to add more memory to my computer"..."Sometimes PCs are working slow"..."Computer was slow and then Roman fixed it – now it is fast"..."Maybe computer viruses make our computers slow"..."PCs are slow and SDS is slow, maybe due to a lot of activity, slowing down our progress and our work – Outlook is slow and Word is slow"..."Definitely some computers, some of them are too slow and often buzz, but this is not the first priority now"..."Anti-virus program ended"..."IT system; anti-virus is blocked!! Get a good translating program"..."All equipment is used in a good way, look to up-grade things next year – software, hardware is fine"...

Speed is of the essence in our line of work, as we are often competing to be the first recruitment company to present candidates to our clients for their hiring assignments. As I conducted the "Tea with Teri" interviews with my staff and management, I spoke immediately with our IT team after any comments about a computer being too slow or making noise, or problems with anti-virus programs or computer memory. Things got fixed right away.

I believe that GOOGLE translate is a good translating program. I use it all the time and it is free. While the translation offered is not perfect, it gives me the gist of what is in a CV or resume, and what someone is writing about; enough so that I can respond adequately to it.

Employees want:
- Their computers to be fast, not slow;
- Their computers to run quietly, without noise;
- Their anti-virus programs to work;
- Good translating applications; and
- Adequate memory for their computers.

CLEAN OFFICE

"Clean up, no complaints, I do think that the office needs a good tidying up (spare tables and computers in sight, etc.) could be a problem if clients visit"...

After we down-sized the office in terms of headcount and space, we had some spare tables, chairs and computers, and related hardware, which were temporarily stacked up in the hallways. I made a note to see what else we could do with them for the time being - until the market picked up and we needed them again.

I am a big proponent of clean offices and clean desks so I was onboard with finding a solution to this issue.

Employees want:
- Offices which are clean and tidy.

RECEPTION

"All is good, Candidates and Clients need to feel comfort, music was a great idea in reception, and cookies for clients and candidates"...

When we updated the office, I bought a sound system for the reception area with the idea that we would play nice, soft, relaxing music, like jazz, to make our guests feel welcome. It was pleasant, although once or twice I did have to instruct our receptionist to "turn that crap off" when she would switch to her own CDs with "thumping" club style, hip hop music.

For clients that interview candidates at our office, we always provide a plate of cookies for their interview rooms, as they can get a bit hungry if they have several interviews in a row and are there for a long time.

Employees want:
- Guests of the company to be made to feel comfortable;
- Welcoming music to play in the main reception area; and
- Cookies or other snacks to be offered to guests.

PAPER TOWEL HOLDER

"Towel holder in the bathroom is broken"..."Paper towel holder needs replacing"...

This was brought up in a previous chapter as well. We had it fixed within a week.

Employees want:
- All bathroom hardware and fixtures to be in proper working order.

COPIER

"Copier is old and does not make the best copies – maybe after the crisis we need to up-grade"…"None, Xerox was broken but now it is OK"…

Similar to the issues with the printer earlier in this chapter, the copier also needs to work well. I made a note to check into it.

Employees want:
- Copiers and other office equipment to be in good working condition; and
- Copiers and other office equipment to be fixed or replaced if broken.

INTERNATIONAL CALLS

"I have limited telephone access to make international calls to a client – I need access or part-time access"…

To control our expenses, and to ensure no one abuses the privilege by calling friends and relatives long distance or overseas, we restrict international telephone access. However, I do appreciate that we have clients to whom we need to make an international call. I made a note to organize a free desk with an open handset for international dialing.

Employees want:
- The access and ability to make international business related telephone calls.

WIRELESS PHONE

"Equipment is fine in St. Petersburg – would be great if we have a cordless phone as it would be helpful to do admin stuff with Feodor and get our remote office working better"…

Our St. Petersburg office would like to have a cordless office phone so that they can speak with our Moscow-based Systems Administrator while walking around the office troubleshooting and sorting out other matters. This is a perfectly reasonable request and I approved it immediately.

Employees want:
- A cordless phone for the office: to be able to freely walk around and access various rooms while speaking, if needed.

Chapter 23

What Can You Say About The Way You Are Managed? On A Daily Basis And On A Month-To-Month Basis?

This was an important question for me as it is always difficult to gauge how management are performing and how much they are liked or disliked by employees; and employees typically feel anxiety about discussing any issues they may have about their superiors.

ALL FINE

"Happy, adequate"..."Likes the style and approach, good balance – has main direction but she is choosing how to get there"..."Good to have one-on-one meetings and feels Nadya's authority and professionalism with clients with issues and in the office – she is very clear with telling people where they need to improve and Diana's management occasionally"..."Fine, James is a good supervisor – they asked him to be flexible and not a micro-manager and he isn't"..."Perfect with Margarita – she is open and honest with good and bad work, she corrects Uliana and guides her. Quarterly meetings and "Teas with Teri" are good – makes everyone feel connected"..."Lucky to have good managers, Polina and Directors on different projects, Directors have to deliver for clients, Diana too but she is in a general role (quarterly reviews)."..."Happy – likes James and Teri"..."Diana: great, and more management"..."Happy to work with James on how to work with clients and write difficult emails, also happy to work with Sofiya as valuable advice"..."SDS is a wonderful manager, James is a great manager"..."Directors update work regularly, likes working for Nadya – she does not cause anyone stress, but also is clear with targets and goals – likes her style of management"..."Directors do a great job day to day – all know what she is doing"..."Results are managed in a democratic way, not bureaucratic - but still controlled"..."Very wisely – encourages best results and goes over mistakes"..."Likes it, Diana and Boris are supportive and communicative. But thinks KPIs need to be looked at"..."Angela is a very strong manager and puts exact goals, aims and priorities and she is very helpful – not just giving orders"..."Likes Angela – very happy and she learns a lot"..."Likes Nadya as a manager, she is loyal to everyone and explains why to do it"..."Monday meetings and Friday reports are good and push him – he is self-motivated"..."Likes it, likes that it is fast when needed"...

I was very pleased to hear that the majority of our team is very happy with our management and the style of management within the company. This is a very important element in attracting, and keeping, good people with us, and grooming others to join our management ranks in the future.

Overall, I think it is fair to say that our management team is very open and hands-on and that they approach all issues and meetings with care, preparation and research, and professionalism. It is also good to hear that some of our managers have been flexible in their approach to supervising the team in the way they need to be. We have always had, and tend to hire, a mature team, in terms of their attitude, style and approach to their careers and their responsibilities at Staffwell, and I think that the responses here illustrate that.

Employees want:
- One-on-one meetings with their management;
- Management to not over manage, when appropriate;
- Management that guide, and are open and honest with criticism and praise;
- One-on-one meetings with the company's CEO, on occasion;
- Help from management on how to work effectively with clients, and how to write proper e-mails - internally and to clients;
- A good digital CRM system that is capable of holding them to task;
- Their management and colleagues to keep the team on top of on-going projects;
- A style of management that combines control with democratic aspects;
- Supportive and communicative management;
- KPIs to reflect the current market situation;
- Strong and helpful management that deliver clear goals and priorities with a lucid rationale;
- Management that are loyal to the Company and to the team;
- Management that are quick to respond to issues or inquiries; and
- Pro-active management that push an individual or the team to deliver, when needed.

FREQUENCY

"Weekly, Friday meetings – Director updates"..."Contact with Diana several times a week –all is good"..."Month-to-month or weekly – do not need day-to-day"...

Frequency of meetings is an important aspect of management, and meetings that are either too frequent or not frequent enough, can be de-motivating to staff. It is vital to find the right balance.

If we are doing things correctly we should be running the following types of meetings: a weekly meeting regarding client updates on projects currently running; a monthly sale's meeting; a monthly Consultant's team meeting regarding their results and their work-in-progress; and a quarterly meeting to review, assess, and track their annual progress-to-date.

Daily management is not needed and I decided to speak to management to ensure this was not happening. The recruitment business is quite fast-paced and the team and management need time to focus on their work in order for us to provide the required results to our clients on their projects.

Employees want:
- Weekly, monthly and quarterly meetings; and
- To not have daily meetings.

NOT MANAGED

"Day-to-day not managed, month-to-month is just review but not managed; would like more dialogue and discussion, but is also self-motivated, but would love to share more with someone"..."Managed fine, fills in reports, given freedom, does not need management – just room to deliver"..."Prefers day-to-day management. For team members and Polina needs weekly results meeting on her results"..."In all honesty I do not feel that I am managed, I know what needs to be done and get on with it. I do believe I have a lot more to offer in a wider real sales management role"..."Polina for banking, nobody for pharma – feels lost, but system is clear overall"..."Very efficient but not clear who manages (Directors, Polina or Diana?); perhaps several managers?"..."Updates system works well but Staffwell has autonomous team that can work independently and without a lot of supervision which she thinks is very good"..."Does not see Albert as a motivator or leader – she is self-motivated"..."Guidance, not management – likes this soft approach"..."Not managed, but happy"...

In a few topics addressed above, it was satisfying for me to hear that the team felt they were managed well. However, here there are one too many comments that point to our lack of good management in certain areas, and this raised a real cause for me to be concerned.

We have several people commenting here from our front office team, who do not feel they are managed at all by their supervisor, and two people who do not even seem to know who their direct report is. A few people also feel their monthly meetings are just reviews of their results without much discussion, motivation, guidance, or leadership. These are training and development issues that I made a note to look further into.

As CEO of Staffwell, these are issues in which I must share some of the blame. We spend a lot of our time, focus and money on training the professional staff, but overlook the corporate need to have properly trained and developed management. At times, we falsely assume that if people have had prior management experience that they will be proficient in that task - often without regularly assessing their performance.

I made a note of all the comments here and decided to personally look into options for improving the performance of our management team. I also noted the desire of one of our top Directors to move into Sales Management for us – something to take into serious consideration as he has done well and I believe he is ready.

Employees want
- Managers to be prepared for review meetings and to offer sound professional advice, guidance and leadership during monthly reviews;
- Management to pay equal attention to each individual on the team, not just a select few; and
- To be promoted when they feel they are ready and have earned it.

BETTER NOW

"Great! The only bad manager was Robert"..."Trust, mutual respect, at first thought Diana was too much on the side of the Consultant's team (Nastya and cheating) – all is good now"..."Adam had a different management style but he liked that too – he was very demanding and watched every step and move – which kept Ivan at attention, but now the style of Diana is more democratic and more successful for our company"...

Robert was not the greatest General Manager for us, and we let him go before his probation period ended. I gave Robert very simple tasks to carry out while I went on my annual extended Summer holiday: learn our business and about our clients by going out with our Directors team on a bi-weekly basis; sit among the front office team to watch over them; and get to know the staff better.

I came back from my holiday and learned from several Directors that not only did he not go out into the field with our Director's team as often as I requested, but he almost never sat with the team. Instead, he stayed in his office with the door closed surfing the Internet for personal use most of the time. He was a nice guy and I am a nice person and a fair CEO, but I also have a business to run.

Adam was a firm General Manager and had a good four-year run with us. Adam's stern handling of the team was a good counter-balance to my friendly, light-hearted and out-going personality with everyone. However, I was strict with Adam on a consistent basis, on the goals and direction I wanted for the company, which enabled him to carry out his responsibilities - without confusion as to what needed to be done, or any bureaucracy in getting it done.

Diana is our current Commercial Director in charge of leading our front office team, having been promoted from a Director role in our Sales Team. I like her and believe in her potential, but fear she is over-loaded - as she has taken on some areas of responsibility outside of her direct remit. I also need more time to work with her and to get to know her better. However, I am glad she is well-liked and viewed as having a democratic management style.

Employees want:
- General management that are visible and truly work hard for the company, not sit behind closed doors and attend to their personal matters;
- Management that treat all members of their team fairly and with respect; and
- Management that is firm but also democratic in style.

COULD BE BETTER

"Albert is the manager, but he is not right for the Consultants – they need to be managed by a top Consultant or higher. Polina would be a great manager for Consultants, she understands all"...

Our Directors work independently in selling our recruitment services to clients. They then update our clients on any work-in-progress, and many other areas of the sales cycle that we have. They are also responsible for: managing and leading any junior Directors under them and in their industry areas of expertise; managing and leading the Consultant's team working in the same areas of expertise; and managing and leading any Consultants in the company who might be assigned to work on various recruitment projects in other industry or occupational areas of focus.

On occasion, the Consultant's team feels that the Directors are not the best overall managers for them, and this is not the first time I have heard this. Perhaps it is time for a change. Polina is one of our top Directors and she wants to move up and contribute more. Also, she was formerly a Consultant, so she knows that job and the issues the team encounter. Our Commercial Director manages both our Director's and Consultant's teams, but I feel there is room for everyone, and there is room for change.

Employees want:
- Management that is suitable for them (and sometimes the current management is not suitable); and
- Management that have come up through the ranks and who really understand and respect them, and understand their role and issues.

Chapter 24

How Would You Change The Expectations/Objectives (Or Absence Thereof) That Are Placed On You And Why?

I thought this was another good question; one that would tell me more about how the team feels about the corporate goals and expectations that I have set, our management and their performance, and probably other areas, as well.

DIFFICULT

"Never had minuses – hard to reach these numbers now"…"Sometimes Feodor feels he is treated like a child – sometimes good ideas are not listened too, such as to get rid of Lev and use out-sourcing"…

Employees in the front office team are all given a decent base salary, based on their past annual performances, which acts as a draw when figuring out their quarterly and bi-annual commissions and bonuses. At the time this question was posed, it appeared more than likely that many would be unable to cover their base salary for the current fiscal year and, perhaps, beyond. This was acceptable to me as I had already planned to fund base salaries by re-investing into the company – for a period of up to three years, if required. This was contingent on the team doing the work required of them, and working hard at it with good attitude. They were aware of this re-investment commitment but, perhaps, they did not have full faith in it given the market uncertainty.

I committed to invest more into the company for several reasons: to keep our best people employed and have them be able to provide for their families; to maintain our strength and market position through the recession; and to emerge from the recession in a strong position and with the ability to quickly grow. It was made very clear to me that targets and KPIs needed to be adjusted to meet market conditions, out of fairness, but also as it would reduce stress and anxiety in the team.

Feodor is our IT Specialist and Systems Administrator that we had somewhat recently hired. He is very young and, therefore, our management may not have given great attention to some of his recommendations. Our former IT Director, who was more mature in age and experience, and well regarded, had recently left us and strongly and confidently advised that we promote into his role a programmer working for us, called Lev. Feodor was opposed to this promotion, as he did not think much of Lev's abilities.

We soon enough discovered that Lev was highly incapable of not only performing the role of IT Director, but also his own programming role, and we had to dismiss him from the company. We were very disappointed with our former IT Director in giving us such poor advice about Lev and also for leaving the IT department in a real mess at the time of his departure. It is a real shame for him that he is no longer well-regarded by me or other management at Staffwell. We do live and learn all of the time and now Feodor is given more credence in regard to his opinions and thoughts on issues in the IT department and other areas.

Leaving a company on good terms is so important, especially as most people tend to change jobs fairly often. Not leaving on good terms, without stellar references from the Owner and CEO of the company, can potentially cost someone a future job offer they have interest in.

Employees want:
- KPIs and targets that reflect prevailing market conditions; and
- To be listened to and have their ideas and thoughts be taken into consideration.

IDEAS

"Targets and our numbers are impossible to achieve today, recognizing top achievers in the company –maybe $. One of our competitors is offering bonuses?"…"We discuss results every six months but do not discuss goals or aims – this is absent"…"Make functions wider – Key Account Management and New Business Development for Consultants"…"Would love more client work – willing to work on anything now. Looking forward to more responsibilities when the market picks up"…"New projects, new customers, to do something extra"…"Trainings, train herself, more meetings and communications with the clients"…"Yes, but wants to do more on the BD side but lacks the confidence – needs training"…"Open to additional work to help the company – she helps with redundancies too, now accountant and office administrator"…

Ideas are great to hear, especially if they make sense, and a lot of these make sense to me.

Our targets and KPIs were impossible to achieve at that time, and we did need to review and recalibrate them to reflect existing market conditions. We kept our old targets and KPIs from 2008 and going into 2009, as we just did not know how bad things would look or get - so I was not sure where to set them. Although the targets were not enforced, the team did not understand exactly what was expected of them at that time, and some people really wanted and needed to know this in order to make them feel more secure and stable.

We have always recognized top achievers through company-wide announcements, awarding small gifts, inviting them attend our annual President's Club Trip and by paying a higher commission and bonus percentages on their billings. More recently, I have had the idea to also introduce profit and equity sharing to our employees - obviously, where the best performers would be rewarded the most from the pool. Perhaps, it is now time to surprise them with this additional benefit.

A competitor offering bonuses does not concern me - nor does gossip about any other competitor's compensation and benefits. I know our plan. I know it is one of the best, if not the best, plan on the market. Furthermore, we always pay as promised, according to our plan, which is somewhat unique on the market in our industry. "The grass is not always greener on the other side", as the saying goes, and many people have found this out the hard way after joining a competitor and facing a reality that was far different from what was promised them, or as they heard via gossip. However, it is apparent here that we need to get this point across better and more often, so that it is clear and understood.

It is not acceptable that goals and aims are not being reviewed and discussed at bi-annual meetings, or any meetings for that matter. This is a management training issue that I myself have to drive, and I will. Simply reviewing someone's work with them is often times boring, useless and a waste of time for the person, as they already know what they have done. However, what makes review meetings useful is when they are given sound professional advice and direction on exactly where the company and management want them to be by their next meeting, and how and why they are to get there.

Many of our Consultants desire to have Key Account Management roles (KAM), to help with new business development and take on a partial Director's team role. This is a very positive situation and helpful to the company. I made a note to review our structure in order to plan for the creation of the new roles, and to plan and prepare for Director's training for Consultants interested in expanding into this area of our business.

Employees want:

- Targets and KPIs that reflect current market conditions;
- More financial rewards and accolades for the top achievers in the company;
- Fair market compensation;
- Management to discuss the goals and aims they should have at all review meetings in a clear and professional manner;
- To broaden their roles, allowing them to expand their abilities and to help contribute more to the company's success, if and when they are ready;
- To have more direct work and contact with the company's clients;
- To be busy and useful at work;
- Frequent trainings to advance their knowledge and abilities, for the benefit of themselves and the company;
- To be trained for a sales role, so they are able to help the company bring in new business; and
- Additional work, if they do not have enough to do.

HIRING

"Everything is fine now – but in the future would prefer to hire a Chief Accountant"...

The quote above is from our Financial Director, who also has a dual role as our Chief Accountant. What she is telling me here is that when the market picks up, and we expand again as a company, that she is ready to step up and take on more responsibility. She is also saying that she is ready to groom and manage a Chief Accountant, a role that she has held close to her and has not wanted to delegate in the past.

This is all good news: for her career and for the Company.

Employees want:

- To be promoted and to delegate their role to another, when they are ready.

ALL FINE

"No changes – understands role here, bring business, motivate and drive the Directors team and have work, etc., out-staffing, out-placing, franchise the company, maybe branch out later, and executive search"…"No, all is reasonable – would not change, all makes sense"…"OK"…"Expectations and objectives are reasonable, JD (job description) is reasonable overall"…"All fine (x 15)"…"Entire system is just, understands all and it is clear and fair and built on performance – clear goals"…"I wouldn't change them, I think all the expectations are fair and the company requires from me the things we all need"…"Objective is to bring the results, dependent on Directors – likes this business"…"All is OK, the objective is to bring the results – very clear"…"I do not think our goals should be changed"…

Most of our team feels everything is fine right now regarding the objectives and expectations which we place on them. This is good to hear. I noted the ideas for new lines of business in the future, all of which we have taken under consideration in the past, and will continue to do so in the future.

Employees want:
- Sometimes no changes to the objectives and expectations which are placed on them;
- The company they are working for to consider new lines of business expansion; and
- Clear, fair and reasonable objectives and expectations put on them.

NOW AND THEN

"Crisis now, then move forward"…"For now all works well but when things pick up I imagine the system will change"…"We had a very strong leader in Moscow, in my opinion he was excessive in his leadership style bordering on bullying at times, however standards were high and things got done (mostly from fear). I feel that we have gone too far in the other direction now (as you know). I believe that sales-driven companies need to be led by experienced sales people, who understand how to get the best from individuals and teams. You would not expect me to say anything else because this has been the story of my entire career, and why? It created highly skilled and motivated people who can achieve great things"…

The current situation is due to a global economic recession, which also impacts Russia and the recruitment industry. We will change as the market changes and improves. Our expectations and objectives will amplified as we do well when the market does well, and our rewards are greater when we push ourselves to achieve more.

On balance, I am a fan of our former General Manager. He was tough, firm and strong, and that is how I wanted him to be then. He got things done and we achieved a lot as a company during those years. However, he, and some members of the team, did have issues with each other, and did not get along well together. It was what it was.

One of the people quoting above feels like our Commercial Director is too relaxed now in her management style, as compared to our former General Manager. What he is saying here is that he thinks the current CD could be better at her job. I hear him, but I am not completely convinced in what he is saying.

First, Russians comprise 95% of our team, and not all of them speak English fluently, and most office communications are in Russian. The person quoted above does not speak Russian. Second, our Commercial Director has taken on more responsibilities, on her own initiative, than just the front office team - so there is a lot that she is doing for the company that he does not see or know about. In addition to a language barrier, there is a lot that our Commercial Director does and contributes, that this Senior Director cannot even witness or observe, or hear and understand, due to his language limitations.

However, this person was one of our two top Directors last year and is set to have another great year this year, and I do like to promote top Directors, just as I did with our current Commercial Director. I also think this Senior Director could add value in a sales leadership role.

I decided that I needed to give this more thought.

Employees want:
- For things to change and the Company to move forward and expand once market recessions have ended;
- Management to not lead and manage by using bullying and fear tactics;
- Strong leadership that drives companies to succeed; and
- To be promoted when they feel they are ready to be, and are confident they will be successful in their role and for the Company.

MOTIVATION

"KPI expectations – updates would be good, expectations, would love to be positive, more Teri speeches, and sharing successes is very motivating as it helps with competition"...

Updating our KPIs to match current market recession conditions has been mentioned in previous chapters, and it is an area we will review. I also clearly hear that the team wants to hear more from me personally - as their CEO and the owner of the company, on how we are doing, my view on the market and our industry and our outlook for the future.

My natural disposition is very positive, in general, and I understand that the team want me around them more now, as I motivate them and make them feel good and optimistic, especially when business is down due to recession. I made notes to myself to spend more time with the teams in both offices and to give more regular updates to them.

Sharing successes (i.e., information on the deals we have closed), is a great idea for the reasons mentioned: they are motivating as they parlay positive news the company is experiencing, and they drive competition within the team which, in turn, drives everyone to perform better and work harder to succeed.

Employees want:
- KPIs to be updated if needed, to match current market conditions;
- Frequent updates and communication on how the company and market are doing;
- Communications from management that are positive in nature;
- In-person communication from the CEO of the Company; and
- To be able to publicly share their successes with their colleagues - as a motivational tool and to drive friendly, positive competition between them.

Chapter 25

What, If Any, Ridiculous Examples Of Policy, Rules, Instructions, Can You Highlight?

I thought this was a great question because if there is anything that the team feels is truly ridiculous I really want to know about it so I can consider making changes.

CLEAN DESK

"Clean desk policy with Adam; accounting offices have a lot of papers!"..."Adam's clean desk policy was impossible for the finance team – he was too micro-managing them on that – they were fighting with him about it- then they won – now all is OK"..."Clean desk policy is understood – she is messy though"...

The clean desk policy was the initiative of our former GM. He was very neat and well organized, which are common traits of strong operations professionals. I supported him in it as it made sense to me: our employees' desks should be clean as it not only looks nice, but we have a lot of office guests, and it forces people to become more organized, caring and responsible.

Everyone else having a clean desk also encouraged me to become tidier as well, which was good for me.

The accounting department is a different story. It is Russia and they have to deal with a lot of paperwork, as most of their work is not fully automated, and they work very long hours. If our accounting team was making a lot of mistakes, I might see a clean desk policy as a possible way to improve their performance. However, they are really good at what they do, are extremely hard working, and almost never make mistakes.

Had I known that the former GM, in pushing a clean desk policy on them, was causing them so much stress at the time, I would have intervened and asked him to back off of them. However, everything seems to be fine now.

I am a big fan of the clean desk policy, for most employees, and we have kept this initiative active in our office and always will.

Employees want:
- To not have clean desk policies if they work in an accounting department; and
- To not be pushed or micro-managed with policies they do not agree with and which are difficult to conform to.

ALL FINE

"All fine (x 21)"..."None, very little bureaucracy and very little report writing – all is fine"...

Twenty-one employees felt we did not have any ridiculous policies, rules or instructions – a sufficient number to substantiate that we were doing most things correctly in these areas.

I am not a fan of bureaucracy at all. I make very quick decisions and implement good ideas without hesitation and I believe this is one of the reasons that we are a successful, fast-paced company. In addition, we are very focused on continually optimizing all of our processes and procedures so that we can be more efficient in everything we do, including reducing the amount of time and information needed to put into reports.

Employees want:
- No changes to be made sometimes, because everything is fine to them;
- Very little bureaucracy in the company; and
- Reporting that contains only the most necessary information.

IT PROBLEMS

"None, but when we moved from the old office to the new, had IT problems – but this is not policy, just difficult"...

Offices moves are never without difficulties and IT, and everything related to it, is usually the most challenging aspect. Our St. Petersburg team has moved offices several times; expanding in good times and contracting during recession. They do not have a dedicated IT specialist working for them locally, and so they have had to make do with remote help and occasional visits from our Moscow-based IT team.

When the market picks up, we will need them to expand operations once more. However, before that happens we will try to learn from our past experiences in order to ensure a smoother and less problematic move.

Employees want:
- Office moves that are less problematic and challenging regarding IT issues.

COMMUNICATIONS

"Albert communicating via e-mail, instead of talking to me when he is only one seat away. Plus Margarita's way of dealing with Consultants"...

I understand this person's frustration with her more senior colleague, who sits very close to her, communicating to her by e-mail. However, there may be a good reason behind this: such as she may have been absent from her seat when he wrote a note to her; or he wanted to document the message so he could refer back to it in the future if needed. For instance, if he asked her to do something and then she did not do it, and then claimed he never asked her to do it, he could then refer back to his e-mail and say "well in fact, yes I did, and here is the email to prove it."

I think the best thing for me to do in this situation is to speak with both of them about it in more detail and then bring them together to discuss it, resolve the situation and move on.

Margarita is a young woman, but she is more senior and successful than the person commenting on her. She is demanding of the Consultants working on her projects, but she is also extremely helpful to them and keeps them to task, which makes them more successful.

The person responding here has commented a lot in this book in the same fashion. Unfortunately, this person has the inability to appreciate varying styles of working, management and leadership, and the broad dispositions of people, in general. This made me start to believe that this person may not fit in long-term at Staffwell.

Employees want:
- Verbal communication, instead of e-mail, if in near proximity; and
- Their peers to act and communicate as they do.

INTERNAL

"Old slogans on PCs were annoying – but we took them down"...

Our HR Director had the idea and then implemented an initiative to put different, famous quotations on everyone's desktop computer screens every week. The problem was that the text was huge, covered the icons and just looked terrible. I was also horrified when I saw it on my computer and immediately ordered it to be deleted and to restore our simple Staffwell logo with reasonable size in the center of our screens, so that icons could fit nicely around it.

Our HRD was just likely trying something out, and thought it would be fun and fitting with our office art that consists of branded motivational posters. It did not work, but there was no harm in her trying.

Employees want:
- A clean, small, and simple corporate logo on their desktop computer screen, so that they have plenty of room to organize their icons around it.

MANAGEMENT

"Diana has tendency to support weak team members, not our strong ones – either competing fair system – justice, or we are all just nice to all, including non-performers. Wants one system - and all to follow it. James is very disciplined, this system can help"..."Vacancy distribution, sometimes Diana does not consult the Directors on this, Real Estate and Construction positions were given to Tamara and she did not inform Margarita or Uliana. Boris was the Director on this."..."When Adam prevented eating at the workplace"...

Diana was a former Director in on our banking team who was then promoted to Commercial Director for being our top-performing Director at the time. She also had management experience prior to joining Staffwell. Unfortunately for me, and the company, I have not spent a lot of time with Diana and failed to groom her into the type of manager I would like her to be. However, this is precisely one the reasons why this entire exercise is so useful to me and the company, as it allows us to significantly improve ourselves.

I am a staunch advocate of real fairness. I have been that way all my life and so I sympathize with the first person quoted here. Of course we need people to be treated fairly and ensure that they feel they are fairly treated. Due to the fact that we are a sales organization, we do need to give more attention, in the form of respect and further motivation, to our top performers – but, also, attention in the form of assistance, discipline and encouragement to our under-performers.

Diana is a good person and has taken on a lot in terms of other responsibilities in the company. Accordingly, she may not even be aware that some of our top team members might feel neglected or unfairly treated by her. I decided I needed to speak with her about it and was sure that she would, on her own, improve things in this area.

James is highly disciplined and his style of working can help when we make changes to the company based on this exercise. All in good time.

The matter of vacancy distribution is a problem that we need to sort out and, again, is an issue regarding fairness and respect. At Staffwell, we break our front office business into industry sectors and occupational areas - all staffed with teams of Directors to bring in and manage the clients, and Consultants to find and manage the candidates.

The situation that is being explained here is one in which our Director who focuses on IT, telecommunications and industrial clients, brought in a real estate position and, instead of our Commercial Director distributing it to our real estate team to work on, she gave it instead to a Consultant who focuses on industrial placements. She also failed to inform or consult the real estate team of her decision prior to it happening. This caused a lot of stress and a feeling of unfairness from our real estate team.

We are not perfect. We can only try to become perfect. For me, this is a simple issue of creating new rules in our operations manual. Namely, that if a vacancy is be considered for distribution outside of a sector or division where it would normally be assigned, the Director of that division must be consulted and the matter discussed and agreed upon by both parties prior to it being distributed. Matter resolved.

Our former GM set out a policy in our Moscow office that no food should be eaten in our office. He did this because when people were eating at their desks they were leaving a lot of crumbs on the floor and quickly after we started to have a mice and roach problem. I was obviously in agreement.

Our building is an old historic one that, while lacking a cafeteria, is centrally located around hundreds of eating establishments. By refraining from eating food or snacks at personal workspaces we also avoided associated odors as well.

Employees want:
- A system that instills fair treatment of all employees;
- Better treatment given to top performers;
- Respect by being consulted prior to any decisions that are made that may affect or involve their area of business within the company; and
- To eat at their work stations or in their office.

METINGS AND START TIME

"8:30am Monday morning meetings were too early"…"Under Adam surprised by rule to come at 8:45am – then realized it was fair and more productive for all"…

As an American, I am used to getting to work early and having early meetings. Out of habit and training in the U.S., I like to get up and get right to it and Adam, our former GM, was very good at supporting me on this. While we officially start the workday at 9am, we ask everyone to arrive at 8:45am in order that they can have their coffee, smoke, chit chat, etc., and then get right to work at 9am. In order to not detract from our main hours of productivity we start out internal meetings at 8:30am.

I may decide to be more flexible to some degree during the recession - but when things pick up again, it will be full speed ahead, and the discipline of getting to work early and on time, is key to our success.

Employees want:
- Meetings that are not too early in the morning (i.e., before the start of company working hours).

IDEAS

"Need fee share guidelines, and change of password on computers every month is annoying"..."Changing PC password once a month is annoying"...

I have learned during this exercise that the current fee-sharing guidelines are not as thorough as they could and should be. I decided to personally take this project on to ensure a very fair system, where there will be little room for debate in the future.

I agree that having to change our passwords every month is very annoying and decided to speak to our IT team about this.

Employees want:
- Very fair and thorough fee-sharing guidelines or rules; and
- To not have to change their computer password every month.

INTERNAL PROCEDURES

"When signed Staffwell hiring documentation with Vlada, signed a job description that did not fit the role"..."Splits not so good for Consultants – would prefer to meet all candidates herself and present them herself (50/50) – review splits! - and get Consultant's buy-in on decision before making it"..."Not many companies where IT people wear business clothes – I am not complaining though"...

We should have people sign the correct employment documentation that corresponds to the role for which we have hired them. I decided to look into that to ensure it was only a one-off mistake and not one we are repeatedly making.

Regarding splits, which refers to the occasional situation when Consultants share candidates and then when one is placed, they need to share in the fee and any subsequent paid commissions. We will always employ splits as we are a team and, at times, need to closely work as a team. However, I concluded that I should review how fees splits are decided and how to improve them, if needed. Consultants should absolutely be referred to before any decision on a split is made and all parties involved should be in agreement on the split before such is made. If it is not already in place, this should be a rule contained in our operations manual.

We are a professional company and our clients and candidates are mostly white-collar executives and professionals. Accordingly, I expect everyone to dress in a professional manner.   Our IT team sits amongst our front office team and, therefore, (even more so, I believe) must also dress professionally, and act the part as well.

Employees want:
- To sign new employment documentation that matches the role they have agreed to take;
- A system of fee-sharing, or splits, that is fair and attractive to them;
- To be consulted prior to any decisions made that would affect them, their earnings, or their business at the company; and
- To dress in casual clothes, if allowed by the company.

MOVING SEATS

"Moving seats too much is confusing, I do not know new extensions or know where someone sits"...

Over the past several years we re-arranged seat locations for employees due to the fact that we were continually expanding and needed to re-organize where teams of people sat. Recently, we moved some people's seats again as we contracted and down-sized our offices a bit.

The moves are confusing, but they do not need be if we prepared better for them by promptly distributing everyone's new extensions and creating a seating chart to help everyone learn and find their new location.

These things, among others, need to go into a new operations manual specifically for office moves or office seat changes. I added this to the list of things to do.

Employees want:
- To not move their work station location very often; and
- To have an up-to-date seating chart of people in the company, and to know the current extension of all their colleagues.

Chapter 26

What Examples Of Ridiculous Waste (Material Or Effort), Pointless Reports, Meetings, Bureaucracy, Etc., Could You Point To?

As efficiency and optimization within our Company are very important to me, I was hopeful that the responses to this question would fill in any gaps we may have.

REPORTING

"Last year's flash report with Adam was a waste of time, with too many things on it"..."SDS updates are time-consuming but hugely important"...

Adam was a very organized General Manager, which I really liked about him. He started something called a flash report, which were brief, written updates on 5 to 7 key areas of work and areas of responsibility, and were meant for the more senior team members. This report was submitted to him on a weekly basis. He would then create a summary report from it and submit his own flash report to me. I loved it and it really kept me constantly up-to-date on things and prepped me for any major decisions I needed to make, issues we needed to resolve, or ideas we needed to consider.

For some of those in the team who were quite busy, and not the types to like report writing, it may have seemed like an added burden that took away time from producing more - especially as they needed to frequently report and separately update into our CRM system.

Recently, we have not kept up with the flash reporting system. However, it is something that I miss and will likely re-instate in the near future again – keeping in mind some of the team's concerns.

SDS updates, which are the updates the front office team makes into our CRM system, are very important and must be done no matter how time consuming. This is because it enables us to store and track all of our project and work history, our KPIs, and our progress, on an individual, team and company basis.

Employees want:
- Simple, quick and efficient reporting systems, that are not overly time- consuming.

NONE

"None (x 21)"..."None or very small, likes it like this – One of our competitors spends 50% of their time making reports and time-wasting"..."Now is a lot less, we have a system but simplify it"...

Nearly half of our team felt that we had no problems with ridiculous waste, pointless reports, meetings or bureaucracy, which is really good to know and shows that, overall, we are pretty good at managing these areas.

One of our front office team members formerly worked in recruitment at one of our market competitors. I was quite shocked to learn that he spent half of his time creating reports and wasting so much time with them. However, this is all the better for us in being more efficient, as it also can only help us to recruit more people to join us, and to attain higher levels of performance and results.

Employees want:
- Sometimes nothing, because they feel everything is fine; and
- To spend as little time as possible on report writing, and more time on trying to attain results.

PAPER

"Copy paper"...

Because we are a recruitment company specializing in executive search and management selection, we use a fair amount of copy paper, particularly to print out resumes for interviews. The team is aware that they should try to conserve paper, when possible and appropriate, by printing on the other side of an already printed page no longer in use or need. However, I suppose we let that slide a bit on occasion.

The occasional reminder should help with this, and also I needed to double check to see if it is in our operations manual.

Employees want:
- To conserve and recycle paper as often as possible.

MANAGEMENT

"Albert is too much of a time-waster, and he can be strange when he is very busy"...None now – only when Adam was here"...

Albert is a very good Director of ours. He has delivered good results, is quite smart, and cares very much about the business, our company and the team. I feel that, given time, he is going to develop into a really top-rate and top-level Director for us.

Albert can be a bit strange and high maintenance at times. However, he is also a highly interesting character with a lot of potential, and I like him as a person - as I enjoy all different types of people.

Please note that the person commenting here is a peer of his, and someone who is under-performing in comparison to Albert. Accordingly, I decided to take all of this with a grain of salt and, instead, try to get her to focus more on herself and her own performance.

We are a bit more relaxed these days as compared to when Adam was here, but that also is due to the fact that the market is slow and we are in a transitional phase with regard to our management structure. Things will very likely change some when the market picks up or when I implement changes to our structure and operations. However, the efficacy of the business will always be my priority.

Employees want:
- Their colleagues and management to not waste time or act strange; and
- To work for an efficient company.

MEETINGS

"Some Director's meetings should be shorter"..."Sometimes Director's meetings go too long, but info is good"..."None, one person complained about weekly meetings but she does not agree"...

We need to have meetings, but they should only be highly useful and very to-the-point. This is something that needs to be in our operations manual, and I need to make it clear, in a quick meeting with the team.

I think nothing is more useless or de-motivating than having to sit through a boring meeting, with mostly irrelevant information, that drags on much longer than necessary.

Employees want:
- Meetings that are short and to-the-point; and
- Weekly update meetings.

BREAKS

"Human Connection is limited, or increase breaks"...

I do not really agree with this comment. Work is for working. We sit in mostly open-plan office space for which one of the purposes is to promote human connection, and we already extend a fair amount of breaks. My opinion is that this is a personal issue with this particular employee who may have a harder time making friends with people in the office.

I am hopeful that some of the other ideas that have come to light in this exercise, such as more team-building activities and peer-organized lunches, will induce greater connections between employees.

Employees want:
- To get to know other employees in the company better, on a friendly, personal basis.

COMMUNICATIONS

"Too many useless e-mails from colleagues, them sending CVs to all – waste of time. AmCham and AEB letters – they send the same letter five times"...Now market is stressed, but info from company is important, on changes and plans – communications regarding the company often"...

I am on the main corporate e-mail list, so I do receive a lot of the e-mails that go around the office to the entire group. To me, the volume seems reasonable as, on occasion, we do need to send around a CV of a candidate who might be interested in many different industry and occupational areas. In such cases, many, if not all, of our front office team should quickly review the CV. However, I recognized that I needed to pay more attention to this and speak to management about it, in order to individually address any employee that may be a repeat offender, or abuser, in sending useless e-mails to the team.

I also find it very annoying to receive the same, constant barrage of mass marketing e-mails from AmCham and AEB (local business clubs) and made a note to mention it to them.

The team wants and needs more information from me on what is happening with our company and in the market. In somewhat uncertain times, people need more frequent information in order to help them feel more comfortable and secure in their job.

Employees want:
- Their colleagues to send e-mails to them that are only highly necessary;
- Business clubs and other companies to not send the same e-mail more than once or twice; and
- Frequent information from their executive management on conditions in their company and on the market.

TRAINING

"But maybe highlights training was not useful because I already know how to write them (Sofiya did this) but I feel her highlights are not great – Ozzie gave a great training on this (more on communication with the client when the client is new). Clients are judging our company on highlights – our professionalism and image, need to have perfect grammar, proof-reading and spelling – anyone but Sofiya should do this training"...

I made a note to check Sofiya's highlights (i.e., interview notes). If she is training in this area then she herself should have perfect highlights. At the same time, the person writing about this is not a fan of Sofiya – stemming from a disagreement over a fee split that, in the end, favored Sofiya, and left him quite disgruntled with her.

I feel that Sofiya is a real talent and will undoubtedly become a superstar. I would be quite surprised if she did not have very good, if not, near perfect, highlights. However, I decided to look into it because it is not beyond the realm of possibility. I decided to review the highlights of the person quoted, because if his are very good-to-excellent, then perhaps he should be doing the training in this area of our business.

More importantly, I hear him clearly in that he did not feel it useful to be trained in an area he was already proficient in - which makes a lot of sense to me. Only people who need the training should be in the training class.

I was happy to hear that he did have a useful experience in being trained by Ozzie on communicating with new clients.

Employees want:
- To not waste their time being trained in areas in which they are already proficient; and
- To be trained in areas they do not already know; or to be taught to look at things they already do and know, but in a better way.

SMOKING

"Strange rules when Adam was here –smoking"…

When reviewing the productivity of the company, our former GM concluded that those who smoked cigarettes during working hours were less productive than those that did not. At first, he wanted me to approve a rule that would completely ban anyone smoking during the entire workday. Later he deferred to my suggestion to simply limit the length of smoking breaks.

Smoking is still very popular in Russia. Cigarettes are inexpensive, it is not seen as completely unfashionable to smoke, and smoking is still permissible in many, if not most, public and private places. Most smokers are somewhat addicted to cigarettes and so I understand that they may truly need to smoke.

In general, people have anxieties, and we have had all types of people working for us over the years with different issues: some smoke a lot; some we feared, and occasionally, discovered were drinking alcohol, or abusing the internet (e.g., social media, porn, or non-work related blogging); some snacked a lot; and some just talked a lot - more than others.

Of course, on the harder abuses, we took measures to deny access to the addiction, especially when related to the internet. With others, we watched their performance and conduct very closely, and if it was truly affecting their results or the company's performance, we parted ways with them.

For our smokers, I did not want to deny them their needs, but just limit the time they spend doing it during prime working hours. Therefore, where typically they may have stepped outside every hour or two with a fellow colleague and chain smoked three cigarettes each, we asked that they each only had one cigarette each together, and then return to work. As a result, the frequent 20 minute cigarette breaks were reduced to 5 minute breaks, and they ended up smoking fewer cigarettes during the day, which is obviously healthier for them.

It was a good compromise that I thought was fair to everyone.

Employees want:
- To smoke cigarettes during the workday, if they are smokers.

WORK DUPLICATION

"In SDS (our CRM system) we have to do progress reports – we should also explain to Directors but then it is a double effort (now) – will tell Director about it and then also have to write it, which is time-wasting"..."Updates and Directors and Consultants –sometimes they both put the same info into SDS – double entries"...

Duplication of effort is a poor use of company time and obviously makes us less efficient. I think it should work in the following way: Consultants should create their updates in SDS on a weekly basis regarding the status of the recruitment projects they are working on; Directors should then read them and then sit with the Consultants only if they have any questions on it or need more information from them; then the Directors should report the final weekly updates to our clients.

I have a feeling that what is happening here is that: 1) the Consultants are late in inputting their information, 2) Directors want their updates from Consultants too early, 3) Directors are not reading the Consultants' updates in SDS, or 4) all of these things. This problem is easy to fix by clarifying our procedures regarding this, by speaking with the team about it, and ensuring that our operations manual clearly details these procedures.

Double entries of the same information into our CRM system, SDS, does not make sense to me either, as it is a waste of time, and is something I needed to look further into.

Employees want:
- Corporate procedures to be followed;
- To not have to duplicate their efforts; and
- To not have others duplicate their efforts.

BAD EMPLOYEES

"All is fine but pity that we spoiled three months of our life with Lev"...

Hiring, or having inadequate, under-performing or bad employees in your company is never a good thing and can adversely affect everyone around them, including the company itself.

Lev was a programmer for us, whom our former IT Director, when he was leaving us, insisted we promote to take over parts of his role. We did this as we trusted the opinion of our former IT Director, as he had been a decent and respected employee of ours over the years. However, you learn sometimes, as we did, that when people are leaving the company, they do not always extend the same level of care that they had while they were a seemingly committed employee.

It took us three months to unanimously conclude, without reservation that Lev was a complete idiot, who had absolutely no idea what he was doing. We also discovered, after hiring a new and very adept IT Programmer (who would later be promoted to our IT Director), that not only did our former IT Director leave us in the hands of someone incompetent, but that he also never documented, with accuracy, anything regarding our systems and how they worked.

Our new IT team was shocked to discover this when they started their new roles with us, and set out as one of their primary initial tasks to learn everything about our systems and to document it all for us.

Employees want:
- To only work with competent, capable and proficient employees; and
- Only top-rate and highly-functional IT management and specialists in their company.

Chapter 27

How Could The Company Reduce Stress Levels Among Employees Where Stress Is An Issue?

The global economic crisis and subsequent recession have created a lot of anxiety. Anything we can do to identify and minimize the stress levels of our staff will surely result in a more healthy, happy and productive company.

STRESS FROM EXTERNAL SOURCES

"I have only external stress – the Tax Authorities, etc. Sometimes they send mistake letters to her asking her to pay US$100 and this causes stress to prove we don't have to pay – that it was their mistake about the mistake"...

Our Finance Director (FD) and Chief Accountant is a perfectionist and she takes her job and performance very seriously. Her work is primarily scrutinized by the Russian Tax Authorities, who seek to identify errors, assess fines and collect such fines. In 10 years of business in Russia, we have not had to pay one fine, which is pretty amazing given the amount of paperwork required and the, often, vague rules set forth. However, I understand the stress our accounting team is under every time they receive a fine and then have to spend days trying to prove they did nothing wrong.

Unfortunately, there is nothing we can do to change how things are done, as it is part of a system in the country in which we operate our business.

Employees want:
- The Tax Authorities to not make mistakes when scrutinizing their company's submitted reporting, and then erroneously fine them.

CRISIS

"Must have stress to perform the job – stress for job security was there and different. Now everyone loves the team. Stress of Directors is a lot of calls with no results. Boris is lazy but a brilliant sales person"..."Most of the stress was over redundancies"..."Everyone is afraid of redundancies"...

Being a front office member of Staffwell, as either a Director or a Recruiter, is always somewhat stressful to a degree, due to the nature of the roles. The recruitment business is a fast-paced environment with a lot of pressure put on everyone to find the ideal candidate for companies in the shortest amount of time. To succeed in recruitment, you must be able to handle a certain level of stress and exhilaration.

Stress related to job security was different during the 2009 crisis and ensuing recession. In total, we had to let about 30 people go and that was really hard on everyone. The remaining staff were still concerned about themselves; happy they had their jobs, but very nervous that they could lose them at any time, due to the depressed market economy. On the other hand, this stress also brought everyone closer together than they had ever been - one of the silver linings from the crisis.

Our Director's team is responsible for new and current client development. It was very difficult for them to have to make call-after-call-after-call, only to mostly hear "sorry, there is nothing we have for you right now". However, it had to be done and the calls had to be made, because occasionally when they made the call they would find vacancies for us to work on. I was committed to covering the remaining core team's compensation for as long as I could - provided that I could see that the effort was being made on their part to perform their responsibilities and an attempt to reach their targets and KPIs.

Boris is a brilliant salesperson but also lazy and stubborn. If you are lazy in a down market, you are never going to get to prove that you are still a brilliant salesperson. There is nowhere for slackers to hide during a recession as the numbers alone (KPIs) speak volumes.

Employees want:
- To work with a team that really get along well together; where there is respect, helpfulness, fairness and hard work;
- To sell in a strong market where there is a higher closing rate;
- The company's sales team to not be lazy; and
- There to not be redundancies related to poor market conditions.

OPEN COMMUNICATIONS

"Good when policy is open and clear for all staff – good when team is prepared for bad news (forewarned), love your Blog, all our team reads and discusses them – learn from this about company, CEO ideas and thoughts"… "Communications from Teri are good if even bad news – all news is good. Positive speeches"…"Information sharing – people need to find their own ways to handle stress on a personal level"…"More meetings and info about the current situation and future, maybe out of office meetings"…"Teri communications"…"Now market is stressed, but info from the company is important – changes and plans – communications regarding company often"…"Share info, Teri's letter last Summer to the team"…"Communicate clearly – goals, decisions, situations – be open and honest"…"More communications from Teri"…"Direct communications like you are doing ("Tea with Teri")"…More one-on-one meetings with Teri – shows trust in team and interest in knowing their opinion and desire to improve and plan through the crisis and come out on top – very strong signal that care about company and personal development. This helps him to reduce the stress – meet Teri often, give attention, even if critique – is better than no communications"…"Monthly meetings between Senior Consultants & Consultants – like the Directors have. I think the stress is reduced when there are no rumors, so the staff should be aware of all the issues that could influence the staff and the company. Recently, the most stressful issues were redundancies and the rumors these redundancies bred"…"Consultants need to know what is happening with the company and the market"…"Everyone being more open with each other"…"An idea is to have meetings every 1-2 months on company plans"…"Later salary payment to tell team – best is communications for team, cannot avoid tax authority stress, etc…Know you are needed is best stress reliever"…

The gist of these comments come across to me loud and clear, especially as it is how the majority of the team feel: namely, that the best way to relieve the majority of stress amongst the staff is for me, the owner and CEO of Staffwell, to speak and communicate more often with all of the team regarding the company - and I will. I always come through as positive and straight-forward (in delivering both good and bad news), as it is my style. The keys element here is more information from me, more often.

We do have open policies but they likely could be made clearer in our operations manual. I did forewarn all of our team regarding the redundancies we were going to make and I think I did a really good job with that; I was extremely sensitive, informative, and supportive.

I am glad the team like my Blog (work360.ru), read it and find it interesting. The advice and information I give there is both for the market and our team, and it is another way for me to connect with them, as they get to find out more about how I think and what I have to say. They also get the opportunity to communicate with me when they leave comments to the blogs.

"Tea with Teri", these one-on-ones I have had with staff, have had a huge positive influence on both the team and on me. I really got to know the team better and their thoughts and ideas regarding the company. But I also got to know them better personally, as at the beginning of every session I spent time asking them some questions regarding their personal life, interests and hobbies. In turn, they got to spend genuine quality time alone with me and were able to speak their minds about the company.

We have monthly Director's meetings, where the Directors get together and go over their results, deals, issues and ideas. However, we do not have the same type of monthly meetings for the Consultant's team, and we should, if even only on a quarterly basis. We have always given our sales teams more direction and attention vis-à-vis our Consultant's teams, but we should not, as they are equally important to the entire recruitment process and cycle.

Rumors are very stressful for the team. Every company has them and everyone, on occasion, likes to spread them or gossip. They can be destructive and divert time and attention from people trying to perform their duties. An idea I have is to put a page up on the server, where anyone, anonymously, can write down the latest rumor spreading around the team or office, and I can then respond to it, in order to put everyone at ease by stating the actual truth on matters.

To my knowledge, we have had only one salary payment made late to the team so far during this recession, which I think is pretty good. I thought we did forewarn the team on that, but I decided to check with our accounting division to ensure that we always do it. I understand that people do need to know this in order to organize their financial commitments.

I could not agree more with the concept that knowing you are needed is the best stress reliever. Both myself and management need to do a better job at making the team members feel that they are needed. I also need to ensure that our management feels needed by me. I would love to feel needed in this way too but when you are at the top of the company, you are all you have. Fortunately, I do feel that our team really like and appreciate me, and my role in the company.

Employees want:
- Open and clear company policies;
- To be forewarned about major news (good or bad) affecting them and the company;
- To hear or read the thoughts and ideas of the company's CEO, via a Blog, articles, or other means;
- Frequent communications from the company owner or CEO;
- Occasional one-on-one meetings discussing corporate and personal matters with the company CEO, or owner;
- Goals, decisions and situations regarding the company, to be communicated clearly, openly and honestly;
- Critique of their work (the good, and where improvements are needed);
- Individual monthly meetings for all divisions;
- To not have redundancies;
- Any office rumors to immediately be addressed;
- To be forewarned regarding any late salary payments; and
- To feel and to know that they are needed.

REWARDS

"Loves the rewards"..."Encouraging letters to team members on their good results – this gives positive feelings to the Consultants – serious or funny"...

At Staffwell, we have given out rewards in the form of cash, wine, gifts and trips to top performers in our front and back office teams. Rewards really improve the mood of an office and give employees extra incentive to work hard, achieve and win. During this recession we have had to reduce our rewards budget, but we will still have them, and soon enough they will be back to full budget.

We are also send congratulatory and thank you letters to our team, highlighting members who are performing well. This sends a message to the employees of the company that we do care about them and notice their good work, and it works as a motivational tool for those who also want to be successful.

Employees want:
- Rewards; and
- E-mails congratulating them on their successes.

TEAM-BUILDING

"More socializing"…"Team-building, fun events"…"Bowling competitions, pizza, play poker, entertainment"…

Employees need and like to have fun and social, corporate-sponsored times together. We work very hard, and having the occasional fun, team-building activity or event together with one another is a great way to get to know each other better and to just have a laugh together. I agree that we need more of this, especially during difficult market times.

Employees want:
- Frequent corporate-sponsored team-building activities to provide more casual and fun opportunities to socialize.

NONE

"Not stress here now but was with Damian and Adam, very happy now – motivated, feels good"…"Stress is normal in sales so all is OK"…"Buy a punching bag ☺, all is normal"…"Currently no stress"…"Level of stress is OK – not high, not low, depends person-to-person, I also would like to wear casual clothes on dirty job days (IT)"…

Adam was a tough, but highly effective, General Manager for the company. Damian was a mostly ineffective and corrupt Commercial Director who worked under Adam for a time - for just under six months before we let him go. We are a happier team now, partly because of the change in management, but mostly because in times of economic recession, we are not as rigid with the team regarding requirements in attaining certain targets.

Buying a punching bag for the office is actually a great idea, as everyone would probably find it funny, use it occasionally as a joke (when they have a difficult recruitment situation), or some may occasionally use it to just blow off steam, or even to exercise.

Our IT Systems Administrator here is requesting that we allow him to wear casual clothes on days he needs to work on or near the floor – places where he cannot help but get dirty. We have a professional looking dress code in our offices, but this makes sense, so an exception can be made.

Employees want:
- Management that do not drive their stress levels above what may be considered normal;
- A punching bag or another humorous way to relieve stress in the office; and
- To wear casual clothes on days their job requires them to dirty their clothes.

BREAK ROOM

"Room to rest, kitchen/hang out"..."Good idea for sales to have a room to rest in when tired"..."Have a relaxation room to visit for five minutes every day"...

In theory, I think this is a good idea as the team would not disturb others working near them while they are taking a short break. We would just have to monitor people to ensure it was not being abused. Unfortunately, we just do not have an available room for it at present – but it is something to consider for the future.

Employees want:
- A dedicated break room.

FREEDOM

"More trust, more room to maneuver"...

We give trust and room to maneuver to people who have earned it: those that hit their numbers and achieve results, or at least work very hard trying to do so. The majority of people in our company are given space and the trust they deserve. The person commenting above will not be given it as he has not yet earned it.

Employees want:
- More trust and less supervision.

FLEX SCHEDULES

"Schedules being flexible"..."Flexible time schedule"...

We had a very rigid work schedule prior to the crisis: 9am to 6pm, and overtime when required, with no exceptions. During the first set of "Tea with Teri" sit downs, I learned that some of the team really wanted more flexible schedules and I acted on it immediately, as it made sense to me. Now we have starting times at either 8am, 9am or 10am, and it really helps those that prefer to beat the rush hour traffic in the morning and get home earlier at night - or those that prefer to start later in the morning and work longer into the night. This being done we have some very happy team members right now.

Employees want:
- Flexible time schedules at work.

NOISE

"Working in open space, try to reduce noise levels of open space room – please get me (Albert) a headset to make that better"...

It can get very noisy working in an open-plan workspace, and the acoustics in the big rooms of our old historic building do not help matters. If Albert wants a headset in order to help him hear his clients better when on the telephone with them, we will get him one. I also decided to ask the rest of the team if they required headsets.

Employees want:
- Telephone headsets, if they are working in noisy rooms.

PERFORMANCE

"Stressed when there is low performance or placements are not made – nothing we can do but start again and plow through, work hard, not just luck. Mentor would not work here as does not like sharing bad news"...

This person is a super star Consultant and she has a one-track mind for success. It has been difficult for her to make her numbers and targets due to the crisis and recession, which is not her fault. Much of her stress will be alleviated as the market improves over time.

Employees want:
- To be working in times when the economy is strong.

WORK

"None, more vacancies"..."Does not think that there is stress now, only when there are tons of projects"..."Winter was stressful with redundancies and slower in client work, now things are stable and picking up client work"...

I completely understand that our team would be less stressed if we were able to bring in a lot more vacancies. When the team has more work to do then they will have less stress regarding job instability.

When times are good, a different type of stress sets in: that associated with positive anxiety, which is a result of potential success and even, at times, too much work. There is not much we can do here but work very hard doing whatever we can do, while we wait for the good times to return.

Employees want:
- More work to be brought into the company; and
- Market stability.

TRAINING AND DEVELOPMENT

"If people are trained and developed properly, there will not be stress"...

I thought this was an excellent point. However, I believe that the reality of the situation is that while there may not be as much stress, there will always be a certain amount of anxiety in our lives at work. When people are not trained and developed properly it causes everybody stress: the people themselves; the people that work with them; the people who manage them; and the clients who may receive their work. Training and developing employees thoroughly and effectively is crucial to a company's success and an employee's potential.

Employees want:
- To be trained and developed in a proper and thorough manner.

Chapter 28

What Things Do The Company Or Management Do To Make Your Job More Difficult/Frustrating/Non-Productive?

This is a very important question to me as I know that, to a great degree, our success is dependent on the efficiencies of the company:

NONE

"None (x 24)"..."Relaxed here and supportive, you are in control of your income – no problems. Those who really want to perform will push themselves"..."Nadya and Nika are really on top of everyone but do not take over-strict measures"...

I was pleasantly surprised that more than half of the company feels that we are very productive. From what I hear across the market, we are relatively productive and, certainly, more so than any of our competitors. However, there is always room for improvement.

Employees want:
- Nothing to be improved sometimes, because all is fine with the current system and situation.

TIMELINESS

"Likes things to be done on time and likes things to move"..."Spoke about getting here late"...

Due to the nature of our work in recruitment, we have a lot of deadlines associated with the system we have created that details our workflow processes. When people on the team are slow in getting things done or sloppy in their work and skip a step, it really impacts the speed of our results and our overall performance - not to mention the mood of the team member waiting on the work to be completed.

I am a stickler for timeliness as it encourages discipline, respect, and success, and it motivated others to do the same. We have been fortunate at Staffwell that our employees also share this work ethic and discipline. While it is not a primary motivating factor for staff, some may be aware that Russian Labor Law allows a company to legitimately dismiss an employee without severance, if an employee has been documented to have been late to work for a total of three days, where those three days need not be consecutive.

At Staffwell, we only use such a termination option as a last resort – in the case where an employee may really be continuously under-performing, and also does not show up to work on time on a frequent basis. I decided to send out an e-mail to all company employees reminding them of the importance and necessity of arriving to work on time.

Employees want:
- Everyone to get their work done in a timely manner so that the company can be more successful; and
- Everyone to be at work on time, which promotes equality, fair competition and a more professional and successful team and company.

MANAGEMENT

"Be more accurate with planning and checking this. Needs a real manager on top of sales team – someone really focused on it and prioritizing meetings"..."All is good, just does not want to report directly to Albert – Consultants should not report directly to Directors"..."Would be difficult to work under stress management, but we do not have that here"..."Nothing major, just sometimes too pushy and gets over-loaded (IT)"...

Managing a front office team is a demanding job that requires focus. Meetings have to be prioritized and the team has to be continually motivated and driven to achieve their KPIs and targets. Our current Commercial Director, who formerly was a Director for us prior to her promotion, develops new and current business for us. She has taken on more than just the proper tasks of a Commercial Director, which could very well explain why people think we should do more on the front office side of the business. I saw the issue as a priority for me to look into once I finished all of the "Tea with Teri" meetings.

Regarding the second comment, our Recruitment Consultants report on an individual basis to every Director whose projects they are working on at any given time – but also to the most senior Director in their industry sector or focused occupational area. In addition, they report to our Commercial Director on their monthly, quarterly and annual results. Albert is the Director in charge of the occupational focus area that this Recruitment Consultant works in.

Frankly, there is not a lot I can do in terms of having her report to someone other than Albert without also changing her focus area - which I know she would not want to do. I need to speak to her and Albert at more length in order to determine what the real issues are, and try to work with them toward a resolution. In addition, I will consider promoting someone to focus on the Consultants; someone who was a Consultant before, has the respect of the team and would, I feel, do a good job leading and developing them.

IT is definitely an area where the team can sometimes act aggressively, especially when a program, hardware, or the internet are not working well, or is completely down. I decided to speak with the team about being more respectful of our IT staff, and to use caution and consideration when choosing tone and wording in requesting their help and assistance. I also decided to add this to our operations manual.

Employees want:
- A front office team leader who is very focused on the team, holds them to task and ensures that scheduled meetings occur on a regular basis;
- To not report to someone they do not get along well with;
- To report to someone who, ideally, has been promoted through their role and really understands their tasks, issues, challenges and opportunities; and
- To not be spoken to in an abrasive and pushy manner, especially when someone needs their help.

SALES ASSISTANCE

"Telemarketing/cold calling – not doing this. Just all-out calls. Totally cold. Better if he is given leads – names and contacts. Otherwise, management is reasonable"…"If our admin could help putting CVs into SDS, for now Alyona does this, or hire someone"…

Our Director's team is responsible for the full sales cycle, including their own lead generation and cold-calling clients for introductory meetings. Any leads we get from companies accessing and reviewing our website, or directly from me or other executive management, are distributed to the Directors' team in a fair manner.

Our current budget is very tight due to the recession and, therefore, we are not in a position to add telemarketers to our head count. However, I did make a note of the request and will consider it in future, when more fruitful years prevail.

The person writing the second comment is a very hard worker and our top Consultant. She works more hours than most people on the team, is very smart and is an efficient worker as well. Her efforts have earned her the deserved right to have some extra assistance in helping input her candidates CVs and interview notes (highlights) into SDS, our CRM system. For now, we can have the receptionist help her and, later, when the market picks up a bit, possibly hire someone for this task.

Employees want:
- Telemarketers to assist sales teams with lead generation and cold-calling; and
- Dedicated assistance if they are a top performer and have little time for the administrative part of their responsibilities.

DIRECTORS' UPDATES

"Nothing, but Director's updates are too haphazard – would be better if they were scheduled in advance, and I am working on five different Director's assignments now"...

I see no reason why Director's updates with the Consultants should not be scheduled in advance as this makes perfect sense to me. We always try to schedule our client meetings in the afternoons and evenings, in order that mornings may be spent on updates with the Consultants, paperwork (including contracts and client updates), and cold calling for the following week's meetings. I decided to ask our Commercial Director to look further into this matter.

Employees want:
- Scheduled updates and meetings, so that they can maximize their time efficiency in trying to get all of their work done.

SPLIT DECISIONS

"Not much, just debate for % split that took over six months to get a decision on. When Sofiya was on holidays, Alyona placed a Head of Legal (although it was my candidate) – she demanded 30% when she never even met the candidate. Ozzie was postponing the decision for six months, which caused a lot of unnecessary stress for everyone. After Ozzie left, Diana finally made a decision of giving only 10% to me."...

This does not sound like a pleasant situation and, on the surface, it does not seem fair. What's done is done, especially as this Consultant does not seem to be demanding that I re-examine the issue for her. However, these are the exactly the types of things that I do not like to happen as it causes stress and lower productivity in the company.

I wish this Consultant, or the team involved, had come to me at the time this occurred. I would have resolved the situation in five minutes and with an outcome that was fair to all. This is one of my strengths as a manager. My proving to be more accessible to all of the team, especially more junior- to mid-level staff, is needed, and something I will work on.

The over-riding problem here is that our operations manual is unclear, or not sufficiently detailed, in its guidelines regarding all potential scenarios involving fee splits on placed deals, where several Directors and Consultants are involved in a project. I decided that this was something I would take on myself, with pleasure, and guarantee that we will almost never have another fee split issue again.

Employees want:
- To be treated in a fair and timely manner when issues regarding fee splits between staff members arise;
- To have a fee split system and guidelines that cover every possible scenario in a fair manner, so that when issues arise there is no room for subjective decision making.

SLOW RECEIVABLES

"Hard when clients pay really late, and then bonuses cannot be paid – but this is a market thing"...

We have been very fortunate over the years in that most of our clients have paid on time, according to legal contract. Russian companies have been especially great at this, and I really appreciate them for it.

However, in the midst of a major recession some companies struggle to adhere to payment terms. There is little we can do here except, within reason, be patient.

We pay commissions and bonuses to our front office team as soon as their placed candidate passes their probation period that, according to Russian labor law, mostly is 180 days for executive and top management, and 90 days for everyone else. We pay salaries to everyone as well so that our team can always cover their monthly expenses, no matter what.

Employees want:
- Clients to pay their invoices on time.

KEY ACCOUNT MANAGEMENT (KAM)

"Lack of KAM. Sometimes the negotiations between the client and our BD take too much time, not always because of the client, and due to this, our competitors present candidates much faster than we do, at times"...

Speed is of the essence in our business and sometimes the competition simply comes down to who gets their candidate to the client first. Most of the time, we are very fast in our work but I can see how, on occasion, it could occur that a Director takes too much time in getting the process started. Many things can cause such a delay, including illness, laziness, other work they are focused on, holidays, or the client not reverting and confirming in a timely manner.

This is a training and management issue that I decided I needed to look into. If properly structured, Key Account Management could also possibly help, and I took the view that I should consider this as well.

At Staffwell, we abide by our own code of higher professional conduct when it comes to presenting candidates to clients. I believe that this differentiates us and makes us better than our competitors, in that we interview every candidate before presenting them to our clients. I find it amazing that many companies on the market e-mail out a CV, or simply a Bio taken off of public sources, of someone they have never met or spoken to, just to get a candidate to a company first. It is not only a shame and very unprofessional, but also perilous for the person whose CV or Bio has been sent out this way - as it puts their current job in jeopardy should someone call their employer.

This problem within our industry can be corrected if companies, and their HR departments, make several demands within the contracts they sign with recruitment companies. Namely, that every candidate presented to them must have recently been interviewed by the agency; that the candidate give approval to be presented to the client; and for the CV to be accompanied by interview notes, further proving that they spoke to the candidate and discussed the requirements of the role for which the CV was submitted. This would really raise the bar on the professionalism of recruiting firms operating in the market.

Employees want:
- Their colleagues to be fast off the mark in launching projects so competitors do not beat them to it and win the deal; and
- Key Account Management structures in place.

CLIENTS

"Client comments and difficult client requirements"..."Nothing from management but client comments can sometimes make her upset (no feedback on candidates) - no answers make her feel like she is wasting her time"...

These replies reflect one of the struggles in our business. I understand that our Consultant's team can get very frustrated when we do not get timely status updates from our clients. Often, the candidates are close to receiving offers from companies that are not our clients. We run the risk of losing candidates on behalf of our clients if we do not provide the candidates with frequent communications and updates on their status with our clients and any job offers.

Moreover, it is then easily understood that this type of situation can lead recruitment Consultants to, on occasion, feel they are wasting their time. On the other hand, our clients are sometimes incapable of reverting back to us as fast as we would like them to do because of their own internal issues - such as decision makers being unable or unavailable to give feedback, or schedule the next set of interviews.

On rare occasions, our team comes into contact with clients who are rude, or quite frankly, unprofessional. Unfortunately, this is just part of life as there are all types of people out there. Of our clients, 99% are really pleasant to work with and we are grateful for this and for them.

Employees want:
- To work with clients that are nice, friendly, respectful, helpful, motivating, thankful, honest and professional; and
- Clients to give feedback and further instructions to them in a timely manner.

Chapter 29

How Can The Company Make Better Use Of The Views And Experience Of Its People?

Similar to most companies, we likely are not proficient at maximizing every single improvement opportunity advanced by our employees. However, their thoughts and ideas can serve as useful insight and a good launching point.

"TEA WITH TERI"

"More 'Tea with Teri' meetings"..."Tea with Teri"..."The 'Tea with Teri' meetings, one-on-ones or small groups"..."Polls, chats like this will help the management understand the views of all the staff"..."Make informal meetings between people. Likes 'Tea with Teri' meetings"..."The 'Tea with Teri' meetings, likes that the team is open and communicative"...

"Tea with Teri" turned out to be a really good idea of mine, if I may say so, and it occurred at just the right time: when I had the time. However, in the future, no matter how busy I may become, I will periodically make time to repeat this exercise. The team enjoyed it, as I did, it was highly useful for me, the team and the company, and it clearly gave us a very explicit framework, with solutions, on how to make our company as perfect as possible.

What made this exercise successful was that I was on time and prepared for every meeting, with tea in hand. I started with some light personal questions to break the ice a bit, then I asked every question in order and, most importantly, I wrote down every word that was spoken to me. Writing everything down illustrated to the team that I cared about what they were saying, found it interesting and important, and that I was likely going to do something positive and useful with the information.

Writing everything down also allowed me to review and organize the information in such a way that I could make better sense and use out of it later; that is, when I mapped out where we needed to make improvements to the company, and naturally, it was essential for the writing of this book.

I have always interviewed candidates in the same way: asking questions and then writing down everything they said, as well as my responses. I think it shows that I care about what the candidates are saying, but it also helps me remember what was said later when I write interview notes or answer further questions about the candidate from a client.

Employees want:
- Structured and informal one-on-one time with the owner and CEO of the company, to discuss their individual thoughts and ideas on the company; and
- The occasional individual or small group meeting with an executive manager of the company, to discuss their ideas for improving areas of the company.

CLOSENESS

"I love teamwork and sharing ideas"…"Learn more about hobbies and backgrounds of people"…"Mutual lunches, going to social events, LinkedIn events, other"…"Loves the office atmosphere, all work hard to help each other – they share there"…

Trying to keep the team close should always be a priority. This is more difficult as the team becomes larger but this is where various levels of good management should help. We will definitely be thinking of ways to stay closer and get to know each other better on a personal level as well, and will incorporate more social and team-building activities into the company.

Maintaining a very good, positive atmosphere in the company is really important to me.

Employees want:
- To work in teams and share ideas together;
- To learn more about the hobbies and backgrounds of the people they work with and for;
- To have lunch with people in the office they don't know well and get to know them;
- To attend social events and become acquainted with more people in the market via LinkedIn;
- To work for a company with a great office atmosphere; and
- To work in a team with colleagues which are diligent and helpful to each other.

COMMUNICATIONS

"Good communications between offices"..."Meetings, communications, sharing ideas"..."Reports and share more info that sectors know about"..."Create intra-net communications between team members, I want to do this"..."More communication with the Moscow office, recently closed positions and client successes – can be used to give clients good news"..."Round tables, quality circles – for people to share experiences and communicate"..."People should come forward with ideas if they have them, should offer it – their own responsibility"..."More communications, one day per week with management"..."Give more info to staff on the company"...

I think these ideas are all great, and they confirm other comments made in previous chapters. We will do better as a company if we improve our communications and the sharing of information and ideas within our offices, between our offices, and with our clients, candidates, and the market. Staff would like to feel more connected to the company through weekly communication from, and with, the company's management, and by frequent corporate updates.

I am convinced that we can incorporate all of these ideas into our daily workload and schedule. We can do this and remain efficient by keeping the meetings and updates highly focused and to-the-point, and very short in duration.

Employees want:
- Frequent and useful communication between offices;
- To share information amongst departments in order to promote a better educated team that, potentially, may contribute more via expanded knowledge;
- To communicate with the company employees via an intra-net;
- To share positive company news with clients;
- Meetings with clients and the market to share experiences and ideas;
- People in the company to share their ideas with the company, if they have any;
- Weekly communication with management; and
- Updates on current news and the health of the company, as often as possible.

TRAINING

"Internal trainings"..."More people development meetings – develop our talent"..."Master classes, brain-storming"..."Attracting staff to develop trainings/coaching/mentoring, archive of the best and most difficult projects and how we managed to place these people"..."Everyone is really talented, to have them all make trainings on what they are good at"...

For our business, training is probably the most efficient way in which we can make our team more productive; specifically, short, focused trainings on very precise areas of our business by those that are experts on the training topic.

Training has many benefits. Foremost, it develops people in a way that allows them to be better at their jobs which, in turn, enhances company performance. However, it also builds organizational and presentation skills for those conducting the training, and motivates everyone involved.

Employees want:
- To be frequently trained;
- To have master class style training;
- Brain-storming sessions with their colleagues and management;
- The company's experts to conduct trainings and to mentor staff; and
- An archive of case studies on the company's most challenging deals, in order to refer to and learn from them.

TEAM-BUILDING

"Team-building"..."With regard to corporate events, great when the team needs to work on things together, fulfills personal and professional qualities, team-buildings are great – combo of fun and usefulness"...

Team-building events do give management and employees the opportunity to speak to one other in a more casual setting, which can help facilitate dialog and stronger relationships between people in the office. Team-building events have been very useful for me as well, as I get to do things with the team on a peer basis (as opposed to CEO-level), which makes me feel closer to all employees in the company, and vice-versa.

As mentioned, in the past we have had some great team-building events, including our annual trips where we have, among other things: chartered a sailboat and sailed on the Turkish portion of Mediterranean Sea for several days; had a sailing regatta in Montenegro; went white water rafting and river kayaking in Croatia; and toured the area of Chamonix, France. We have also spent quality time curling and bowling together, and numerous other mental and physical obstacle-course-type challenges, and other activities. We will certainly continue to do these team-building events.

Employees want:
- Team-building events.

MANAGEMENT STYLE

"Shift to a more democratic way – thinks Teri is too strong a leader and people won't speak up"…"Meetings, make people communicate in them, ask direct questions to specific people, don't disagree with opinions - say 'interesting' and then move onto other people's opinions"…

I disagree with the first comment made here to a large degree. I consider our company to be very democratic in most everything we do: management is approachable, we have an open-door policy and open-plan seating, and all aspects of our operations are fair, clear and progressive.

Indeed, I am a strong leader - in the sense that I know what I want done, what I expect of people and in the results for the company. One must be a strong leader if you want to have a successful company. After all, it is a business and it must be taken seriously: it is not a pajama party.

I do not consider myself too strong a leader. Rather, I feel that I have the optimal balance of strength, as is required to run a successful company. If people do not speak up then that is their choice, their own issue and their own weakness. There is nothing more that I can do about that, other than what I already have done - by reminding all of our team in e-mails and meetings that if they ever have anything they need to speak to me about then they can just come and see me. My door is always open and I am always ready to listen and help where I can, if that is desired.

I am aware of occasional situations in which some senior members of our team have told more junior members that they should not come and speak to me about their issues. They have explained that I would not want to be bothered by it and would even look down upon them if they did. This is disinformation and could not be further from the truth. It really saddened me to learn that some of my team appears, unfortunately, to enjoy playing these types of manipulating mind and control games with other people on our team.

My door is always open for every single member of our company. I will continue to make this clear in meetings and in e-mails, and will even incorporate it into our operations manual, if it is not already there. "Tea with Teri" has been an excellent exercise to give everyone in the company the opportunity to meet with me one-on-one for genuine quality time together. It has been one of the most personally fulfilling things I have done in the company, and for the company.

I understand and I see the point, to a degree, about the second comment regarding my conduct in meetings where, on occasion, I disagree with this person and disregard his input. However, for the benefit of all at Staffwell, any and all meetings should be to-the-point, useful and efficient. If meetings are not about reporting or sharing of information, then they should be about new ideas or solutions to issues that we have. It is beyond my nature and ability, and as the leader of the company, to not object to relentless and, at times, baseless complaining, or views that constantly refer to past events and not future outlook, or discussion that that gets off track from the topic being addressed.

In such circumstances it would be insincere for me to say things like "interesting" or "'thank you for your input". That would be a lie. Sometimes I disagree with people and I have to let them know that - even if it is in front of a group of people. I believe that the best they can do in such situations is simply to listen and learn and try to answer the following question for themselves: "What am I saying to them?"

This is a very simple matter and I will repeat it once more and ensure it is in our operations manual: If meetings are not about reporting or sharing of information, then they should be about new ideas or solutions to issues we have. Views should stay on topic, only be forward-looking into the future, and not be centered on relentless and baseless complaining.

My final point here is that you cannot make all people communicate in meetings. Not everyone is out-going or a natural-born communicator, especially in a group setting. For this reason, we conduct, on occasion, one-on-one meetings, where people are encouraged and given the opportunity to speak their mind on various topics.

Employees want:
- To share their thoughts and ideas with the Owner and/or CEO of the company;
- To not have any of their thoughts and opinions rejected by the Owner and CEO of the company, or anyone else (*TL: but this is unrealistic*); and
- For everyone to speak up in meetings.

FEEDBACK

"Collect anonymous feedback from employees. Thinks a lot of people want to talk about something"..."Creating electronic poles and then arranging tables and info from it"...

In this modern world, I think it is nearly impossible to create and collect anonymous feedback of any kind, as anything can be traced back to its original author or source. However, I do believe that people in the company do want to speak out, comment or share ideas, and reach out to me, the Owner and CEO of the company.

Continuing with "Tea with Teri", or an abbreviated version, every 2-3 years, is a way for me to do that. In addition, this may be accomplished by me sending a personal e-mail to each employee on an annual basis letting them know I am available to meet with them privately, in the office or for lunch, or just to review their thoughts and ideas in e-mail form.

Creating electronic polls for market research is something we could, perhaps, revisit for external marketing and PR purposes in the future. For internal purposes, where the polls would be more fun or entertaining in nature, it may be better to consider spending time looking at it only after the market picks up and we are growing at a significant rate.

Employees want:
- To share their thoughts and ideas on the company, and their role, with the Owner and CEO of the company, in a private setting; and
- To have electronic polls created to gather the thoughts and opinions of employees.

PROFESSIONAL DEVELOPMENT

"Change payment system for people, professional development – more discussions on goals and targets, people want great positions and growth and development"…"Need to grow BDs out of Consultants – Consultants are ready for this, some of them"…

We have a great earnings system in place for our front office team, which especially works very well when the market is good, as it is a no-cap, unlimited earnings system. In the current down-market, our system can result in some team members incurring debts to the company. This happens if they have not covered their base salary with the sales they have generated. What our team was unaware of the time, but would discover over the ensuing few years, was that I had made provisions to cover the salaries of all remaining hard working staff through the crisis period. As a result, they will not end up in debt, and any debt they accrued will have been written off the books.

Hard work and a great attitude are the key elements here. I will support my team during the tough times as long as I see them put in a great effort. Accordingly, we will not change our earnings system right now, as it truly is a great one, but we may make amendments to it at some point in the future if necessary.

The other comments made here were things that I noted and will develop over time.

Employees want:
- An earnings system that is achievable and provides comfort and stability, especially during challenging economic times;
- More discussions about their professional development and strategy to help them best achieve their goals and targets;
- Good business flow into the company so that they can work on interesting and lucrative projects; and
- Their colleagues to outgrow their positions and move into new roles, where they can take on more tasks with greater responsibilities in order to help the company develop further and faster.

THE WORK

"For top and senior level vacancies, have more than one Consultant on it"..."Individual people on different recruitment projects"..."As for experience, sometimes, in my point of view, it could be good to believe in an employee and give him or her a chance for more responsibilities like starting a new branch or give them more senior positions to place"..."Brain-storming of Consultants and Directors"..."and offer more brain-storming discussions in groups"..."If Directors and Consultants have interesting stories or case studies to share that would be great for the company, and we can share the presentations, especially problem cases – very specific true stories will be very interesting"...

I think each of these ideas is reasonable and that, over time, we will certainly incorporate them into the company. At times, we do need more than one Consultant working on important searches for clients and we do need to give some of our potential rising stars some bigger projects to work on so that they gain more experience.

When we do open new branch offices in the future we will, without question, first consider our own incumbent employees to spearhead such expansion. In the very least, we will assign priority in their involvement, if they are not actually leading the effort. In addition, we will immediately start to devote more time to brain-storming and sharing ideas and issues regarding recruitment projects. This is for educational purposes, is easy to organize and would be highly useful in further developing the team.

Employees want:
- To share their more difficult work with others, to ensure better quality and faster task completion, for the benefit of the company and the client.
- The opportunity to take on work that offers a higher level of responsibility; and
- To brain-storm and share stories in group settings, in order to further learn and develop.

RESPECT

"The main thing is mutual respect and we have that at Staffwell"...

We do have mutual respect for each other at Staffwell. This is another corporate element that is very important to me and will always be an area that I will focus on, especially as we grow.

Employees want:
- Mutual respect between all employees, both management and staff.

WORK360

"The blog is great and full of experience and views on the market, maybe good for the team to write articles about achievements or have meetings on this"...

I am really glad that the team enjoys my blog and it brought some needed excitement to the company, and to my life, at a time when the market was particularly discouraging. I think it is a great idea for the team to become involved with the blog: to write something if they would like or, in the very least, provide information for the articles that I will write in the future.

Employees want:
- Their company to have a really great blog site; and
- To be involved with their company's blog by writing articles for it or providing information for it.

Chapter 30

How Strongly Are You Attracted To Committing To A Long And Developing Career With Staffwell?

I thought this was a great question for planning purposes and to gauge the mood of our team toward our company and what we have to offer.

LONG

"Long time"…"I would like to spend the rest of my career with Staffwell. I really enjoy the industry and fully intend to stay in it for the rest of my career"…"I hope to stay a long time and to grow"…

This was encouraging to hear and I made a note on these individuals, as they will likely be some of our core pillars now, and in the future.

Employees want:
- To build long-lasting careers within the company they work for.

NEW OFFICE

"Wishes to have a very long career with Staffwell. Very interesting and difficult work now – hard work will pay off – wants to help open a new office in the future"…

Several people have mentioned that they would really like to be involved in opening new offices for us. I think this is great as we do have expansion plans in our future. This is an easy way for us to motivate our more senior, and successful, team members by adding new and more challenging tasks to their current remit.

Employees want:
- To be involved in opening new offices for the company.

DEVELOP

"Committed, wants to develop"..."Loyal to good employers – not a job hopper. More responsibilities and more difficult responsibilities. Monotonous job. Recruitment is interesting – pure sales is not as interesting. Surveying, analyzing and understanding what the issues are, etc. Likes to see the overall picture and strategies. Tactical is finding the right task – but not wanting to be a manager, monotonous manager, micro-managing. If opening a new office – to do that. Manage things strategically, maybe general management"..."Professional growth, difficult projects and difficult tasks – thinks career promotion is limited, take part in strategy, want Staffwell to be a leader"..."To develop career will need to sell as well – so anxious to do this"..."Very excited to be here and want to develop inside the company – Zhanna is a great example and so is Angela"..."Very long, wants to stay and develop and grow to team leader or other"..."Strong enough. Is a company person and does not like job-hopping. You have to work for quite a while to perform and grow – should only leave if no room for development and growth"..."Hopes after the crisis we will grow quickly – have big personal development"..."Hard to realize vertical growth, but about professional growth is still learning and growing – would like to understand the HR market better – yes, committed to develop"..."Interested in a long career and placing candidates and developing my career"..."Staffwell is very strong and with a strong corporate culture and people. Hopes when market grows and is hiring, would love to train new people and become an account manager and BD – long!"..."Likes to work here, loves this company and likes to know people here like me too and sees when I am developing"..."Wishes to be here a long time and to develop –in Staffwell and in training – not only consulting"..."I am a committed person – I do not like changing jobs, but need to see perspectives"...

I hear clearly that the majority of people want to develop at our company and that this is the most important thing for them. We promote on merit, so those who work hard in their current roles and achieve success in them, will likely grow and develop in the ways they desire. Others who are not successful in their roles may never achieve the career growth and development they desire with us. This is life. Nonetheless, I acknowledged what everyone said and noted their individual interests.

The second person quoted here is a Director on our sales team. He is expressing his interest to work in more strategic and general management areas of the company: that is, as long as such tasks are not monotonous and he would not have to micro-manage anyone. He also somewhat expressed his disinterest in sales. I appreciate that he is being honest. However, it is not likely that any role we will ever have to offer will satisfy him. It is important to point out that the role of Director is not a pure sales position. In fact, only about 40% of a Director's role is sales-related.

All work can be monotonous at times, regardless of role or position. If you are promoted into management then you are required to actually manage people. We are also a sales organization and, frankly, if you hope to ever take on a management role with us, then you better love sales.

Within our industry, career promotions are somewhat limited but we can and should offer interested team members some involvement in our on-going strategic development. More input and ideas can only help us.

Some of our team members have been with the company in excess of 10 years and I am glad that others really look up to them and respect them for that, and aspire to replicate their longevity and success.

Employees want:
- To commit to their employer and develop with them;
- More challenging responsibilities;
- Work that is not monotonous;
- Work that involves more than just pure sales;
- To figure out what role they would enjoy doing the most;
- To be involved in opening new offices;
- To take part in developing corporate strategy;
- Their company to be an industry leader;
- To push themselves out of their comfort zone and into more challenging roles, in order to develop and be promoted within the company;
- To stay long-term with their employer;
- To not job hop;
- Their company to grow quickly during good economic times;
- To understand their entire industry better;
- To train new people; and
- To see career prospects that they can realize for themselves at their company.

NEW OFFICE

"Wishes to have a very long career with Staffwell. Very interesting and difficult work now – hard work will pay off – wants to help open a new office in the future"...

Several people have mentioned that they would really like to be involved in opening new offices for us. I think this is great as we do have expansion plans in our future. This is an easy way for us to motivate our more senior, and successful, team members by adding new and more challenging tasks to their current remit.

Employees want:
- To be involved in opening new offices for the company.

MAYBE NOT

"As long as I am comfortable here and have goals and aims. Would love to be a jewelry designer. Would love to be more successful at Staffwell. Has a ton of hobbies, would love fun time and to learn things – training, loves to learn"..."Strongly! Next 2-3 years then we will see, studying to be a yoga teacher – got her first certificate in Goa, India in Yoga teaching"...

The two people commenting here obviously do not have their heads and hearts devoted to a long-term career at Staffwell, and I accept that as a business professional.

The first person is fairly new with us, has many interests in life and, ideally, would like to become a jewelry designer. She is testing herself in one of our Director's roles to see if she likes it. However, my gut feeling from her entire "Tea with Teri" interview with me is that she will likely not last very long with us, so I will keep an eye on that.

The second person quoted above is a Recruitment Consultant in the legal sector and is a nice, steady performing member of our team. She loves yoga and I respect her passion and wish her all the best in becoming a yoga instructor in the future. She is saying that she will be with us for 2-3 more years before she will likely leave to begin teaching yoga as a full-time career. This is useful for us to know so that we may implement a succession plan as that time approaches.

Employees want:
- At times, a completely different career path than the one they are currently on.

COMMITTED

"Committed to the work now during the crisis – as long as we are committed too. Miron likes results"..."Very excited for the future and market to pick up – very committed and excited"..."Strong enough, attracted, committed – the question is to Teri"..."YES"..."Sure about development in Staffwell and strong position on the market and caliber of colleagues"..."Strongly here during the crisis. Trust Staffwell and feels trusted which gives great comfort for me to Staffwell – was even promoted to now Senior Consultant – will work hard and it will lead to more promotions and awards"..." I like this company a lot, the team, the way we work, my candidates for whom Gleb and Staffwell are synonyms. So I am strongly committed to a long and developing career here"..."Very attracted due to good management, interesting communications, excellent staff, strong active stars, intelligent, great reputation, understandable industry/topic and clear plans for future growth"...

I am really pleased to know that most of the team feels a strong commitment to the company. The answer to the questions directed to me is: yes, I am very committed to all of our employees, financially, career-wise and personally, and it is just really nice to know that this feeling is reciprocal as it further motivates me to do more for everyone and the company.

Employees want:
- To be committed to the work they do and to the company they work for, and to feel that the company and its owner are committed to them;
- To work for a fast-growing company with top-level employees;
- To trust the company they work for, and to feel they are trusted by the company;
- To work hard in order to receive promotions and rewards;
- To really like the company they work for, the team they work with, the work style, and the products or services presented by the company;
- To work with good, communicative and intelligent management and staff, and top-level performers; and
- To work for a company that has a great reputation and clear growth plans.

THE WORK

"Likes it here, I am in the right place – can make a difference. It is not about making everyone happy – it is about closing the business with team members who can do this"..."Not a very career-oriented person – most interesting is stable, interesting work that I do well. Loves recruitment – clients, candidates always changing, would love to expand my sector work (worked in a hotel before) become a small expert in banking. Happy!"..."This is the second job I have had, and I can compare my life here with a school of development and life growth. Yes!"...

The work itself is a sound reason to want to stay at Staffwell over the long-term. I feel that we have such great clients, recruitment projects and candidates; all of which really make our job enjoyable and fun - and because they are always changing, it also makes our work highly interesting and challenging.

Employees want:
- To be at a company, and in a role, where they feel they can make a difference;
- To work with competent team members, who can close business deals in a quick and successful manner;
- Stable, interesting work that they can perform well;
- Work that frequently changes;
- To expand their roles into new areas; and
- A role that also gives them a sense of being educated on the job.

MANAGEMENT

"As long as the business is there and people are assessed fairly; number one is good management"...

I keep driving the point home about good management being critical to a company's success. Throughout the economic recession, I think that we have had in place very good management that has left the team very happy and satisfied. In addition, I am confident that our current management team, supplemented by a few others that will likely be promoted through the ranks, will do a fine job in leading our expansion and growth when the markets pick up and we are back at full speed.

Of course, business flow is very important and we are very fortunate in that we have built a strong reputation on the market as an extremely reliable recruiting company that delivers results. We always try to assess our employees fairly and have benefitted from having very good Human Resources Management work for us, as well as by having advanced, modern procedures in place for years.

Employees want:
- Good management in place;
- The company to have strong active business flow; and
- All employees in the company to be assessed in a fair manner.

SUCCESS

"Wants to be more successful at Staffwell after the baby will be born"...

The period of economic crisis conveniently allowed some of our people to go on maternity leave. When the market picks up again, they should be refreshed, eager and looking forward to getting back into the crazy, busy life of recruiting in Russia during good economic times.

Employees want:
- To work really hard and achieve greater levels of success after their maternity leave has ended and they are back at work.

Chapter 31

What Can The Company Do To Retain Its Best People?

This may not be a pressing question for me at present given the on-going global recession. However, I was still very interested to hear the responses as they can be useful in the future, when the markets recover and show strong growth.

COMPENSATION SYSTEM

"Different for different people, – for me, I am happy – you are generous. Maybe new bonus system for sales team, we don't calculate for team who leave – then we have debts and we need to calculate this. Maybe increase base and decrease % - will work on this and other things including confidentiality agreements"…"Monetary comp – material and non-material. Non-material it is great – one of the best places. Total money plus splits is harder. Interesting job and good compensation here"…"Direct communications, recognition, President's Club and fair bonus system. Thinks we need to work on the splits – and what is fair – has heard we have the best bonus system on the market"…

It is likely that we have the most competitive bonus system on the market in our industry as we have no caps and, thus, allow for unlimited earnings potential. For the front office team, an increase in base salary and accompanied decrease in commission percent would simply result in top performers earning a lot less than they are used to making and deserve, and poor performers making a lot more than they should. This would be a system that is unfair and not based on merit and, therefore, something that I can never favor or approve.

At present, we have a flaw in our bonus system, stemming from the fact that we pay commissions to the team at the end of the quarter in which we receive payment on the invoice. A problem arises if a team member leaves after receiving such a commission and, subsequently, the candidate fails during their probation period. In this case, a different Consultant will be paid another commission on replacing the candidate. This does not happen often but when it has the company has incurred some additional losses.

I resolved this problem immediately after having my 'Tea with Teri' chat with the first person quoted above. I implemented a new policy whereby we only pay commissions due to the team after the client has paid our invoice and the placed candidate has passed their probation period (6 months for executive/senior level placements, and 3 months for all others, as per Russian Labor Code). This does necessitate slower payments to the team but we are fully covered in terms of financial risk as a company.

Likewise, I need to re-evaluate the system of splits, which determine who deserved credit for working on various parts of a recruitment project. I feel confident that reform in this area will alleviate stress the team feels stemming from the problems and arguments they encounter with their colleagues regarding this issue.

I plan also to take on the improvement of confidentiality agreements as another project. In the past we have had a few very unethical employees who stole, or tried to steal, company property - including clients, deals and parts of our databases. I hope that by requiring all employees to sign confidentiality agreements we can avoid future potential indiscretions in the future.

Employees want:
- To not have the company incur debt when employees leave;
- To have a compensation structure that provides a feeling of stability, as well as proper motivation, in order that they can work hard and earn more;
- Good monetary compensation and good benefits;
- An equitable and detailed system of guidelines regarding commission splits;
- Good communication within the company, recognition for above-average performers, and company trips for top performers; and
- Confidentiality agreements to help deter any employee that may consider stealing company property.

BENEFITS

"Have insurance, extra day holiday for long-term employees, trainings, listen and communicate. Last year was salary level – now not an issue."..."Plus we pay bonuses – great for office to know!"..."Create interesting perks such as yoga, one day a week work from home, create a more fun culture, make it a super desired company to work for – create culture and below the line ideas"...

We have always paid due salary, commissions and bonuses to all staff members, including those who have left the company. This is what we have always done as a company and is something that is critically important to me and my reputation with our team and former members of our team. We always stand by our employment agreements and our commitments to our staff.

I am all in favor of creating a more fun culture within the company and will try to engage the team to come up with some good ideas. Yoga is an easy one as we have a yoga teacher-in-training on staff. However, I am less inclined to offer staff one day per week to work from their homes. The reason for this is that I feel that people will likely only work 10-30% of the time when they are at home, as there are too many other distractions to pull them away from working.

Employees want:
- Standard benefits and perks such as insurance, an extra holiday day per annum for every year worked (for long-term employees), trainings and respectful communication;
- Salary levels that are appropriate for the level and quality of work they produce;
- To be paid the bonuses they earn according to the company plan; and
- Fun perks such as yoga classes, and to work from home one day per week.

TURNOVER

"Try to help our teams as when some leave is tough as relationships can go – maybe consider different structures – especially for when hiring"...

We definitely need to give more attention to the issue of employee turnover. We need to give more support to the people we let go, in terms of job search assistance and moral support. This will also encourage them to think well of us in the future, should they ever be in a position to provide business referrals to us.

We also need to give more attention to the remaining employees who were close to those that left the company – as they can experience depression and loneliness if left on their own without others to fill in the gap. These are all HR issues that we need to further develop within our company, and we will.

Employees want:
- Their company to help staff that are let go, by assisting them in a new job search; and
- Their company to give time, attention, and support to the employees who were good friends with employees that were let go.

TEAM-BUILDING

"Small budget for events"..."Would like team-building events to continue"...

Team-building activities are certainly something we will continue to do; no matter how depressed the market economy ever gets, as they are highly motivating, fun, and can be organized on any budget (even no budget!).

Employees want:
- To have frequent team-building events in their company, at any budget level.

CLOSE TEAM

"Our St. Petersburg team have all been there more than 2-3 years, since inception, I am in close contact with the team and help them develop their skills"..."Keep a great atmosphere and team – very helpful people"..."Mutual respect is the main thing"...

Having a close team is an excellent way in which to retain staff. This takes constant effort, care and mutual respect between all management and staff members. We must always evaluate the closeness of our teams and team members and do everything we can to foster a close company environment.

Employees want:
- To work in a close team environment with a great office atmosphere; and
- To work with great, helpful people where there is mutual respect between everyone.

BRAND

"At the HR management fair they talked about building an HR brand – building a better brand."...

In truth, I had to research this topic before commenting on it, and I did not find much value in it. Building an HR brand seems to me like merely a lot of hype in trying to find ways to re-configure the commonly-used term, "Human Resources", into new jargon, such as Human Capital, People Capital, Human Talent and People Talent.

None of the research available on the internet proved beneficial. Therefore, we are sticking with "Human Resources", which seems to me superior in that it is already widely recognized, understood, accepted and even preferred. Furthermore, there are far more important matters for us to focus on as a company than a discussion about re-vamping standard industry terminology.

Employees want:
- Their company to explore new things, like building an HR Brand.

TIME OFF

"Understand their motivations – for me it is time. Additional days off or less work schedule"..."Vary work hours (extra vacation days)"

I come from a sales background and I was always a top performer at almost every company I worked for - and always one of the highest paid. I also lived a great life and was allowed to take the occasional day, or week, off whenever I needed or wanted. But this was directly attributed to the fact that my results for the companies I worked for were so great.

As a result, it just boggles my mind, that the first person quoted above, who is still fairly new to the company and has not proven to be anything more than a below-average performer, has the nerve to request additional days off, or work fewer hours per day, and all without a pay cut.

While I appreciate his honesty, it is clear to me that he is not cut out for our work ethic at Staffwell and, consequently, it is not likely that he will ever become a top-tier performer for us, or even be above-average for that matter. I decided that we needed to monitor him more closely, and that if his performance did not improve very quickly, we will would cut our losses, sooner rather than later, and ask him to leave.

I would note that, as a result of these "Tea with Teri" meetings, we did implement flexible work schedules for the employees.

Employees want:
- To work less for the same pay, even if they are a below-average performer;
- Flexible work schedules; and
- Additional vacation days for long-term employees.

REPUTATION

"Have top performers and best people, continue with fair treatment and good treatment and make people inside and outside happy with Staffwell – we have a great reputation as a great employer – lots of trash talk about other agencies from employers, clients and candidates"...

I do agree that a great way for us to retain our best people is to keep hiring and developing other great people who can potentially be top performers for us. Successful people admire and like to work with other successful people. It is motivating and stimulating, and it brings greater results to the company.

From my position downward through the organization, we will also always continue to treat our employees well and in a fair manner, and do everything we can to give the best service possible to our clients and the candidates we represent. We have worked hard to build our strong market reputation and we will continue to improve upon it and never lose focus.

Employees want:
- To have a lot of top performers in their company;
- Everyone to be treated well and in a fair manner;
- Everyone in their company, and on the market, to think positively about their company; and
- To have a strong reputation as a great employer.

COMMUNICATION

"Update people regularly, lots of communication. Find out everything going on with our people. Maks is great at letter writing!"..."Communicate a lot with people that they are doing a great job (for those who actually are), – verbal communications"..."Communications"..."First thing is to discuss with them why they are not satisfied, not to press them but to try to provide them with what they really need, within due limits of course"..."Communications is number one – being very closely in touch with our team. Creating a great atmosphere"..."Awareness about company plans, communication and openness"..."Sharing through career opportunities, talk about future prospective and future development of company – Important to feel stable and know the plan"...

Having strong communications in the company is very important to the team. We have communications, but they are nowhere near the level where they could and should be. My focus will be to improve the situation and make it one of our more important initiatives going forward.

I agree that we need to talk more with our people: to offer praise, when deserved; constructive criticism, when improvement is needed; to listen to our team and their ideas and issues; to update the team on company news and plans; and communicate to everyone about their career potential and how that fits in with the company's plans.

Employees want:
- Frequent communications from their employer;
- Their employer to have conversations with them and to get to know them better;
- Praise from their employer if they are doing a good job for the company and deserve it;
- To discuss their thoughts and needs with their employer;
- Executive management to have very close communications with the team; and
- To feel that the company they work for is stable, and to know about the company's future plans and how their careers fit into that plan.

MORE RESPONSIBILITIES/PROFESSIONAL DEVELOPMENT

"Offer new responsibilities – project manager, team leader"..."Sometimes nothing you can do. Sometimes offer new career options or responsibilities"..."Likes our structure but knows as we grow it will be more varied – and more levels of management, etc. Would like a group of recruiters under her – would love to manage them. More responsibilities, comp package and grow professionally"... "Professional skills development, not only sales skills, career growth opportunities, clear system of professional career growth – this will keep people for a long period of time. If I do this, I can achieve this (example)"..."Question of motivation of future prospects"..."Developing new challenging projects"..."Material and non-material and results-oriented. But people can need promotions and other responsibilities (non-material) – but motivating (managing, coaching, training, creating systems, projects, etc.) and when we promote people we need to document changes and new responsibilities. No difference between Consultant and Senior Consultant – need to differentiate this – need to work on this. In an ideal world, each individual person will have career growth and build along this (HR)"..."Show that the people are really important to the company and improve and develop their own talents"..."Thinks we have a great group of people here – who really want to work here and develop here – professional growth and the number of vacancies is the best way to retain"...

From these comments, it is clear that on our Recruitment Consultants Team we need to create one, or a few, new supervisory or managerial levels, dealing with projects, key accounts, and/or people management. We also need to differentiate in documentation between the various levels of specialists we have on both the Director's and Consultant's teams.

Human Resources will play a key role again in our company in helping to turn a lot of these requests into reality, and we will work on making this happen.

Employees want:
- To gradually take on more responsibilities;
- More levels to be added to the organizational chart so that they can have more opportunities to grow professionally;
- The opportunity to supervise or manage people;
- The various levels of occupation roles in the company to be clearly delineated and documented; and
- A lot of business to be brought into the company.

TERI

"Make them feel a real part of what is being created. I would like to see you spend more time with people, client visits, attending interviews, generally getting close to you. I am very fortunate in this way of course, others are not. I would be very motivated if shares in the company could be an option, given my comment above"..."Very good idea with share option plan"...

Months prior to starting this "Tea with Teri" exercise, I mentioned to the person quoted above that I was going to provide 20% of all future company profits to the employees and, in the event that the company was ever sold, I would distribute 20% of those proceeds to the employees (shares and profit sharing). No one asked me to do this prior to my doing it. I just decided I wanted to do it. I wanted the team to feel more a part of the company and to receive more rewards from the company for helping to build and grow it, and make it more successful.

The team was very happy and surprised when I later officially made this announcement to them. They did not expect it and, most likely, did not believe it, but it is real and now a part of our compensation and benefits package. As there is a major recession, it may take several years and lots of hard work before the team realizes these benefits. However, they will come and it will be a very nice perk for everyone employed when those payouts occur.

It was also fun for me to create the criteria associated with future distributions: success levels; years employed; employment levels; attendance; who read and commented on my blog when asked to; and a host of other variables like teamwork, helpfulness and attitude. I am really looking forward to their first disbursement and the pleasure they will derive from it.

Regarding me spending more quality time with the team - I know I need to do this and I know how beneficial it will be for everyone, especially key people and top performers. I am also aware that I have a lot to offer everyone and that I am somewhat of an interesting and creative person, and that the team would love to get closer to me because of that. However, I am only one person and I have a lot on my plate, almost all of the time - so the best I can do is to just commit to do more and put a plan in place to do that.

I also understand that by being more accessible I can clearly help Staffwell retain its best people.

These "Tea with Teri" meeting have been huge for me, and the team, and I have learned so much about our employees and our company. Already, we have made a lot of changes to the company as a result of the feedback and we will continue to do so until we complete the adoptive suggestions.

Foremost, this book is for all of my employees, and for them to learn from me: for them to spend time with me; to read my responses and to learn from my thoughts. It has been a wonderful exercise and one of the best things I have ever done in my life. It also is one of the most important things to do as a businessperson, which is why I am sharing it with a broader audience in the form of this book.

Employees want:
- Their CEO and executive management to spend time with them, teaching them and sharing their knowledge; and
- To be offered a corporate share option plan.

SUPPORT

"Feels the support of the company when he is in need (financial and time)"...

It was glad to hear this comment. I always give people the time when they ask for it, and have always tried to help employees who needed financial assistance in the past. It is important for me to help others, it is a part of who I am and it makes me feel good to do it.

Employees want:
- To feel the support from their company when they really need it, in terms of financial assistance and time off.

TRAINING

"A lot is done. Trainings, ongoing trainings, maybe trainings abroad"...

Training is a proven and effective way for us to help retain staff as it makes the team feel like they are learning and developing. Trainings abroad are something we may look into when the market recovers and we are back to high, pre-crisis earnings.

Employees want:
- Frequent and on-going training; and
- Training in international locations.

MOTIVATION

"People leave the company because of unjustified expectations – but Staffwell is always open to discuss issues, but to do more of this, talk to people and find out their issues is good"..."Need to create successful motivations for them – to try to understand people and why they leave"..."Financial motivations are great but also important is non-material things, trainings, things that make people feel like they are developing and makes people feel grateful to the company – people develop together with the company"..."Build career paths for people (from when they start) with targets, etc. So people work hard to reach goals plus different motivation systems for different people – single people, people with families, etc."..."Understand what is important to individuals – all different"..."Build a great atmosphere inside the company. Have health insurance and is thankful for that –that we have fresh water, as others don't in the building. After crisis money will be better. "Everything: social package, insurance, mobile, trainings, and listen to the people and opinions and ideas"..."Monthly results – awards, achievements, team-buildings, opportunity to earn money. Plus, very important is non-material motivation (communication, a pat on the back, a thank you and some good words. Russian companies don't do this and it is very stressful (that she worked for) – the communication there is very different as no feedback is given"..."For me all is good but for others maybe more attention to their needs and more bonuses or something like that"...

I feel that these responses provided some very good suggestions and that we do need to focus on these things as part of our retention program. Communications, trainings, career paths, a mix of motivational systems, office atmosphere, team-building events, benefits, praise and a pat on the back for a job well done, are all things we will work to perfect.

I think it is very easy for companies operating in times of recession to take the attitude that employees should just be thankful that they have a job. However, I believe that companies must always push forward and work to improve their businesses and I have discovered that, through this exercise, a lot of that starts with the employees of the company, and what their ideas and needs are. If a company can get it right in terms of what its employees need, within reason, then I feel it is inevitable that staff will want to stay and work hard to make the company and themselves more successful.

Employees want:

- Their employer to talk to them and find out what their issues are;
- Financial and non-financial motivation, like trainings;
- Different motivational systems to be created for different types of people (married, single, etc.);
- Career paths within the company to be structured for them;
- Great benefits, awards and recognition, and to be listened to; and
- Praise and appreciation if they have performed well at a job.

MANAGEMENT

"Have authority – strong authority who can motivate and negotiate with people, thinks the team is strong and very professional and the management – yes!"

We do have a very good, strong management team that is motivating, driving, and diplomatic. However, management especially need to constantly reflect and improve on who they are, and about how they lead and motivate others, as they are ultimately accountable for their unit and/or company-wide results.

Employees want:

- Strong management, with the authority and the ability to motivate them and successfully engage with them; and
- A strong and successful company comprised of top professional executives and management.

THE WORK

"Need more recruitment projects"...

I agree that one of the very best ways for us to retain our team is to have a lot of good work for them to do. This is the reason, first and foremost, our focus must always be on driving our front office team.

Employees want:

- The company to win a lot of business so they are busy and can be successful.

Chapter 32
Have You Anything To Say About Your Treatment From A Discrimination Or Harassment Perspective?

NO ☺

"No (X 48)! - with smiles, laughs and giggles"..."No, happy with equal male/female team – great when this is in balance and harmony"..."Not really"..."No, Thank God"...No, worried Pyotr might say something, lol"..."Have only one man – none! lots of laughs (these questions help all to systemize their thinking about work and Staffwell) – very motivating"..."Nope ☺"

During the course of the "Tea with Teri" meetings, our Moscow office had an equal amount of men and women, and our St. Petersburg office had one man and about eight women. Most of our team found this question funny and light-hearted and I thought it was a really great way to end this exercise: on a very upbeat note.

I am also very pleased to know that no one in our company had ever felt sexually harassed or discriminated against by any other member of the team. This does occur in the work place at other companies. I have heard candidates we interview talk about it over the years and it certainly must be an incredibly horrible thing for anyone to go through. We have hired well, and have very strong rules, operations, values, and management. This matters and it makes a difference.

Employees want:
- To not be discriminated against;
- To not be harassed, sexually or otherwise; and
- To have gender balance in the team: an equal amount of men and women.

OTHER

"No, we need a sign in reception room 312"..."No, we need to create a customer satisfaction questionnaire and what else we can do to improve our services and also one for placed candidates"..." Many companies are jealous of Staffwell because of Teri – because Teri is a person who is really concerned about the company and the people in it – fantastic for a business owner – always wants more for and from us. Very creative – very few owners are like this. Monthly awards you started, the focus on PR, feels PR initiative very smart things the PR is very good, also useful is new website and advertising campaign (Headhunter, Vedomosti, Kommersant newspapers) Also LinkedIn but they are seen mostly by foreigners"..."No, likes the idea of getting origination fees and get computer analysis updated"...

Here everyone again answered no to the question - but they also used the time to get in their last remaining comments and ideas. I thought some of them were good, such as the idea of a reception sign, which we did need outside of our reception room, and which I immediately took care of.

Creating a customer satisfaction questionnaire for both clients and placed candidates was also a great idea. We had used them before in the past but had dropped the practice when we got really busy and did not have the time for it. However, I know their importance and they are consistent with our objectives to always improve our business and increase sales.

At the beginning of the economic crisis, we did move away from traditional marketing and, instead, relied solely on our Director's team to generate new business for the company. We developed our first PR initiative for the company and hired a PR Manager, who focused on working hard to get our name out there in the market. It turned out to be a very wise move on our part as the initiative worked out well for us.

We also completely redesigned our website, creating a more clean, modern and simple design with easy functionality, and started to really network a lot through various business networking sites, such as LinkedIn. In addition, we instituted a company-wide rule that any employee could earn origination fees, should they bring a valid lead or referral to the company. This turned out to be really motivating for many and made people feel they had the ability to be more helpful.

The comments about me above are very sweet. I have been very fortunate to have a team that has always seemed to appreciate me and what I contribute to the company. It feels good, and owners and CEOs also need to feel appreciated at times, if deserving.

Employees want:
- A reception sign outside of reception;
- Customer service questionnaires for clients that employ the company's services;
- Monthly awards for top performers;
- Their company to engage in strong PR efforts;
- Their corporate website to be well-designed and easy to navigate;
- To receive origination fees from the company if they generate new, valid business leads or referrals; and
- An owner and CEO who really cares about the people in the company, is creative, and who really motivates and directs them to achieve more.

WANT IT ☺

"I would like to receive some sexual harassment but realize it is unlikely to happen ☺"…" No, unfortunately ☺"…

The smiley faces are included here as these comments were made in a joking manner with great laughter. The men in our office are really great, very funny, and actually very sweet.

Employees want:
- Other people in the office to find them attractive; and
- To be funny sometimes.

AGE

"No. Finds Staffwell great at anti-age discrimination, we hired her when nobody else would (as she was a PA before and of a more mature age) plus Lika looked very young to be hiring for us – older candidates complain about 20-year olds at competitors interviewing them"…

We always hire for proven or potential ability. Therefore, I am glad to know that our team does not use age as a criterion in our screening process. Age discrimination is not an issue explicitly addressed in our operations manual but I feel it needs to be and it will be included in the future. At present, we have front office employees that range in age from the early 20s to the late 50s - and, hopefully, they will still be working for us when they are in their 60s and 70s!

I am glad we hired Alyona when nobody else would. I feel really good about that decision, and she has proven herself to be a very solid performer and contributor to our success.

Lika was young when we hired her. But she was also very effective, mature in disposition and had a highly professional appearance. I think you are only as young, or as old, as the age you act.

I am aware that some of our competitors have very young and very immature people working as recruiters for them. When such people interview more mature candidates on the market, the candidates often do not appreciate the fact that their time is being wasted on people who, themselves, have almost no valid work or life experience, and can be completely silly in disposition. Their doing this only makes us better and gives us a competitive edge.

Employees want:
- To not be discriminated against due to their age, when applying or interviewing for new jobs; and
- People that are mature, and look and act in a professional manner, to be involved in the recruitment and selection process at their company.

NO, BUT

"No, however, Diana mentioned the GM of our building was too touchy with many of our team – would bring coffee to our team – trying to get in with them!)"…"No. However, the former, gross courier Yuri was making noises like a cricket at her when she would walk by – he maybe had mental problems or was strange – but she immediately ordered him out when that happened"…

The GM of our office building was a good-looking, elderly Russian man, who was very flirtatious by nature. Personally, I enjoyed his delight in seeing me every day, as it made me really happy and happy to be in his building. However, his attempts to touch some of our team members is inappropriate behavior and I am sorry no one mentioned this to me before. Had they done so I would have spoken to the building management about it and put a stop to it.

He would also touch me at times - holding my arms when he asked how I was and how Staffwell was doing. But I found it endearing and quite friendly in a very Western way, as I quite often do the same thing with other people.

The GM no longer works in the building so the problem no longer exists. However, we still need to insert formal harassment and discrimination rules and procedures in our operations manual and encourage people to speak up, including all the way to me, should they ever feel they are experiencing it.

The other comment refers to a the very strange courier we had working for us, back in the day when we were publishing the print version of The Well, our corporate and career magazine, which he delivered around Moscow for us. He was somewhat disturbing and I could not stand him either and would order him out of the office whenever I saw him there. Thank God that era is over and he is no longer working for us.

Similar to all companies, we have had some real "winners" working for us at times, but we have really stepped up our game now and hire only top class people.

Employees want:
- To not be touched, in any way, by people in the office or building, that they do not want to be touched by; and
- To not have to work with, or near, odd people that act in strange ways.

REGIONS

"No, and better is that people don't treat him like he is someone from the countryside. People from the regions feel very alone in Moscow"...

Being from the United States, I had only really thought about discrimination as it mostly related to race or age. It never really dawned on me that in Russia people can feel discriminated against because they come from a different city within the country. It saddens me that people from the regions feel very alone in Moscow, and I hope it is something the citizens of Russia will try to address and change over time.

I am really happy that we have a diversified team of people from Moscow and St. Petersburg, other Russian cities, former CIS countries, and other countries. We also are open to, and hire, people of differing religions, ages, sexual orientations, and also have someone with a limiting, physical disability on our team. Treating all people well and with fairness and respect, is the right thing to do, and the goodness of it comes back to those who give others such treatment.

Employees want:
- To not be discriminated against because they originally come from a city or region that is different than the majority of their co-workers.

Summary

Founding Staffwell in 2000, and then driving it forward as its CEO until now, has been a lot of fun and a great experience for me. I believe I have been a true entrepreneur in the sense that I have been a strong leader with a clear vision and direction, enjoyed a degree of risk and challenge, and have been a highly creative "do-it-yourselfer". In fact, I have never had a personal assistant for the sole reason that I preferred to do everything I needed to get done, myself.

I have made good and bad decisions over the years on behalf of the company, and I take full ownership of those, as I rarely conferred with anyone on the team or outside of the company prior to making them. I thought I knew best, and because we were growing and making money, I rarely doubted my directions or decisions, instead I just steamrolled ahead, as typical textbook entrepreneurs tend to do.

What I learned from this exercise of meeting with my team individually to get to know them better and their thoughts on the company, is that, in a nutshell: forty-eight heads are better than one. In fact, even though I knew, as the saying goes, that "two heads are better than one", I learned that I may have missed a lot of opportunities by never really, adequately, incorporating the concept in my owner/CEO role, or used it to the extent I should have.

"Tea with Teri" gave my team the confidential forum alone with me, which they needed, in order to feel comfortable to speak about themselves and their real thoughts and feelings on the company. The funny thing about it is that I didn't know at the time I was initially creating the exercise that I really needed to know what they were going to end up telling me, but I sure found that out. I had no expectations going into it other than to get to know our team better as people. Without a doubt, it has been the most enlightening and useful experience of my career.

There is a lot covered in this book: my employees unloaded an immense and widely varying amount of important information and ideas on me. Employees have a lot to say; the key is finding a way, or a forum, to get them to say it. Having structured one-on-ones, "Tea with Teri's", was what worked for us. It was a success and we will continue to use the information in this book, as an important resource, for many years to come.

This book was really important for me to write. I knew almost immediately that what I was learning from my one-on-one conversations with my staff had to be shared with the public and business community, so that others could also learn what I learned, and put it to use for themselves and the companies they work for, or own.   I also wanted the book for myself and for my team, so that we would always be able to review it together to ensure that we were staying on top of the core things that our employees want from their workplace.

Finally, it is one thing to have structured and meaningful one-on-ones with your employees, but equally important is the appreciation they feel in being asked to share with you their thoughts and opinions on all aspects of the company they work for, and to know what, if anything, you did or were going to do with the ideas and information they gave you...

Concluding Chapter

So, what did I do with all of the information I was given from my team during the "Tea with Teri" chats?

2009

The first thing I did, almost immediately, was take care of all of the quick fixes: I bought that mirror for the accounting department, fixed the paper towel holder in the ladies' bathroom, bought wine bottle openers for each room in the office, got headsets for those that wanted them, and authorized Uliana to try the up-graded version of Linked-In. I tasked our IT department to check and clean everyone's PC, set up a separate cordless phone for the team to make international calls from, and set up SKYPE for everyone in our front office team.

Regarding office equipment, I authorized the purchases of a new printer, color printer and copier for our Moscow office, and a wireless phone and a coffee machine for our office in Saint Petersburg. For our receptionist in Moscow, I formally introduced her to her new direct report, our Commercial Director, and got her tasked to help the front office team by inputting CVs into our database.

Then I moved on to what was, for me, the most important action I needed to take in the Company at that time: changing the organizational structure to incorporate new levels of management. If you will recall, in our Moscow office, the Consultants team wanted a dedicated leader of their team to report to, and several people had mentioned/nominated Polina, who was a former Consultant herself and a top Director. Polina also wanted this role as she felt it was needed and that she was ready and the right person for it.

James, who was also a top Director, felt he too was ready and the right person to lead the Directors team. Our Commercial Director, Diana, was leading the entire front office team in Moscow at the time, after being promoted from a top Director's spot in 2008. However, through her own initiative, she was also unofficially leading and managing all of the back office operations at Staffwell as well (no small task).

I immediately sat down and started to work on new, formal job descriptions for everyone, including the current Head of our St. Petersburg office. In the new structure I promoted Diana to General Manager of the entire company, James to Head of Business

Development in Moscow (the Directors Team), and Polina to Head of Recruitment in Moscow (the Consultants Team).

I sat with Diana and laid out my decision to promote James and Polina into their new roles and to promote her to General Manager. With her, I then went through the new job descriptions I had created for all of them, which were very detailed and reflected a lot of what the team had desired in my "Tea with Teri" meetings, to get her input on them as well, prior to us rolling them out.

Then, Diana and I went through all of the new roles with James, Polina and Nadya, and everyone understood their own and each other's new responsibilities, goals and targets. From that moment on they started working together as the newly expanded front office management team.

I then prepared a presentation, which I delivered to all of the employees of the company, which covered the results of my "Tea with Teri" chats/project, and what had been done, changed, and fixed already, and what was still to come. I announced the changes in management and introduced the new leadership team and went over their roles briefly with everyone. Then I announced new corporate benefits I was rolling out which included flexible work hours, one extra day off per quarter for anyone with children or grandchildren, and one extra day off per year for every year over 5 years that an employee has been with the company (for some this ended up giving them an extra week off per year).

As a surprise for the team, which nobody was expecting or asked for, I went on to announce that I was going to give 20% of all future net profits in the company to the staff employed at the time of any distributions (profit sharing pool), and should I ever sell the company, 20% of the net proceeds would also go to the staff employed at the time. I then detailed a matrix I put together that explained how these future payouts for the employees would work based on various criteria that were important to me, such as: performance, rank in the company, years with the company, attitude, teamwork, attendance, and commenting on my blog postings. The team was extremely surprised, touched, grateful, and motivated, and some, maybe, unbelieving.

I did this because it made me feel good to give something significant back to everyone who works hard every day to help make us successful. I wanted our team to feel even more a part of the company they worked for and to take more ownership of their future performance for the company. It also made me feel really good to do it and I knew it would make them feel good to receive it. Now we were really in it together, as a team, to succeed

We then rolled out some improved initiatives in the company that included new short and to-the-point, frequently scheduled meetings between management, departments, teams and offices, in order to improve communications and sharing of projects and stories. We also started a focused and intensive long-term training agenda for employees that covered every single training request mentioned in this book (43 training areas in total). Our own proven Staffwell experts of each area of training were tasked to create their own practical-style master classes, and to then train the other team members on it, on a continued basis. This proved to be highly effective and has resulted in our team being, according to me, and client feedback, the best on the market.

We did not have a budget for formal teambuilding activities in 2009, the hardest hit year of the crisis, but I was turning the "Big 40" and decided to dip into my savings and throw a birthday party for myself, inviting all of Staffwell's employees and my close friends - some of whom were also our clients. The party was held at an outdoor venue in Moscow, and the staff and I spent a really fun day drinking, eating, and creating hysterical theatrical performances, all centered around recruitment themes. We had a great time and were joined later in the evening by our other guests. It was a great time and a mood-booster for everyone.

If you will recall, throughout the book we had a Director named Miron, who was a below-average performer and desired to work part-time from home and to have me hire telemarketers to do his cold calling for new client meetings for him. Well, almost needless to say, things did not improve and we started putting pressure on him to leave. To our advantage, the day we were to formally dismiss him, he resigned before we had the opportunity to talk with him. I was grateful that we did not end up having to pay him any amount of severance.

Boris was our next departure and a bittersweet one for me at that. I liked Boris and he was a talented salesman and always one of our top 3 Directors prior to the crisis, but he was not assimilating well under the depressed market conditions or under our new management regime. James, as our then new Head of Business Development, was to drive the Directors team to make their KPIs, which included, among many things, making a set number of cold calls to clients and new clients, daily, in order to get client meetings arranged. Boris did not like to, want to, or want to be made to, make the calls.

Cold calling in a tough economy is a really hard thing to do. You must adjust to hearing a high percentage of rejection responses, and continue to make the calls, as there are always active clients to be found. Boris could not bring himself to make the calls and soon thereafter he resigned. Thankfully, our budget was getting lighter and more manageable, with some of these departures.

I then created a little of my own fun, and launched my blog Work360.ru. Designing it was a lot of fun, as was the writing. This was one of my solutions to communicate more with my team. I wrote articles on general business topics, and updates on the market and Staffwell. They were all opinion pieces so my team got to know me a bit better, as did the market, and they also had the chance to communicate back to me via the comments section on the blog. It was fun, stylish, and a good marketing tool for Staffwell, and still is today.

Along with some strategic and personnel moves, there was a physical move for us as well. Our landlord in Moscow then recommended that we move out of the building. We were in an old, centrally-located historic building, which was managed by the City of Moscow, and every year for the previous 10 years, the Federal Government took the City to court over the management rights of the building. The City won the case every year, however, for this particular year, (late 2009) they did not feel as confident. Machine gun carrying OMON (equivalent to a SWAT team in the US) even started to camp out in the building's reception area, which was sort of a thrill for me, but sent shivers up and down the spines of all of our staff. Our City landlords strongly advised us to find new space immediately, as they were certain we would not be treated well under Federal landlords, and then they wished us well.

We ended up finding a great office space: the building was modern with a great lobby, and we were able to take the entire top floor, which had wall-to-wall, floor-to- ceiling windows that looked out over a park - so for most of the year we feel like we are working from a country dacha. The space also had a really perfect open-plan layout for us as well, and our Staffwell branded career-themed motivational posters were properly showcased throughout the office, and look great.

For our main reception area, I purchased 2 coat closets that had full-length mirrors that covered their doors. This enabled our staff and visiting candidates and clients, to be able to view their entire appearance, easily and conveniently, prior to working, having an interview or meeting, or at anytime throughout the day.

What a difference moving to this new office made to our mood, spirit and outlook! It was new and it was a positive change, and we needed it at the time and were really grateful for it. Clients and Candidates visiting our office have all remarked on how impressed they are with it, and that it is by far the best recruitment and executive search company office in town. These little things all matter and we were very fortunate that circumstances enabled them to happen for us, in the most difficult year of the economic crisis, when our revenues dropped 80%.

Regarding Albert, and the finance recruitment team he supervised - who were not getting along well together, all seemed to sort itself out through a natural course of changes. Asya, who had quite a negative disposition throughout my chat with her, and had not proven herself to be a strong performer for the team, resigned. Following that, Zhanna and Kira both went on maternity leave, giving Kristina the opportunity to handle most of the finance recruiting projects on her own.

2010

We started 2010 by establishing new KPIs and targets for the front office teams, which were more in line with market conditions, now that we knew where the bottom was. These helped the team to feel more confident and optimistic in their roles and abilities.

On the PR side, we focused heavily on getting our names mentioned in the media and speaking at conferences and round table events, and having our front office team contribute with analytics and research related to changing compensation and benefits, and hiring and redundancy practices on the market. Our focus on PR during the crisis, really helped us to keep our name and brand going strong in the market, even though our activity had decreased, due to the stagnation of client hiring needs.

During this year we also purchased the lighter and smaller laptops for the Directors' teams to use on their client presentations, improved our highlights form so that our interview notes we provide to all clients would be in a better format - and with more useful and targeted information in them, and we made numerous improvements to our SDS system: Staffwell's Digital (CRM) System.

Our top Senior Consultant in the company, Sofiya, also made a move to take on a dual role; combining the responsibilities of a Director and a Consultant. We were very happy that she exhibited the confidence and drive to do this, as she was a very multi-talented professional with a lot of future potential. Her pushing herself to take on more, and experience more, would only be good for Staffwell.

This particular year was Staffwell's 10th anniversary year of successful business operations in Russia, and well, the last and most recent one being more accurately a successful "survival" year. As much as I would have liked to have thrown a huge party for clients and placed candidates, to help celebrate with us, our revenues were still dramatically low, albeit better than 2009. I was nervous, financially, and decided that at the end of the day, the market would understand my decision to keep it smaller and lower budget.

We made it into an anniversary/team-building party only for Staffwell employees and held it at Moscow's Curling Club. It was a huge hit. We started the morning off with a Tai Chi instructional session, and then half of us went curling while the others played challenging mind/trivia games with each other, and then rotated activities. This was followed by an afternoon of funny and creative skits we came up with - and then performed theater-style for each other, dinner, and ending the night with night club style dancing.

Just like at my 40th birthday party the year before, it was really nice having our St. Petersburg office staff there, to enjoy time together and to build stronger relationships and communications. Although the entire day and night were fun, curling was really a highlight for all of us. It is such a great sport and brings a lot of teamwork to it, friendly competition, and laughter. I highly recommend it.

We ended the year on a good note. We did not break even, but our revenues were up and growing. I dug back into my personal savings, again, and reinstated our holiday gift giving to top clients - to thank them for choosing Staffwell for their recruitment/hiring needs. I also decided to reinstate our President Club Trip, so our top performers and management of the year would spend a fun, long weekend together with me at some point the following year. I was confident and optimistic that we would make it through and continue to grow and stay on top in terms of market reputation and revenues.

2011

As usual, we started the year focused on budgets, KPIs and targets. Things were looking encouraging on the market, so I decided to go full steam ahead on hiring and rebuilding our team, which would also increase our revenues.

It then came to my attention that we had a problem on the team regarding a split/fee share, which is what we refer to as the decision with regard to who on the team gets what percent of a fee for work done. Of course, I remembered from my "Tea with Teri" chats that a lot of people mentioned having issues with our splits system; however, I had just not had the time to look into it yet, but did then so immediately.

As it was a very touchy area with the team and management already, I decided to take on this project myself, as I already had the solution in my head. Our current split system broke down the recruitment process into about 7 stages that the team could allocate toward themselves. My solution was to increase the stages to about 20, as I felt there were a lot of grey areas in-between, which were not accounted for in our current system, and this was very likely what was, and had been, causing the tension all along.

I made sure I covered every base and felt confident that we would almost never have another split issue again. I introduced my new system to the Management and then the front office team, then put it officially into our operations manual and made it formal policy. I then moved on to other things I was working on, like overseeing the company and writing this book for instance. To this day, June 2012, we have still not had one new split/fee share issue.

In addition to continuing our focus on training and development of the team, improved communications in and between offices, and shorter more to-the-point frequent meetings in the offices, we also started scheduling more management visits to our St. Petersburg branch office. Also, we gave more frequent rewards, encouraging words and announcements for our strong performing team members, for jobs well done. It goes without saying that these things all had a positive influence and effect on the team.

We had a great first six months of the year and were up 100% on 2010 revenue figures. Then the financial turmoil unfolded in Greece, dragging most of Europe into a significant economic downturn, which naturally impacted our business in Russia. We hunkered down for some rough months ahead, as Client recruitment/hiring mandates went on hold temporarily, one-by-one.

When I returned from my annual summer vacation, James, our Head of Business Development in Moscow, had informed me that he had some ideas to improve the front office team and scheduled time with me to show me his presentation on the subject. I was very happy and impressed that James had done this, and done it on his own, and that it was good.

What James had done was identify some of the main reasons the Consultants and Directors teams in Moscow were not working well together and, more importantly, he identified viable solutions to the problems. Also, very important, was that his management team colleagues also bought into his ideas, vision and solutions, which made it easy and efficient for all of them to then work together to roll out the proposed changes to improve the overall team dynamics for the Company.

The management team and I developed a newfound respect for James after that. He had spent his personal time outside of the office to reflect and think of what was good for the team and the company. I was thrilled and looking forward to seeing more of what he could contribute, and what his actions might inspire in our other management in terms of creative ideas to help us going forward.

Then, in late September, it was time for our Presidents Club Trip, which entailed 3 days of sailing on the Turkish Mediterranean. Along with me, our 12 top performers of 2010 enjoyed an amazing time together: sailing, swimming, diving, jet skiing, banana-boating, fishing, eating great food, drinking, dancing, and sleeping out underneath the stars. We lived on the boat together for three days in fairly close quarters and just had the greatest time, and a very relaxing one too. We needed it and enjoyed our time together, and our top performers deserved it.

Our new PR Manager, then organized for me to have my own personal Blog platforms on Forbes, Harvard Business Review, and FINAM, and I became a member of Forbes Women's Club. Our team, including myself, also started to write more for the print media, guest speak on Radio and TV, and present at networking events and conferences.

We also started our "Get To Know You" project. This was an idea of mine that stemmed from the e-newsletter idea that came from the "Tea with Teri" chats. I thought that if we did not have the time to do a full newsletter then, in the very least, we could make an effort to get to know each other better in a different way. So we created a short questionnaire that covered professional and personal areas including hobbies, travel, and things more prosaic things like "what's in your refrigerator?"

One by one, our employees would fill out the form, attach a few fun photos of themselves, and then it would be sent out by email to everyone in the company, to get to know the person better. These were also saved on the server, so that new or current staff, could always access them to review more about their colleagues, at anytime.

They were, and still are a lot of fun, and highly useful, as people discovered many common interests that they did not know about.

Toward the end of the year, I conjured up another new project for myself as well: 360 degree top Management Team Assessments. Ever since my "Tea with Teri" chats I felt that a real gap existed in developing our senior executive team. Our top team trains everyone underneath them, but who trains our top team? Personally, I did not really have the time to develop my own trainings for them, nor did I feel confident in being able to give them everything they might need from it. We also did not have the budget to hire external trainers and, again, I was not entirely convinced they would be effective even if we did.

We started the preparation for the project with the intent to roll out the assessments during the first quarter of 2012.

2012

We closed out our books for 2011 and confirmed that we broke even, and had a 60% increase in revenues over 2010. Not bad overall, given the Greek and European crisis that affected our growth from August through November.

I had also made a decision to promote 2 top performing front office team members to our Executive Management Committee, which I had just created. Albert who was our top Director for 2011, and Sofiya, who was our top Consultant and a Director for several years running, would join myself, our General Manager, the Head of our St. Petersburg, and our newly titled Commercial Director (James) and Operations Director (Polina), in Moscow. I was especially happy that Sofiya was moving up due to her success as a Consultant, which would hopefully give the rest of our Consultants team confidence in the company treating them fairly and with respect and deserved consideration.

A nice surprise for me was starting the year with my General Manager, and Moscow Commercial and Operations Directors, all wanting to deliver their own private presentations to me on what they saw were the accomplishments for 2011 and what they planned to achieve in 2012.

I was so impressed. Each presentation was different, and packed with great views, ideas and solutions. They were extremely well put together, informative, and showed a really high level of professionalism and maturity. Afterward, during the next week or two, they presented to each other, and came away with newfound respect and admiration for one another. This, in turn, created an excitement to work again together this year at a higher level - with the common goal of accomplishing more and achieving higher levels of success.

I then dived back into the top Management Assessments. First, I went through all of our Management's job descriptions and put them into similar new formats with common wording and language. I started with James, and using the part of his job description, which detailed his role as Head of Business Development, I created the assessment form. For each and every responsibility he was tasked with, I asked the assessor to comment on his performance for 2011 and then comment on what improvements they would like to see James make regarding each task in 2012.

For each top manager, there were anywhere from 10 to 20 responsibilities/tasks in which to assess them on. I also added in the person's target for the part of the business they managed and what resulting number they had at year-end, their annual attendance level, and more general things to comment on at the end, such as professionalism and teamwork.

Each top manager was assessed by the direct team they managed, their management team colleagues, our General Manager, Finance Director and HR Director, me, and finally a self-assessment. I can tell you in no uncertain terms that this was the best experience my Management Team had ever gone through professionally, according to them. It was the best training they could have ever had in their life because they were told exactly what they were doing right and wrong, and given concrete examples on how to improve themselves, and they were being told from all angles by different levels of people in the company, and even telling themselves too, in certain instances, in their own self assessments.

Staff was really appreciative to be given the opportunity to partake in the exercise: they felt respect from the company for being included, and they felt useful. Some of the staff told me they worried their jobs could be threatened by their manager they were assessing, if they honestly were to share their true feelings, as they potentially could read their comments and hold it against them. We talked through this privately and I assured them that this would not be the case as the people being assessed really want to know how they can improve themselves for the good of the team and team members. I also said that, in the worst case scenario, I personally have everyone's back in this at the end of the day; meaning I would not let anyone get treated unfairly for speaking the truth and how they really feel, especially if it was meant to help the person being assessed and the company.

As a precursor, I did then speak to the Management team being assessed and prepared them to hear and swallow gracefully and constructively, any degree of negative feedback they might receive. Of course this then made them a bit nervous, but in the end, the comments they received from everyone were outstanding in terms of being useful and constructive – many, in fact, were also very complimentary. As I mentioned earlier, our management team felt it was one of the best experiences they had ever had professionally.

These customized and personalized assessments gave our top management team the tools they needed to effectively lead and manage their teams and carry out their responsibilities to the highest degree of success. They are also a resource tool that these managers can review throughout the year and over years to come: to review and reflect as to whether they are performing to the standards the team, their colleagues, their direct reports, and me as their CEO, are expecting from them.

We made a very small profit in 2011 and, notwithstanding the debt I have outstanding with the company, or the stagnation of hiring decisions in the first quarter of 2012, I still made the decision to pay out to the team their first profit share-related bonus in April 2012. It was enough for everyone in the company to go out and have a nice meal, or buy something special for themselves that they might not have done otherwise. The team was surprised and really appreciative, as it was quite unexpected for them, and the whole experience and positive responses made me feel really good to do it, and excited about there being much more to come.

Coming back to Albert's finance recruitment team: Zhanna and Kira had both returned from their maternity leave, and together with Kristina, all seem to be working much better together. The time away from each other was likely needed, and our more comprehensive system of determining fee splits between colleagues surely helped lessen any possible tensions regarding fee calculation disputes that they had occasionally anticipated or had experienced.

Regarding our entire Consultants team, we began highlighting, praising and rewarding those with the most number of placements (not only revenue amount) and those with the highest number of placements are also now invited to join our annual President's Club Trip (a historical sightseeing trip to Samarkand, Uzbekistan in 2012 for the 2011 winners). We also implemented Consultants Meetings, much like those we organize for our Directors. In these meetings our

Consultants hear company updates and discuss with one another projects they are working on, ideas they have for the business, and any issues they are facing.

In an initiative to improve our customer service and communications with our placed candidates and clients, we have created a new role within our company to have a dedicated representative call on all of our placed candidates to discuss their experience using Staffwell and to find out how they have assimilated into their new, or already established, careers with our clients. This feedback we will use to update our databases with and then, where appropriate, pass back to our clients for their record keeping as well. We have filled this role internally with a member of our Consultants team, who we felt would do a good job with it.

So, what is left to do?

There was a lot covered in my "Tea with Teri" chats from 2009 and I have been doing the best I can to check them all off and get them done, all while running a company, writing a book, raising three little boys, and having an enjoyable personal life. In addition, due to the normal course of business over these past few years, we as a company, have also taken on and completed a lot of other projects not mentioned in my "Tea with Teri's", which were necessary for us to focus on.

From my point of view, almost every idea mentioned to me in my "Tea with Teri" chats were worth developing and implementing in our company - in order to make it as perfect as we can for our employees, our clients and the market. We will continue this year and next, to complete all of the outstanding ideas and initiatives which include: creating our key account management (KAM)/team leader function and mentoring roles for our Consultants team, Intranet newsletter, staff confidentiality agreements, new customer satisfaction forms for clients, new career growth plans for all employees, and to further improve our CRM system, and to rework and update our operations manual along the way.

I am personally committed to giving more of my time and attention to my executive management team as well - to ensure that the company's vision, goals and targets are being focused on and realized, and so that they have ample access to me whenever they need or want my attention. It is important as well, I know, for me to spend more quality time with our team of strong-performing, rising stars in the company who will, hopefully, also be promoted into our executive management team in the near future as we grow.

Having the "Tea with Teri" chats with my staff was one of the most important and influential things I have ever done at, and for, Staffwell. It gave me most, if not all, of the answers to the question: "what would make our company perfect?" What would make our company perfect may evolve somewhat on an annual basis, but the exercise brought to light most of the fundamentals that we, as a typical service business, need to always stay focused on for the company's success and the team's happiness, and...

I hope the information in this book, as was the intention, also gives you, the reader, many ideas to help you with your business and career.

And now, just one more thing: the grand finale!

In October 2012, while I was preparing this book in its final stages to be published, we learned that we (Staffwell) were nominated for Russia's 2012 Company of the Year Awards and were invited to attend the awards ceremony later that month. We had entered the competition under the category of unique business model and our industry classification was business services industry, and we put a lot of work and time into the presentation we submitted.

We attended the ceremony with great enthusiasm but with very low and humble expectations of placing. When the lights dimmed, Ernst & Young was announced as the company of the year winner for the business services industry. This made sense: a huge company, huge profits, their presentation was probably amazing, and they likely had a team bigger than our entire company working on it. They then announced that Staffwell was the second place winner. They had our huge logo up on the screen and we went up to accept the award with great surprise and true feeling of honor and accomplishment.

We did not expect to win because we are a small company, and the recruitment industry overall, has been hit quite hard during this recession, so our revenues of better market years weren't there. But that wasn't what was important or interesting to them regarding Staffwell and our application and presentation. They saw a unique business model better than any they had seen in our industry and for all but one in others.

Listening, over a cup of tea, to my team in 2009 and engaging with them more over the past few years, has definitely contributed to the improvement in areas of our business model. It is "almost" perfect!

Acknowledgements

I would first like to thank my family: Timur, Vovi, Leo and Savva Lagutin. They have all been really understanding and supportive of the time I have needed to put into writing this book over the last three years. I really appreciate that and the excitement and encouragement they have expressed over having me accomplish it. Thank you: I love you guys!

This book could obviously not have been written without the sixty to ninety minutes that each of my Staffwell team members gave me of their time - to get to know them better and to find out their thoughts on the company and how we could make it better. I was impressed and really appreciative that most of the team took the exercise very seriously and came to the one-on-one meetings prepared, communicative, and excited to possibly make a difference; and they did.

So a very big and grateful thank you to each and everyone of the Staffwell team who was employed and enjoyed a cup of tea with me in April 2009 (in alphabetical order): Ekaterina Aberemova, Julia Aleshkina, Inna Alpaidze, Mark Amelin, Victoria Chayka, Jamilya Emirbekova, Marina Filatova, Olga Filatova, Ksenia Golovina, Tatiana Gracheva, Alexander Khadyakov, Svetlana Kharitonova, Elena Kolkova, Victoria Korneeva, Michael Krupenin, Elena Kutishenko, Natalia Kuznetsova, Lada Lazareva, Olga Leonova, Galina Lozovan, Anton Manyakin, Marina Mareeva, Julia Onuchak, Elena Petrova, Victoria Seleznova, Vyacheslav Shaposhnikov, Kirill Shiryaev, Ekaterina Shuster, Elena Sidorenko Sergey Sklyanin, Alexey Smetanin, Julia Smirnova, Allan Sullivan, Natalia Suvorova, Idris Tulparkhanov, Irina Uvarova, Irina Vereshagina, and Elizaveta Zaitseva.

Karen Cernek, a good friend and highly experienced real estate professional in Asheville, North Carolina, where I like to vacation, was my first reader. She joined me at my house on Lake Lure one day, where I was writing, and read through some of the first ten chapters. She then talked non-stop for several hours, as we floated in the water, about her impressions of what she had read and how the stories and information applied to the corporate world as she knew it at her current and past employers. I loved that it made her think about, and want to discuss, her own work experiences, and about the issues the companies she worked for had, as it was one of the main outcomes I wanted for the book.

I knew at that point as well that this book had the potential to be a book club favorite: so much to discuss and so relevant to everyone's life, for those who hold or have held "white collar" jobs, at any level. I hope that book club book idea/fantasy of mine takes off. Thank you for being my first reader Karen.

Jennifer Eremeeva and Beth Knobel were my second readers and are, among other things, writers themselves. They were given my first ten chapters and came back with the echoing comment that they thought the content was great, but that readers would want more of "me" in it giving the CEO's viewpoint. So they advised that I expand my part/responses to what my team was commenting on.

Most entrepreneurs don't like to be given advice or told what to do, and I'm no different. Their comments gave me writer's block for about a year, until I finally realized that what they were saying was correct, positive in nature, and even highly complimentary. Thank you Jennifer and Beth.

Before I continue with acknowledging those who helped me during the process of writing this book, I would like to thank my brother Fred Lindeberg, and friends Allan Sullivan and Stephen O'Connor, for offering to help me with potentially helpful editing and publishing contacts or being an initial reader, even though I did not take any of them up on it. I really appreciate their support and interest and am grateful they accepted my occasional stubbornness, paranoia and controlling behavior, when it came to my book.

Thank you very much to my friends Melinda Rishkofski and Lisa Giroux for allowing me use of their dwellings in Moscow to write parts of my book. Sometimes I needed a change of scenery in order to write and their generosity really helped me with that during certain times.

There was one section in the book where I had a really hard time trying to figure out what my position was going to be. It really irked me and inhibited me from writing for several months. I mentioned it to a friend of mine, and fellow entrepreneur, and although I cannot remember exactly what he said to me, as it was more of an abstract thought, it triggered me to decide my position on the subject I was stressed over and allowed me to push forward and write about it. That exchange was with Michael Sito. Thanks Mike.

Thank you as well to Julia Kaliakina, Julia Smirnova, and Marina Filatova for assisting me in organizing the translation, production, and publishing aspects and process of the book. Your enthusiasm and dedication is highly appreciated.

Finally, I would like to thank Michael Sassarini for editing my book and writing the forward. I will never forget when Michael first read the book, before formally agreeing to edit it. After composing himself he said to me "You are not a good writer. I mean your command of the English language is terrible and your grammar is atrocious...but...however...you wrote a book?...you wrote a book!...and it's good, it's really good."

What I appreciate about Michael is that (while cleaning up my atrocious English), he kept the book in my style and voice, and he made the process really fun for me. Thank you Sass: for editing the book, writing the foreword, and for your endless patience, advice, humor, and most importantly, for your friendship.

Author Interview

Sunshine Publishing House (SPH): Have you always wanted to write a book?

Teri Lindeberg (TL): Yes, I have always wanted to write a book, and have tried several times in the past but never really made it past two pages. I did not succeed in the past because I was trying to write about my life, and I do not think I was ready to write that story then: I was too young and my mind was not mature enough, or focused enough for it.

SPH: How did you decide on the structure of the book?

TL: I decided that each chapter should be one of the questions I used during the interviews with my team, and they were already in a logical order so I stuck with that. Then, based on how my team answered the questions, I further broke down the chapters into topics. I then wanted three things for the book: to read exactly as my team had said it to me, with their personal views, in order that readers also would have true and accurate information. Then I wanted the reader to have the CEO point of view, my view in this case, relative to what was being said. Finally, I wanted topical summaries ("Employees want…") that would act as a "quick check" business tool for companies to use.

SPH: What was your writing process?

TL: It took me a while to start writing as I first had to make sense of all the research I had conducted and then act on some of it immediately; making some quick changes in the company. I then decided on the structure I wanted for the book and began to organize it by chapter headings, topical headings, and the staff quotes that went under each of them. Finally, I added in my part; the voice of the CEO, and the topic summaries of "Employees want…".

SPH: Was it difficult to write this book?

TL: Writing the book was not difficult due to the natural structure of the book taken from the questionnaire I used to interview my team. My part was also not difficult to write as, in almost all cases, I knew exactly what the positions were or how I felt about what my team had said to me. Therefore, I knew what I needed to write in response to them and to the book's future readers.

It was difficult to motivate myself to type and think at the same time. I am, and always have been, a big daydreamer so I had to constantly get on myself to stop talking to myself about what I was going to write, having the conversations in my head, and get right to typing it.

SPH: In your acknowledgements you claim your English is atrocious, is this true?

TL: Well, I didn't used to think so as I did a lot of article writing and edited that on my own. However, I really noticed the difference when my writing for this book was reviewed and edited by someone with a higher command of the English language.

SPH: Who do you want to read the book, who is your audience?

TL: Making Perfect is intended for a wide audience. It is for every level of employee, from entry level professional staff to CEO and shareholder, but also for university programs and students geared toward business degrees, and anyone else interested in business and workplace issues.

Of course, Making Perfect is ideally suited for the Russian market as the story takes place in Russia. However, the reader will quickly find that the story they are reading could have taken place at almost any company anywhere in the world.

Making Perfect will also, I believe, be highly useful and entertaining for every recruiter and human resources professional working around the globe, at recruitment firms, and internally as part of the human resources departments of companies.

SPH: What do you want readers to get from the book and what do you want them to take away from it?

TL: First, I want readers to feel they are reading a good book, albeit quite unorthodox; that they are reading something very special - a company's true secrets, issues, and ideas are being revealed and the minds and thinking of its employees and CEO are being shared.

It also represents an almost complete case study to learn from. There are a lot of patterns to identify throughout the book as well as lots of views and decisions to that were discussed. I want this book to make readers think - about the story they are reading, but also to think about their own work lives, careers, and the companies they work for.

I would also like for readers to use the general summaries at the end of every topic ("Employees want...") to ask themselves; "are we doing this at our company?" And if the answer is no, I hope they will try to get some ideas and recommendations implemented. I really enjoy the practice of improving businesses and I hope that by reading this book others will also become more interested and engaged in it, and have some new successes of their own.

It would also be great if this book inspired more employees to speak up and give their thoughts and ideas to their companies rather than keep things hidden. While I would like to see employees drive this initiative themselves, I would also hope that the book helps motivate management to spend more time with their staff and to listen to their issues and ideas, and act on those that make sense.

Lastly, I hope that readers will view Staffwell and our team as I view them; smart, innovative, positive, results-oriented and committed to continually perfecting our performance - for ourselves, our clients, and the market; and that readers will see Russia, the Russian workforce, and the potential for investing in and doing business in Russia, with the confidence and enthusiasm that I have.

To read an extended version of this interview or to ask the author additional questions you would like to have answered, please visit the Author Interview section on the Making Perfect website at www.makingperfect.ru.

About the Author

Teri Lindeberg is the founder and CEO of Staffwell, a Russia-based recruitment and executive search firm specialized in placing top management and professionals with their client base of Russian and Western companies. In addition, Staffwell also provides a range of consulting and training services to companies.

Prior to Staffwell, Teri worked in Moscow, London and New York, for a UK-based international recruitment company. Before relocating to Russia in 1996, she worked in recruitment and the publishing, printing and office equipment industries in New York.

Teri began writing when there was a need to create marketing materials for Staffwell, during their start-up phase in 2000. Several years later, she started the company's corporate and career development magazine, "The Well", where she was the editor and lead author of its articles and content. More recently, Teri writes for her own blog on Work360.ru, and is a featured blog writer for Harvard Business Review, Forbes and Finam (Russia).

Making Perfect is Teri Lindeberg's first book. She is currently in the process of conducting the research for her second book and plans to write several more books (mostly business related) in the future.

Teri has a degree in Retail Management from Syracuse University (USA). In her spare time, she spends quality time with her three young sons, socializes with friends, or plays, practices or coaches sports, including softball, baseball, broomball, tennis, Tae Kwon Do, kayaking, golf and walking. Teri also enjoys reading, painting, theater, films and travel. She lives in Moscow, Russia and spends most of her leisure time at her "dacha" near Asheville, North Carolina.

How to Contact the Author

Requests for further information or recruiting/executive search services, as well as inquiries about the author's availability for speeches, book signings and seminars or corporate consulting services, should be directed to her at the contact details below. Readers of this book are also encouraged to contact the author with comments and ideas for future publications.

To send an email to Teri Lindeberg, please write her at
Teri@staffwell.com.

To find out more about Teri Lindeberg, please visit her website at
www.TeriLindeberg.com.

About STAFFWELL

The company founded by Teri Lindeberg, Staffwell, provides full recruitment, executive search, and HR consulting services for companies operating in a wide range of industry sectors in Russia, the CIS and other international locations. Staffwell has offices in Moscow and St. Petersburg, Russia.

In October 2012, Staffwell was awarded 2nd place at the Company of the Year Awards for Russia in the Business Services industry sector.

Staffwell's services include:

- Recruitment and executive search of successful, highly skilled and talented, executives, management and professionals;
- Outplacement;
- Outsourcing (temporary payroll solutions);
- Market, people, and compensation & benefits surveys;
- Induction programs;
- Recruitment Consultant trainings;
- Employee and Management Assessments; and
- Corporate Performance Improvement Consulting ("Tea with Teri")

How to Contact STAFFWELL

To find out more about Staffwell, please visit their corporate website at: www.staffwell.com

For companies needing Staffwell's services, please send a detailed email to company@staffwell.com, and someone from the Staffwell team will get right back to you.

For job seekers looking for new employment please view and apply to Staffwell's daily updated job vacancies on www.staffwell.com, and email them your CV to CV@staffwell.com.

For those desiring to work for Staffwell, please email your CV and cover letter to joinus@staffwell.com.

THANK YOU
Thank you very much for reading Making Perfect!

TESTIMONIALS
If you enjoyed this book and found it interesting or useful to you, I would greatly appreciate hearing from you about it, so that I can read your comments and put them on our website or in a future published edition of the book. You can write me at Teri@staffwell.com

REFERRALS
If you did like this book and know of others you feel might enjoy it and or benefit from reading it, I would greatly appreciate your referring it to them. This book can be purchased at www.makingperfect.ru and other retailers listed on the website.

GIFT IDEA
Please consider Making Perfect as a gift idea for birthdays and holidays for your friends, family, colleagues, management, staff, companies or divisions of companies, students, professors, and or others you feel would enjoy and benefit from reading this book. This book can be purchased at www.makingperfect.ru and other retailers listed on the website. **Multiple copy discounts are available.**

BOOK CLUBS
Making Perfect would be ideal for a book club read and discussion, especially for those who enjoy talking about and debating workplace issues that most of us face. I encourage you to pull your friends and/or colleagues together and to discuss this book with each other. It would also make for a fun and beneficial corporate team-building exercise.

READERS CIRCLE
Please join our online Readers Circle, where you can give your thoughts regarding various chapters and topics covered in Making Perfect, and also respond to what other Readers Circle participants are saying. The Staffwell Team and I will read the entries and enter into the discussions. You can join the Readers Circle at www.makingperfect.ru. We look forward to seeing you there!

Again, thank you so much for reading Making Perfect! More books to come...

TL

8981113R00173

Printed in Great Britain
by Amazon.co.uk, Ltd.,
Marston Gate.